USAF Gunsh

Spectre – Spooky – Stinger – Shadow – Ghostrider

(USAF)

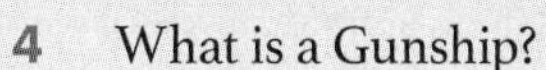

4 What is a Gunship?
8 Profile: AC-47D Spooky
16 Profile: AC-119 Stinger and Shadow
22 Profile: AC-130A
30 Gunships Go to War: Southeast Asia 1964 to 1975
40 Profile: AU-23 and AU-24
42 South Vietnamese, Laotian, and Khmer Gunships
48 Profile: AC-130H Spectre
56 Bushfire Wars 1980 to 89
60 Profile: AC-130U Spooky II
64 Gulf War to Kosovo 1990 to 1999
70 Into Afghanistan 2001 to 2002
76 Invading Iraq 2003 to 2011
82 Profile: AC-130W Stinger II
86 Profile: AC-130J Ghostrider
94 Afghanistan: The Long War 2003 to 2021
102 War against ISIS 2014 to 2024
108 USAF Fixed Wing Gunship: Past, present and future
114 Tracing Gunship History

(USAF)

(USAF)

(USAF)

(USAF)

(USAF)

(USAF)

(USAF)

(USAF)

ISBN: 978 1 83632 021 0
Editor: Tim Ripley
Data and photo research: Fergus Ripley
Senior editor, specials: Roger Mortimer
Email: roger.mortimer@keypublishing.com
Cover Design: Steve Donovan
Design: SJmagic DESIGN SERVICES, India
Advertising Sales Manager: Sam Clark
Email: sam.clark@keypublishing.com
Tel: 01780 755131
Advertising Production: Becky Antoniades
Email: Rebecca.antoniades@keypublishing.com

SUBSCRIPTION/MAIL ORDER
Key Publishing Ltd, PO Box 300, Stamford, Lincs, PE9 1NA
Tel: 01780 480404
Subscriptions email: subs@keypublishing.com
Mail Order email: orders@keypublishing.com
Website: www.keypublishing.com/shop

PUBLISHING
Group CEO and Publisher: Adrian Cox

Published by
Key Publishing Ltd, PO Box 100, Stamford, Lincs, PE9 1XQ
Tel: 01780 755131
Website: www.keypublishing.com

PRINTING
Precision Colour Printing Ltd, Haldane, Halesfield 1, Telford, Shropshire. TF7 4QQ

DISTRIBUTION
Seymour Distribution Ltd, 2 Poultry Avenue, London, EC1A 9PU
Enquiries Line: 02074 294000.

What is a Gunship?

The USAF's deadliest aircraft?

ABOVE: Gunship action. The basic design of the AC-130 has remained the same since the first gunships entered service in the 1960s. Sideways firing weapons allow firepower to be concentrated against a single spot on the ground for sustained periods. (USAF)

Spooky, Spectre, Shadow, Stinger, and Ghostrider. Evocative callsigns from the early days of the United States Air Force fixed wing gunship operations during the Vietnam conflict of the 1960s and 1970s.

The callsigns were coined by Vietnam-era gunship crews, who wanted to big up their missions to hit the enemy hard, with precision night strikes. The idea was to give the impression that they could and would deliver death by surprise, under the cover of darkness.

The crews wanted to use names associated with horror movies or the supernatural. The idea was to terrify their enemies and boost the morale of US and allied troops fighting across Southeast Asia, as US military commanders dubbed the war zone that grew to include North and South Vietnam, Laos, Cambodia, and Thailand.

The North Vietnamese troops on the receiving end of gunship strikes, could easily have thought they were on the set of a horror movie, as their positions were raked by unrelenting fire. There were few survivors from gunship strikes. Those that did survive were often horrendously injured by red hot shrapnel.

RIGHT: The AC-130U Spooky II bristled with guns, high resolution sensors and high-capacity communication antenna. (USAF)

For US and allied troops who watched gunships unleashing their devastating firepower, morale soared. It was massively re-assuring to hear the approaching drone of a gunship and once it opened fire the landscape would be illuminated by cones of tracer fire and then explosions. Amid any pauses in fire, the screams of dying or wounded communist soldiers could usually be heard.

The origins of the USAF gunship lie in the early days of Vietnam as US military advisors headed out into the jungle with patrols of South Vietnamese, or Army of Republic Vietnam (ARVN), troops to take on communist Vietcong guerrilla fighters. As ARVN troops started to build camps to secure ground, they came under relentless night attacks from the Vietcong. The call would go up, 'Charlie is on the wire'. Charlie being the Vietcong,shortened to VC or Victor Charlie in the phonetic alphabet.

Neutralising VC assault teams attempting to overrun ARVN camps was easier said than done. The communists were often hiding in jungle cover, hidden from the pilots of US strike jets sent to help out. It was just too difficult for the pilots to see their targets.

There was a need for an aircraft that could stay on station for extended periods to patrol over the ARVN jungle camps and strike when the Vietcong broke cover to attack.

The answer was to fit World War Two-era Douglas C-47 Dakota transport aircraft with sideways firing machine guns. Enterprising USAF officers realised that if the newly named 'gunships', were banked in a 45° pylon turn, its guns could be brought to bear continuously against the same point on the ground. When firing tracer rounds, gunship attacks created a distinctive 'cone' of fire as the aircraft circled over targets.

It was such a simple idea that at first senior USAF officers refused to believe it would work. However, once the gunship pioneers had carried out tests and proved the idea, a prototype was sent to Vietnam in 1964, and it was rapidly sent into action.

Same Mission, Different Tech

The concept has remained unchanged since the Vietnam era but 21st century gunships incorporate far more modern technology than their 1960s ancestors and the rate of evolution was impressive. Early analogue computer technology was harnessed to create highly accurate sights, which could concentrate fire on target zones only a few metres across.

Early AC-47 gunships had to rely on flares to illuminate targets at night. Soon USAF chiefs wanted to provide their gunships with the first generation of night-vision technology to allow them to find targets in darkness. Once fitted with night-vision devices, gunship operations were transformed.

No longer did gunships have to circle over ARVN camps and wait for the Vietcong to break cover and charge forward. Gunships could now go hunting for the enemy, both striking targets and passing warning of enemy troop movement to friendly forces. This later role was soon dubbed 'overwatch', and it became just as important as actual attacks on enemy.

As the technology evolved, the USAF moved to introduce bigger and more powerful gunships. The AC-47 gave way for the Fairchild AC-119, which was based on the C-119 Flying Boxcar twin-boom transport aircraft. By 1967, the first Lockheed C-130 Hercules had been converted into a gunship and was on its way to Vietnam. Soon the AC-130A was the dominant gunship in Southeast Asia. As well as protecting US and ARVN troops in Vietnam, it was sent hunting North Vietnamese truck convoys in Laos and Cambodia. It was quickly dubbed the Spectre.

The AC-130 was the ideal gunship. Its large cargo hold and rear-loading ramp meant it could be easily modified to carry heavier weapons

BELOW: The new and old. A modern-day AC-130J Ghostrider does a flyby at the Oshkosh airshow in 2021 with a restored C-47 Dakota which has been modified to represent an AC-47D Spooky. (USAF)

RIGHT: Gunship crews have to work as a team to sustain their aircraft's rate of fire, loading rounds and clearing empty cases. It is hard physical and dangerous work. (USAF)

and a large load of ammunition. Its armament was progressively updated, with 20mm cannons being added to 7.62mm mini-guns. It was then fitted with 40mm cannons and 105mm howitzers to create a powerful stand-off weapon system. When combined with thermal imaging night-vision system, the Spectre became the USAF's ultimate night strike platform of the Vietnam war.

Over the following 50 years, the AC-130 was progressively updated to make it relevant to America's wars in the late 20th century and into the 21st century. The Spectre received better night-vision, air-to-air refuelling, computerised targeting, network communications, more guns and precision guided missiles.

A decade ago, a project was launched to migrate from the legacy C-130H airframe to the more modern C-130J, which featured glass cockpits, new engines, and distinctive six-bladed propellers.

The latest Lockheed Martin AC-130J Ghostrider has capabilities far more advanced than those early Vietnam era gunships. One thing has not changed, gunships still depend on their crews working together to dominate the battlefield.

BELOW: Hurlburt Field in Florida has been the home base of the USAF's gunship fleet since the 1970s. (USAF)

ABOVE: The AC-130W was the last USAF gunship variant to be based on the C-130H model Hercules. (USAF)

Enlisted Men

Unlike most USAF combat aircraft, which are crewed by officers, since the early days gunships have been crewed by mainly enlisted airmen, who load, aim and fire its weapons. This is hard - almost industrial era – physical labour, loading shells, clearing spent casings, and then moving ammunition to guns from storage racks.

The crew must work as a team to ensure guns are always ready to fire, with enough ammunition and the night sensors working at peak performance to find targets. On almost every gunship mission something goes wrong. Guns jam, sights drop out of alignment, or communications are lost with ground controllers. Crews must work quickly to find faults and rectify them. On fast jets if a gun jams, there is little chance of the pilot resolving the problem, so he usually has to turn for home. If a gunship suffers a weapon stoppage, the crew set to work to fix it and get the aircraft back in the fight.

Another thing has not changed. The first Vietnam gunships were assigned to 'Air Commandos' squadron. The name originated from the Burma campaign in World War Two, when US Army Air Force transport units parachuted supplies to British commando units operating behind enemy lines. Hence 'Air Commandos'. So, when US President John F Kennedy dispatched special forces, or Green Beret, advisors to Vietnam in the early 1960s the USAF formed special squadrons to provide them with air support. These experts in 'unconventional warfare' were so dubbed 'Air Commandos', in a throwback to those unconventional US aviators in Burma. Even though the Air Commando squadrons and wings were re-titled as special operations units in 1968, the 'Air Commando' name was retained. Even today, all members of the US Air Force Special Operations Command (AFSOC), including gunship crews, proudly refer to themselves as 'Air Commandos'. They take seriously their 'Air Commando' history and heritage. In its mission statement, AFSOC declares: "our Air Commando heritage demands, we remain culturally bound to get the mission done or find a way where none exists."

LEFT: Ever since the Vietnam war, USAF gunships have sported nose art based on their aircraft's supernatural nicknames. Gunships of this generation also had black painted undersides to reduce their visibility during night missions. (USAF)

AC-47D Spooky

The Original Gunship

ABOVE: An AC-47D Spooky belonging to the American Flight Museum in Topeka has been restored to flight as a tribute to Medal of Honor winner John Levitow. (USAF)

As the USAF's first operational gunship, the Douglas AC-47D Spooky set the standard for future development of this unique weapon system.

Its origins stretch back to 1926 when American military fliers first tested the concept of using lateral firing machine guns to strike at ground targets during a banked, or pylon, turn. The idea was resurrected in World War Two as a possible way to engage German submarines during the Battle of the Atlantic.

It was not until the early 1960s that the concept of sideways firing 'gunships' flew from the drawing board into reality. A designer at the Bell aircraft company, Ralph Flexman, is credited with proposing the idea as a way to support US military advisors in jungles of Southeast Asia. In 1961, he met up with a USAF officer, Lieutenant Colonel Gilmour Craig McDonald, who was also looking into the gunship concept. They proposed the idea to USAF chiefs, who were already looking for new ways to ramp up American airpower in Vietnam.

This led to the launching in 1963 of Project Tailchaser which involved the first flight test of the concept, using a North American T-28 Trojan light strike fighter. A team of USAF officers, led by Captain Ron Terry, went to Vietnam to look at how the gunship could be used to help US military advisers and their local allies take on Vietcong guerrillas.

The first flights of the unarmed experimental aircraft took place at Wright-Patterson AFB in Ohio in June, 1963. Its pilot, Captain Harley Johnson, proved he was able to keep a ground target fixed in a gun sight as he banked the aircraft through a

RIGHT: The first generation of AC-47 gunships sported three Gatling guns in two windows and the cargo door. (USAF)

LEFT: A freeze framed photograph of an AC-47D gunship attack in Vietnam shows its distinctive 'cone of fire'. In the background, flares from the gunship are illuminating the target. (USAF)

series of high angle turns. Trials were then carried out using a twin engine Convair C-131 Samaritan to prove that the concept would work with a large transport aircraft. In these early trials cameras were fitted and it was not until the summer of 1964 that the first live firing exercises were carried out at the Eglin AFB firing range in Florida.

The first weapon installed in the C-131 test aircraft was a General Electric SUU-11A 7.62mm Gatling gun, known as mini guns, mounted in a pod, which could fire 6,000 rounds-per-minute. In a series of tests against land and sea targets, the gunship concept proved devastating. In one test, 25 manikins were set up within a three-quarters of an acre area. The C-131 appeared and raked the target zone, easily hitting 19 of the manikins. Within weeks, the USAF top brass had got to hear about the results, and they ordered the test programme to be accelerated. By September 1964, the first Douglas C-47 Dakota, or 'Goony Bird' as it was known to US airmen, was assigned to the test programme and the AC-47 was a step closer. The 'A' stands for attack. The twin engine C-47 was the workhorse of the Allies during World War Two, famously dropping paratroopers on D-Day and flying supplies into Burma.

Capt Terry proved a pivotal figure in the AC-47 story, selling the idea to senior officers and using his operational experience as a fighter pilot to overcome technical problems. He convinced Tactical Air Command that the C-47 was the ideal platform for conversion into a gunship – it was simple to operate, easy to maintain and hundreds of surplus aircraft were available for conversion. His proposals were approved, and work was put in train to carry out a combat evaluation in South Vietnam in December 1964.

In Country Evaluation

The trial involved Terry leading a team of aircrew and engineers to Bien Hoa Airbase, near Saigon, to install three lateral firing 7.62mm mini guns into a C-47 Goony Bird. The aircraft was already in South Vietnam for Operation Farm

BELOW: Some early AC-47 gunships in 1964 and 1965 sported .30cal machines guns because mini guns were not ready to be installed. (USAF)

ABOVE: AC-47D gunships were painted into the distinctive three-tone camouflage to allow them to blend into jungles of Southeast Asia. (USAF)

BELOW: Later versions of the AC-47D incorporated improved mini guns that could be positioned in three windows, freeing up the cargo door. This made it easier to load ammunition and for the crew to escape in case the aircraft was hit by enemy fire. This is a 4th Special Operations Squadron aircraft. Note the 'Spooky' nose art. (USAF).

Gate, as the US advisor mission in the country was codenamed. The conversion also involved installation of a rudimentary sighting system and a flare dispenser. USAF engineers on the air base took only a few days to complete the work and then Terry set about teaching pilots and crews from the 1st Air Commando Squadron how to use the gunship, which were initially designated FC-47s, with the 'F' standing for fighter.

The most important work involved bore-sighting the mini guns so they could be used near friendly forces. A series of test firings were conducted over the South China Sea to make sure the mini guns fired where they were supposed to.

Next, the new crop of gunship pilots had to be taught how to put their aircraft into a turn over the target and line up the cabin crew to start dropping flares to illuminate the battlefield. The gunners then had to learn to spot fleeing enemy soldiers in jungle terrain and keep their weapons on target.

This was all new, even for Terry and his team of instructors, with the Air Commando crews devising new tactics as they went along and working out how to keep their guns firing for prolonged periods. The first gunship crews had to learn how to use the aircraft to best effect on the job. Once on target, the crews would then hold their aircraft in tight orbits to rain fire down on the enemy.

The first gunship mission was flown during daylight on December 15, 1964, with Terry at the controls. His aircraft was directed at targets located by forward air controllers on the ground. Over the next week, Terry attacked several targets, including a building containing Vietcong. After the gunship strike, the air controllers reported that the building "looked like a sieve" and 21 enemy fighters had been killed.

On the evening of December 23/24, the FC-47 carried out its first ever night mission to support an Army of the Republic Vietnam (ARVN) outpost which was under Vietcong attack. During two engagements, the gunship expended 25 flares and fired more than 9,000 rounds of 7.62mm ammunition. The friendly ground troops reported that the enemy rapidly withdrew back into jungle after they came under attack from the aircraft.

This set the pattern for the next few months of the FC-47 trial as increasing Vietcong attacks led to a surge in demand for nighttime close air support. The awesome sight of thousands of tracer rounds from the gunships lighting up night skies across South Vietnam led to the FC-47s being compared to fire breathing dragons. Soon they were nicknamed 'Puff the Magic Dragon' after a famous children's fairy tale, or just the 'Dragonships'.

In a sign of things to come, in July 1965, an FC-47 was fitted with one of the first forward looking infra-red (FLIR) night vision systems to test whether this new technology could help find the heat signatures of enemy troops hiding under jungle canopies.

After nearly six months of operational FC-47 trials in Vietnam, the USAF top brass needed no more convincing that more gunships were needed in Southeast Asia on a permanent basis. Orders were placed for a squadron of 16 aircraft to be in Vietnam by November 1965, under the code name 'Operation Sixteen Buck'.

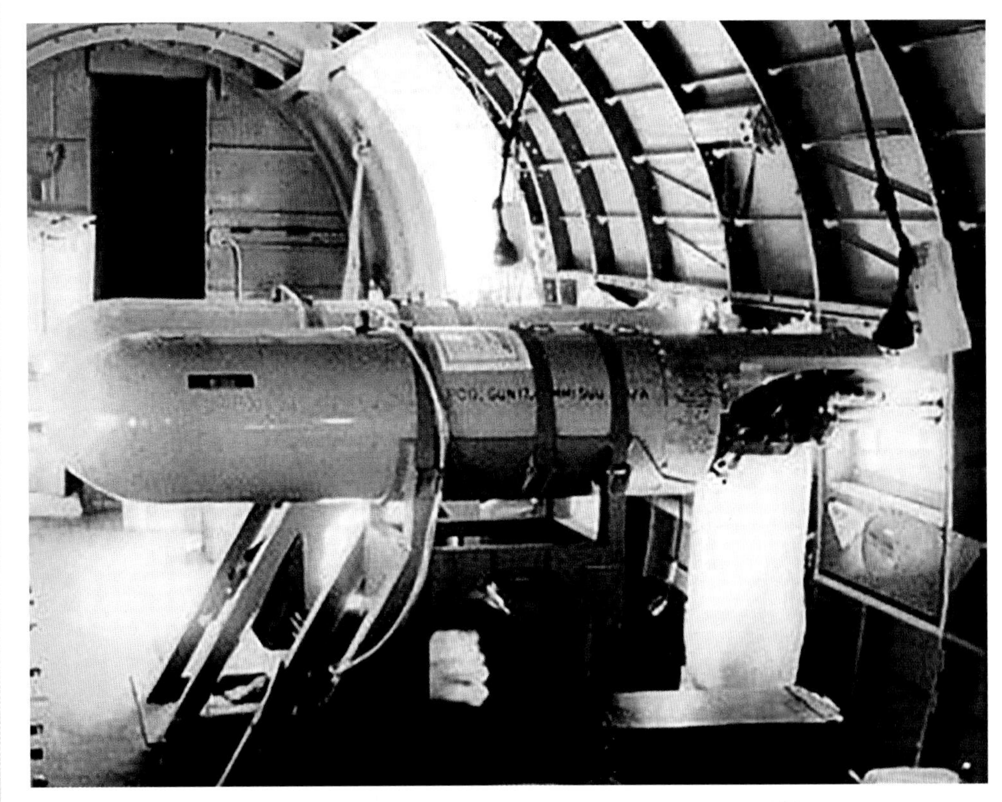

ABOVE: An SUU-11 mini gun in action from an AC-47 over Vietnam. (USAF)

LEFT: First versions of the AC-47D had a SUU-11 mini gun installed in the aircraft's cargo door. (USAF)

The AC Designation

Following much high-level debate in the USAF, the aircraft were designated the AC-47D, with the FC-47 title being dropped after opposition from the service's fighter community.

The new AC-47Ds were to be armed with three GAU-2B/A 7.62mm mini gun pods as standard but there was a bottleneck in supply of mini gun pods, so this new batch of aircraft would initially be fitted with SUU-11A gun pods until the more powerful weapons were ready.

In August 1965, the new gunship unit, the 4th Air Commando Squadron (ACS) started training at Forbes AFB in Kansas. Delays in manufacturing the mini guns, meant the first aircraft had to be fitted with 0.30cal belt fed heavy machine guns as an interim.

The need to fit long distance fuel tanks to allow the AC-47Ds to make the trans-Pacific flight from the Continental US to Vietnam meant

AC-47D SPOOKY
Powerplant: Two × Pratt & Whitney R-1830 Twin Wasp 14-cylinder air-cooled radial piston engines
Wingspan: 28.96m (95ft)
Length: 19.63m (64ft 5in)
Height: 5.16m (16ft 11in)
Max take-off weight: 14,969kg (33,000lb)
Max speed: 370kph (230mph)
Range: 3,500km (1,890nm)
Crew: Seven
Armament:
Three × 7.62mm General Electric SUU-11/A then GAU-2/M134 mini guns

ABOVE: An AC-47D puts down night-time fire on a Vietcong position near Saigon in 1968. (US NATIONAL ARCHIVES)

the aircraft's guns had to be stripped out and flown out on dedicated cargo aircraft. After the arrival of the aircraft at Tan Son Nhut Airbase outside Saigon, engineers had to re-install the weapons and crews had to carry out test firing to bore-sight them. By the end of 1965 there were 20 AC-47s in South Vietnam, which included four attrition reserve aircraft. The 4th ACS soon began using the radio call sign, 'Spooky', which ended up becoming the official name of the gunship.

As the Vietnam conflict escalated in 1966, so did AC-47D operations and crews soon began asking for improvements to the aircraft. Extra radios were fitted to allow crews to talk to multiple ground controllers and other aircraft, during engagements. A image intensifying night-vision device, known as Starlight Scope, was trialled, along with .50cal heavy machine guns. The Vietcong were coming to fear the AC-47D and started to fire back at them, using 12.7mm DShK heavy machine guns. Gunship crews asked for armour to be fitted to their aircraft. At first the AC-47Ds carried 45 flares and 24,000 rounds but combat experience soon led to the ammunition load being doubled to 48,000 rounds, along with 75 flares.

In 1967, demand for gunships was overwhelming the 4th ACS so approval was given for the formation of a second unit, which was designated the 3rd Air Commando Squadron. A new weapon, the MXU-470/A mini gun, was also installed in the AC-47D. This was smaller in size than the old SUU-11A, so all the guns could be installed in the aircraft internally, so it was no longer necessary to mount one gun in the main cargo door space. The new gun also had an improved ammunition

DOUGLAS AC-47D SPOOKY GUNSHIPS OF VIETNAM WAR

Serial	Name	Lost	Cause	After USAF Service	Notes
43-16065				RVNAF July 15, 1969	
43-16133				RLAF May 29, 1970	
43-16159		May 4, 1968	Shot down, 7 KIA		
43-16368				RVNAF December 31, 1969	
43-48072					
43-48263				RVNAF December 24, 1969, then RLAF	
43-48356		March 23, 1967	Shot down, crew OK		
43-48466				RVNAF July 20, 1972	
43-48501					
43-48579	Puff				
43-48591	Git-Em' Bullet	October 2, 1967	Shot down, 7 KIA		
43-48686		September 17, 1971	Written off after accident at Da Nang AB	RVNAF July 30, 1969	
43-48701					
43-48801				RVNAF June 30, 1969	
43-48916				RVNAF July 31, 1972	
43-48921		April 26, 1967	Accident? 7 KIA		
43-48925		June 3, 1966	Shot down, 6 KIA		
43-48929				RVNAF	
43-49010				RVNAF May 29, 1969, then KAF and then RTAF	On Display in Thailand
43-49021		September 1, 1969	Shot down, 8 KIA		
43-49124		January 9, 1967	Shot down, 9 KIA		
43-49211		June 9, 1971	Battle damage and then scrapped	RVNAF	

DOUGLAS AC-47D SPOOKY GUNSHIPS OF VIETNAM WAR				
43-49268	March 13, 1966	7 KIA		
43-49274	December 13, 1968	Air-to air collision, crew OK		
43-49330	March 6, 1968	Destroyed on ground		
43-49339			RVNAF July 30, 1969	
43-49421				
43-49423			RVNAF Dec 69	
43-49492	December 17, 1965	Shot down on transport mission, 9 KIA		
43-49499	August 29, 1968	Destroyed on ground by rockets		
43-49503			RVNAF December 15, 1969	
43-49516			Khmer AF May 1974, then RTAF 1975	On Display in Thailand
43-49517			RVNAF July 30, 1969	
43-49546	May 4, 1966	Shot down, 8 KIA		
43-49770			RVNAF 1969	Medal of Honor aircraft
43-49852				
43-49859	February 15, 1968	Shot down, 8 KIA		
44-76207	May 5, 1968	Shot down, 2 KIA		
44-76290	March 9, 1966	Shot down, 3 KIA on ground		
44-76354			RVNAF 1969	
44-76370			RVNAF 1969, then RLAF	
44-76394			Philippine AF after 1975	
44-76534	March 29, 1967	Shot down, 7 KIA		
44-76542	February 18, 1967	Crash landed crew OK		
44-76593				
44-76606	September 5, 1969	Crash landed at Binh Thuy, crew OK	RVNAF 1969	
44-76625			RLAF	
44-76722				
44-76985				
44-77263	May 11, 1973	Scrapped at Phang Rang	RVNAF July 23, 1972	
45-0919			RVNAF	
45-0927			RVNAF January 1, 1970	
45-1047			RVNAF, then RLAF	
45-1057	November 24, 1972	Lost in crash at airbase, 2 KIA	RVNAF	
45-1117			RLAF Dec !969	
45-1120	December 24, 1965	Shot down over Laos, 6 KIA		

Notes
KAF: Khmer Air Force (pre 1975 Cambodia); KIA: Killed In Action; RLAF: Royal Laotian Air Force; RTAF: Royal Thai Air Force; RVNAF: Republic of Vietnam Air Force (South Vietnam)

ABOVE: The 3rd Special Operations Squadron was activated in May 1968 to be the second AC-47D gunship unit in South Vietnam. (USAF/US NATIONAL ARCHIVES)

ABOVE: AC-47D, serial 43-48801 of the 3rd Special Operations Squadron lifts off from Bien Hoa Air Base in August 1968. (USAF)

ABOVE: The sprawling Bien Hoa Airbase outside of Saigon was a regular haunt of AC-47D Spooky crews during the war in South Vietnam. (USAF)

feed mechanism that reduced the need for crews to deal with stoppages.

An improved flare dispenser, which could be jettisoned in flight if one of the flares caught fire was also installed to improve cabin safety. A smoke removal system was also installed to flush out the toxic fumes from any flares that ignited in the aircraft's cabin.

The AC-47Ds were increasingly being used in Laos in 1967 and 1968 as part of the US interdiction campaign along the so-called Ho Chi Minh Trail, which was used by North Vietnam to move vast quantities of supplies to their forces fighting the Americans in the south. To help detect communist truck convoys, the USAF dropped fields of acoustic sensors, which were a land-based equivalent of anti-submarine sonobuoys, along the trail. AC-47Ds were fitted with receiving devices to pick up information from the sensors to help them on their truck killing missions in Laos.

In 1969, four years after the AC-47D entered service, the USAF began to transition to the bigger and more powerful AC-119s and AC-130s gunships. The North Vietnamese were rapidly improving their air defences, so bigger weapons, with longer stand-off ranges, were needed to keep USAF gunships in the fight. It was just not physically possible to install bigger weapons in the confined cabin of the AC-47D. A new generation of gunships were needed.

The 3rd Special Operation Squadron, as the Air Commando units were now designated, handed

RIGHT: SUU-11A Gatling mini guns in gunships were powered by electrical mechanisms and feed channels to remove spent cartridges. (USAF)

over its aircraft to the South Vietnamese air force in the summer of 1969 and flew its last mission on August 7. The 4th SOS soldiered on until December 1, when it flew its last mission and handed over its surplus aircraft to the South Vietnamese and Laotian air forces, which continued to use them until the end of the conflict in Southeast Asia in 1975. A few aircraft also found their way into the hands of the Khmer or Cambodian air force, which operated until their country fell to the communist Khmer Rouge in 1975. Several surviving AC-47s were evacuated to Thailand in April 1975 and were absorbed into the Royal Thai Air Force.

In total, 53 C-47 aircraft were converted into AC-47D at a cost of $6.7m. Given their impact on the battlefield during their four-year period of combat, it was an amazingly cost-effective weapon system. Records indicate that 25 of these were lost in combat or accidents in USAF or Vietnamese service, with 86 USAF AC-47D crewmen being killed in action during the conflict. An unknown number of Vietnamese AC-47D crew were also lost in the war.

The AC-47D blazed a trail for USAF gunship operations. Spooky crews wrote the book on gunship tactics, proving the revolutionary concept could make a difference on the battlefields of Southeast Asia.

ABOVE: USAF gunships were protected against Vietcong rocket and mortar fire by revetments on airfields in South Vietnam. (USAF)

BELOW: Daytime missions by AC-47Ds were rare over Vietnam because of the threat from Vietcong anti-aircraft gunners. They were usually flown to zero weapons and familiarise new crews with conditions in Southeast Asia. (USAF)

AC-119G/K Stinger and Shadow

The Boxcar gunship

RIGHT: AC-119G crews created distinctive calling cards to give to advertise their capabilities to US and allied troops, promoting the image of the 'Shadow'. (USAF)

Almost as soon as the Douglas AC-47D Spooky started to show its worth in Vietnam, the USAF senior leadership instructed that work begin to develop a more capable successor.

Interest focused on the new generation of transport aircraft that featured rear loading ramps and cargo cabins that could accommodate vehicles or large pallets. These aircraft were ideal for conversion into gunships. Their cabins were wide enough to take larger guns and, perhaps more importantly, they could carry significant amounts of ammunition to sustain high rates of fire.

WHEN UNINVITED GUESTS DROP IN . . .
CALL FOR
"THE SHADOW"

We Provide:
Lighting for
All Occasions
Beaucoup 7.62
Mortar Suppression

We Defend:
Special Forces Camps
Air Bases
Outposts
Troops in Contact

"Who Knows What Evil Lurks Below the Jungle Canopy?
THE SHADOW KNOWS!"

Attention focused on the two-engined Fairchild C-119 Flying Boxcar and the four-engine Lockheed C-130 Hercules. They both had high wing designs, so weapons mounted in their cargo cabin could easily engage ground targets. As well as their large cargo cabins, these aircraft had far more range and endurance than the World War Two-era C-47. The new aircraft could also fly higher, which was increasingly important as the need emerged for gunships to operate outside the firing envelopes of communist anti-aircraft guns across Southeast Asia.

The USAF gunship community were keen to adopt the C-130 as

BELOW: Stinger strikes. The AC-119K was adapted from the Flying Boxcar transport aircraft to provide aerial firepower. (USAF)

LEFT: The 71st Special Operations Squadron adorned their AC-119Gs with their unique 'Shadow' logo. (USAF)

LEFT: AC-119Gs had four 7.62mm mini guns as their main firepower. (USAF)

their future gunship platform but its political head, the then secretary of the air force Harold Brown, was not keen. He wanted to keep C-130s for airlift missions and there were fears the development of a gunship version of the Hercules would take too long. A rapid programme to convert C-119s to gunships would fill the gap until the AC-130 was ready for action.

In June 1967, Brown gave the go ahead to Project Combat Hornet to begin converting C-119Gs into gunships and wanted the option to convert C-119Ks for the gunship mission. The Boxcar had the advantage of nearing the end of its service life, so there were significant numbers of the aircraft that had recently been retired and could be brought back into service without impacting on frontline airlift units.

Work got underway on the detailed design work and concerns emerged that the G model would not have the hot-high performance required in the climate of some parts of Southeast Asia. It was decided to go for a mixed fleet of G and K models. The K model featured two General Electric J85 turbojet engines in underwing pods, which gave the aircraft extra thrust on take-off, so it could lift 25% more weight.

The basic design of the new gunship involved four main weapon stations with a combination of SUU-11A/B or GAU-2B/A mini gun pods mounted on the port side of the aircraft. Directly behind them were 7.62mm ammunition racks along the length of the starboard side of the cabin, containing 35,000 rounds. Gunners could easily re-load the weapons during extended fire missions. In the forward port window, an image intensifier night observation system was installed to find targets. At the rear of the cabin were flare launchers containing 60 flares and a sideways facing 1.5 million candlepower

AC-119G/K SHADOW/STINGER
Powerplant: AC-119G Two × Wright R-3350-85 Duplex-Cyclone 18-cylinder air-cooled radial piston engines
AC-119K: Additional two × General Electric J85 turbojet engines in underwing pods
Wingspan: 33.3m (109ft 3.25in)
Length: 26.3m (86ft 5.75in)
Height: 8.1m (26ft 7.75in)
Max take-off weight: 28,123kg (62,000lb)
Max speed: 330kph (210mph)
Range: 3,110km (1,680nm)
Crew: Eight
Armament:
Four × GAU-2/A 7.62mm mini guns, 1,500 rounds/gun
Two × M61A1 20mm six-barreled Gatling cannon (AC-119K only)
60 × Mk 24 flares in a LAU-74/A flare launcher

RIGHT: An AC-119G on patrol along the South Vietnamese coast from Phan Rang airbase. (USAF)

AN/AVQ-8 searchlight to illuminate ground targets. To protect the crew from enemy fire, the cockpit floor and the floor under the gun position were reinforced with armour. The result was intended to be a far more efficient and effective gunship.

71st Special Operations Squadron

Design work was complete in early 1968 and the first G Model aircraft were scheduled to go through the conversion process at Fairchild-Hillers plant at St Augustine in Florida in May 1968. Work on the K model was taking longer, and conversion was scheduled to start in October 1968.

Test flights of the first G model began at Elgin AFB in Florida in June 1968 but it was dogged by poor results. The aircraft was heavier than expected and this impacted on its performance. A weight reduction programme was launched but this delayed bringing the aircraft into service. It was proposed to convert 26 AC-119 gunships to the K model, with its additional jet engines but there was not time. The aircraft were needed in Southeast Asia in November 1968.

As production was ramping up, the 71st Special Operations Squadron was stood up at Bakalar AFB in Indiana to operate the AC-119Gs. It was formed by mobilising reservists from the 71st Tactical Airlift Squadron. They soon moved to Lockbourne AFB in Ohio for more training.

The squadron began to deploy to Nha Trang Airbase in December 1968 and flew their first combat evaluation missions on January 5, 1969. Initially, the AC-119Gs were allocated the radio call sign 'Creep' but after protests from the crews, within days this had been changed to the iconic 'Shadow'. It was not until March 1969 that the first 18 of the AC-119Gs were in South Vietnam. In June 1969, the 71st SOS was re-designated as the 17th SOS.

Shadow crews found themselves in action across South Vietnam, flying missions to protect US and allied troops, as well as interdiction strikes against enemy supply lines. Crews reported that the guns and sensors were effective, but the aircraft performance limited its endurance and flight profile.

Back in the US, work was well underway on the AC-119K. It boasted far more firepower and better sensors that the G model. This included two M61 Vulcan 20mm Gatling cannons, with six rotating barrels, in addition to the four 7.62mm mini guns, as well as a AN/AAD-4 forward looking infra-red (FLIR) night-vision sensor. This was a very advanced device that could detect heat signatures under jungle canopies but the manufacturer, Texas Instruments, was having difficulty getting it work properly because extensive cooling was needed to stop its electronic components overheating. Deliveries of the K model aircraft and their vital sensors stretched into 1969. It had been hoped to deliver the first AC-119K in October 1968, but this slipped to February 1969, with the final aircraft being handed over in September 1970. As a result, cost for the project escalated from a projected $81.2m to $141.4m.

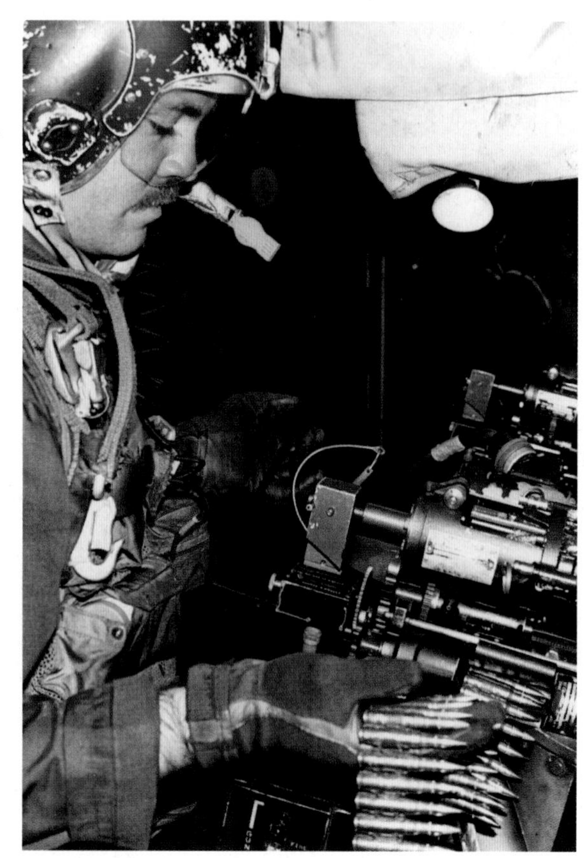

BELOW: A gunner adjusts the ammunition feed of a mini gun during AC-119G mission. (USAF)

18th Special Operations Squadron

The 18th Special Operations Squadron stood up at Lockbourne AFB in January 1969 and it eventually deployed to Phan Rang AFB in South Vietnam in October. However, the first four aircraft left for Southeast Asia without the vital FLIR sensor and had to be retrofitted some months later. All the fully equipped AC-119Ks were not declared fully combat ready until February 1969. It took several months for the AC-119Ks to get their own distinctive callsign when they were allocated 'Stinger'.

During 1969, the two AC-119 squadrons were in action across the region, with the K model taking on the majority of tasking against the Ho Chi Minh Trail in Laos because of their long range, endurance, and hot-high performance. The FLIR system on the

LEFT: The AC-119K sported two turbojet engines as an addition, which significantly improved its performance. (USAF)

K models provided highly effective at finding trucks and troop positions in the jungles of Laos but it was temperamental and engineers from Texas Instruments had to deploy to South Vietnam to keep them working in the hot climate. The K models with their 20mm cannons were much in demand because their extra range allowed to them carry out stand-off strikes against targets protected by heavy air defences. Increasing use was made of the K model's new AN/APQ-133 side-looking beacon tracking radar navigation system to allow it to strike with precision against targets in low cloud and tropical rainstorms. Friendly troops activated a transponder that was picked up by the AN/APQ-133 radar, so the AC-119's gunners could make sure they did not attack them by accident.

The AC-119 continued to serve in Southeast Asia throughout the 1970s and into 1971. When the US presence in South Vietnam started to run down, the USAF decided not to keep the AC-119 in service. It only wanted to keep the AC-130 in its future gunship force after the war was over.

Progressively, the AC-119s were taken out of service and the first aircraft started to be handed over to the

BELOW: An AC-119G Shadow of the 17th Special Operations Squadron flies over the South Vietnamese capital, Saigon, in October 1969. The unit was previously the 71st SOS up to April 1969. (USAF)

ABOVE: AC-119Ks were operated by the 18th Special Operations Squadron right up to the end of the US presence in South Vietnam, being based at Da Nang Air Base from September 1971 to December 1972. It handed its aircraft over to the South Vietnamese Air Force. (USAF)

FAIRCHILD AC-119G/K SHADOW/STINGER GUNSHIPS OF VIETNAM WAR					
AC-119G Shadow					
Operated by 71st SOS, then 17th SOS after June 1969					
Serial	**Names**	**Lost**	**After USAF use**	**RVNAF Unit**	**Notes**
52-5898					
52-5905					
52-5907		October 11, 1969 crashed on take-off from Tan Son Nhut, six KIA			
52-5925	*Charlie Chasers*				
52-5927		Destroyed January 20, 1972, eight KIA	RVNAF Aug 71	819th Squadron	
52-5938					
52-5942					
53-3136			RVNAF Aug 71	819th Squadron	
53-5145			RVNAF Aug 71	819th Squadron	
53-3170					
53-3178			RVNAF Aug 71	819th Squadron	
53-3189			RVNAF Aug 71	819th Squadron	
53-3192			RVNAF Aug 71	819th Squadron	
53-3205					
53-7833			RVNAF Aug 71	819th Squadron	
53-7848			RVNAF	819th Squadron	
53-7851			RVNAF	819th Squadron	
53-7852			RVNAF	819th Squadron	
53-8114					
53-8115					
53-8123					
53-8131					
53-8155		April 27, 1970 crash on take off from Than Son Nhut Airport, six KIA			
53-3205			RVNAF Aug 71	821st Squadron	
53-8069					
53-8089					
AC-119K Stinger					
Operated by 18th SOS					
52-5864					
52-5889		April 29, 1975 shot down by SA-7 SAM over Than Son Nhut Airport	RVNAF		
52-5910					
52-5926					
52-5911					
52-5935		June 6, 1970 crash near Hainan Island, one MIA			
52-5940					
52-5945					

FAIRCHILD AC-119G/K SHADOW/STINGER GUNSHIPS OF VIETNAM WAR					
52-9982					
53-3154	*Good Grief The Peanut Special*		RVNAF Aug 71	821st Squadron	
53-3156		February 19, 1970 crash on landing. Crew OK			
53-3187			RVNAF Aug 71	821st Squadron	
53-3197			RVNAF 1972	821st Squadron	
53-3211			RVNAF1972		
53-7826		May 2, 1972 shotdown by 37mm flak over An Lộc seven survivors out of 10 crew			
53-7830	*Fly United*		RVNAF 1972	821st Squadron	
53-7831		Hit by a Viet Cong rocket while parked in a revetment, date??	RVNAF 1972	821st Squadron	
53-7839	*Black Killer Duck*	March 1, 1973 lost in training accident, one KIA	RVNAF 1971	821st Squadron	
53-7850			RVNAF	821st Squadron	Museum in Ho Chi Minh City
53-7854			Used by VPAF after 1975		
53-7877			to VNAF	821st Squadron	
53-7879			RVNAF Aug 72	821st Squadron	
53-7883			RVNAF	821st Squadron	
53-8121					
53-8145			Used by VPAF after 1975		
53-8148	*Patti's Pride*				

Notes
KIA: Killed In Action: MIA: Missing in Action: RVNAF: Republic of Vietnam Air Force (South Vietnam): SOS: Special Operations Squadron (US); VPAF: Vietnam People's Air Force (Communist)

South Vietnamese air force. First to go were the G models of the 17th SOS which were transferred in August 1971. USAF AC-119G crews became instructors, to train up their allies to fly the gunships, which were the most complex aircraft in their inventory.

The Stingers of the 18th SOS remained on duty for another year and began handing their aircraft over to the South Vietnamese in December 1972, just days before the signing of the Paris peace accords that ended the US presence in South Vietnam.

During the Vietnam conflict, at least nine AC-119s were lost, but only three of the losses were due to enemy action. A USAF AC-119K was hit by 37mm enemy anti-aircraft fire over An Loc at the height of the communist spring offensive in May 1972. A South Vietnamese AC-119K was destroyed by rocket fire in 1972 and another was shot down outside Saigon in April 1975 in the final days of the war. Four USAF and two South Vietnamese operated AC-119s were lost in accidents.

The AC-119 proved to be an effective gunship in a wide range of tactical situations, even if the G model had significant performance limitations. The Shadow and Stinger crews entered gunship folklore, and their call signs lived on in the modern USAF.

LEFT: The Shadow and Stinger proved very effective gunships in Vietnam and their iconic callsigns were passed onto modern day USAF gunships. (USAF)

BELOW: This AC-119K was seen during the final stages of the work up of the Stinger unit, the 18th Special Operations Squadron, prior to its deployment to South Vietnam in October 1969. (USAF)

AC-130A

Birth of the Spectre

ABOVE: An AC-130H Spectre gunship from the 16th Special Operations Squadron conducts a flyover at Arlington National Cemetery during a memorial service for Senior Master Sergeant James Caniford on May 28, 2008. The remains of Sergeant Caniford, a former 16th SOS illuminator operator, were identified more than 30 years after he was listed as missing in action in Vietnam following the shooting down of his AC-130A. (USAF)

After Air Commandos proved the power of the AC-47D in South Vietnam it was not long before the US Air Force started looking for a more capable gunship to take the war to the communists across Southeast Asia.

The obvious solution was to convert the relatively new Lockheed C-130A Hercules transport aircraft into a gunship. It had the range, endurance, and - most importantly - a large cargo hold that could be packed with weapons, ammunition, and night-vision sensors. The aircraft's high wing allowed its weapons to be employed without their fields of fire being impeded.

In the summer of 1966, a USAF study into how more effective night attack aircraft could be provided for the war in Southeast Asia concluded that a better gunship was needed. This in turn led to Project Gunboat that actively sought a replacement for the AC-47D. By November 1966, the Project Gunboat team had selected the C-130 as the successor gunship platform. It was to be equipped with 7.62mm mini guns, 20mm rotating cannons, and advanced night sensors. US Air Force Systems Command then launched an effort to convert a C-130 into a prototype gunship.

A C-130A, serial 54-1626, was selected as the prototype Gunboat and it arrived at Wright-Patterson AFB in Ohio in February 1967 to have its weapons and sensors fitted. Fire power was provided by four GAU-2 7.62mm mini guns fitted above the port undercarriage fairing and four General Electric 20mm M61 Vulcan 20mm Gatling cannons, with six rotating barrels, installed on the port forward and aft fuselage.

RIGHT: The awesome firepower installed in the AC-130 included twin 40mm Bofors cannons, which reached far further than the previous weapons used on early versions of the Spectre gunship. (USAF)

Sensors included a Starlight Scope image intensifier night observation device, a sideways looking infra-red (SLIR) night-vision sensor, flare dispensers, a 1.5 million candlepower AN/AVQ-8 searchlight to illuminate ground targets and a AN/APQ-133 side-looking, beacon tracking radar to identify the transponders operated by friendly ground troops. In a major advance, the aircraft included computerised fire control systems that linked the sensors to the weapons, which allowed the crew to aim the gunships precisely at night. To protect the aircraft, it was fitted with floor cockpit armour and inert fuel tanks so it could take hits from enemy anti-aircraft fire.

The conversion work was complete by June 1967 and the prototype was flown to Eglin AFB in Florida to begin its flight test programme. Although the sensors were early generation technology, they proved highly effective in the tests and a major improvement over anything else in service at the time. The FLIR could detect hot vehicle engines under jungle canopies.

Gunship II

It was decided to send the prototype, now dubbed the Gunship II, to Southeast Asia to see how she performed under combat conditions. The aircraft arrived at Nha Trang Airbase in South Vietnam on September 21, 1967, and three days later it flew its first live mission. The combat evaluation was divided into three phases, with the first segment involving working in defence of US and ARVN bases in the Mekong Delta. Then the aircraft was sent truck hunting along the Ho Chi Minh Trail in Laos. Finally, Gunship II was sent over the Central Highlands, where US troops were locked in combat with North Vietnamese regular forces.

By the end of the evaluation in December 1967, Gunship II had fired 87,720 rounds of 20mm ammunition, 222,800 rounds of 7.62mm ammunition, and dropped 310 flares. In the truck hunting phase, it had detected 94 trucks and destroyed 38. Combat evaluation showed the prototype demonstrated a "three-fold improvement over its predecessor, the AC-47."

The aircraft so impressed the US supreme commander in Vietnam, General William Westmoreland, that he was reluctant to let it be withdrawn from Southeast Asia to be refurbished. In the end, Gunship II returned Stateside for just six-weeks and was back in South Vietnam in February 1968.

Over the next nine months, Gunship II was in the thick of the action across South Vietnam and Laos, flying 246 sorties. A trial deployment to Thailand in February 1968 proved its effectiveness at hunting North Vietnamese supply trucks moving down the Ho Chi Minh Trail in Laos, including sighting 1,000 enemy trucks and destroying 228 of them.

Even before the Gunship II combat evaluation was complete, senior USAF officers were pushing for the conversion of several C-130s into gunships to augment and then replace the AC-47Ds. US Air Force Secretary Harold Brown gave the go ahead in December 1967 to begin converting seven JC-130A aircraft into AC-130A gunships. Ling-Temco-Vought (LTV) Electrosystems, at its Greenville site in Texas, was to carry out the work under a $21m contract.

ABOVE: Daytime photographs of AC-130s in action over Southeast Asia are very rare because of the nocturnal nature of Spectre operations. (USAF)

BELOW: Hercules, serial number 54-1626, was the prototype AC-130 airframe, which was eventually dispatched to Southeast Asia in 1967 to test its firepower in action. Note the incorrect zero in the serial number. (USAF)

AC-130A/E
Powerplant: Four Allison T-56-A-9D turboprops (A model), T56-A-7 (E model)
Wingspan: 40.41m (132ft 7in)
Length: 29.5m (96ft 10in)
Height: 11.73m (38ft 6in)
Max take-off weight: 56,336kg (124,200lb)
Max speed: 611kph (380mph)
Range: 4,023km (2,172nm)
Crew: 11
Armament by Variant:
AC-130A Gunship II: Four × 7.62mmMXU-470/A mini guns, four × 20mm M61A1 cannon
AC-130A Surprise Package: Two × 40mm M2A1 canoon, two × 20mm M61A1 cannon
AC-130E Pave Aegis : Two × 7.62mm MXU-470/A mini guns, two × 20mm M61A1 cannon and one × 40mm M2A1 cannon, one × 105mm M102 howitzer

The aircraft were to be delivered between August and December 1968 to Southeast Asia to stand up a dedicated AC-130A squadron. When the company ran behind schedule, the USAF decide to do the work itself at Wright-Patterson AFB.

These aircraft were dubbed the 'Plain Jane' variant and were essentially like the prototype Gunship II but had some improved systems, including AN/AAD-4 FLIRs, an improved targeting computer and AN/APG-136 moving target indicator radar, which could detect trucks and other vehicles moving at night. This set in train an almost non-stop process of improvement to field new weapons, sensors, and defensive systems on the aircraft.

The monsoon season generally prevented air operations across much of Southeast Asia, but the heavy rainfall also hindered the movement of truck convoys down the Ho Chi Minh Trail, effectively creating a pause in the fighting across much of the region. This window provided the USAF with the opportunity to pull its AC-130s out of the combat theatre to be overhauled and upgraded with new weapons and sensors. A duel developed between the USAF AC-130s and the North Vietnamese anti-aircraft gunners. The gunship crews wanted better sensors and better weapons to allow them to stand-off at safer distances when hunting trucks along the Ho Chi Minh Trail.

The 16th Special Operations Squadron (SOS) stood up on October 31, 1968, at Ubon Royal Thai Air Force Base in Thailand. It initially only controlled the Gunship II prototype, but in a few weeks later the first AC-130A arrived.

In August 1969, work began on an upgraded version of the AC-130A, dubbed the 'Surprise Package', which boasted two M61 20mm cannons and two 40mm Bofors canons, as well as advanced night-vision sensors. These included an AN/ASQ-145 low light television sensor, an AN/AVQ-18 laser rangefinder/designator to guide other strike aircraft to targets, and an AN/APG-17 searchlight. However, when the 40mm cannon was first

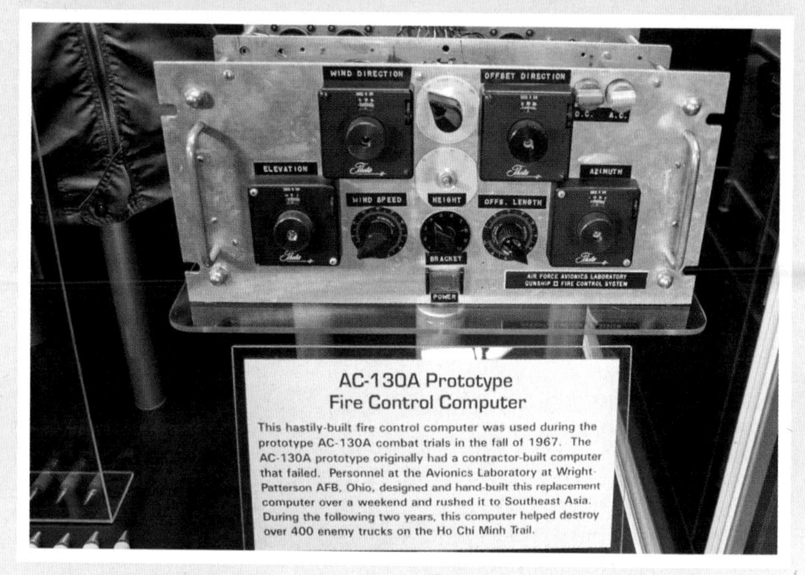
WIND DIRECTION
OFFSET DIRECTION
ELEVATION
AZIMUTH
WIND SPEED
HEIGHT
OFFS. LENGTH
BRACKET
POWER
AIR FORCE AVIONICS LABORATORY
GUNSHIP II FIRE CONTROL SYSTEM
AC-130A Prototype
Fire Control Computer
This hastily-built fire control computer was used during the prototype AC-130A combat trials in the fall of 1967. The AC-130A prototype originally had a contractor-built computer that failed. Personnel at the Avionics Laboratory at Wright-Patterson AFB, Ohio, designed and hand-built this replacement computer over a weekend and rushed it to Southeast Asia. During the following two years, this computer helped destroy over 400 enemy trucks on the Ho Chi Minh Trail.

RIGHT: The electronics used in the AC-130 were cutting edge for their time and paved the way for many of the avionics used in modern combat aircraft. (USAF)

USAF
AH
AF 55 011

BELOW: AC-130A, serial number 55-011, of the 415th Special Operations Training Squadron in 1971. It was the Surprise Package prototype aircraft. (USAF)

test fired on the prototype aircraft, it caused cracks to appear in the wings, prompting a redesign of the gun mountings.

Black Crow

The most innovative additional sensor was a magnetic anomaly detector (MAD) system called the Black Crow (AN/ASD-5). This was a highly sensitive passive device with a phased-array antenna located in the left-front nose radome that could pick up localised deviations in earth's magnetic field and was normally used to detect submerged submarines. The Black Crow system on the AC-130A could accurately detect the unshielded ignition coils of Russian-supplied trucks driven by the North Vietnamese that were hidden under the dense foliage of the jungle canopy along the Ho Chi Minh Trail. It could also detect the signal from a hand-held transmitter that was used by air controllers on the ground to identify and locate specific target types. The system was directly linked into the gunship's targeting computer.

The Surprise Package aircraft arrived in Southeast Asia in December 1969 and a week after arrival it was in action over Laos. Early results were impressive, and orders were placed for the AC-130A Plain Jane variants to be converted to Surprise Package configuration. Nine additional aircraft were also ordered in July 1970 and started to arrive in Thailand in November 1970. These aircraft were refitted and were then assigned the code-name 'Pave Pronto'.

The ultimate Vietnam-era gunship was the AC-130E and it was armed with a 105mm artillery piece that could devastate whole truck convoys with barrages of shells. This was a former US Army weapon that was installed in an AC-130E's rear cabin.

Two prototypes were ordered in April 1970 under the Project Pave Aegis and a year later nine more ordered. These aircraft benefited from the E models improved performance, longer range, enhanced endurance, and

ABOVE: The Pave Pronto configuration aircraft, 56-0490, was nicknamed *Thor*. She was shot down near Pakse in December 1972, with the loss of all 14 crew. (USAF)

LEFT: Crewmen on a Spectre clear away empty cartridges with a shovel after a fire mission. (USAF)

ABOVE: The inside view of the AC-130's twin 40mm Bofors canons. (USAF)

other avionics improvements. These meant the gunship variant could stay on station longer and carry more ammunition.

Gunship specific improvements included a first-generation digital fire control computer, which permitted faster target engagement. Target detection was enhanced by the installation of an improved version of the AN/ASQ-145 low light television and newly developed AN/AAD-7 FLIR. The self-defence capabilities of the aircraft were improved by the AN/ALQ-87 jamming pods mounted on wing pylons and SUU-42 chaff and flare dispensers were also installed on the wings.

The complex sensor and weapons systems installed on the AC-130E resulted in the way the crews worked together being changed dramatically. It had two weapons cabins, one forward with the two 20mm M-61 cannons and two MXU-470 mini guns, and one aft with a 40mm Bofors gun and the 105mm cannon. In between, were the sensor operator's stations. These included operators who monitored the low light television camera, the FLIR sensor, the electronic warfare systems, and night observation devices. This was a new arrangement for the USAF and the crews had to establish slick procedures to rapidly pass intelligence to fire control officers, who selected targets for attack.

Spectre

These improved aircraft were dubbed the Pave Spectre variants but soon they were just known by their callsign 'Spectre'. The name stuck, and eventually this became the official USAF name for the AC-130E/H gunship.

The AC-130E first saw action in February 1972 during the air campaign to counter the spring communist offensive when the AC-130 crews claimed several tank kills.

In 1973, the USAF decided to re-engine the remaining 10 AC-130Es, with Allison T-56-A-15 engines to bring them up to H model configuration, resulting in the fleet being re-designated as AC-13Hs. These aircraft started to arrive in Southeast Asia in early 1973 and saw action over Cambodia and South Vietnam in the run up to the US withdrawal from these countries in April 1975.

During the war in Southeast Asia, the AC-130 was credited with being the USAF's top truck-killing platform, despite only flying a small fraction of the number of sorties flown by fast jets. USAF statistics indicated that AC-130s destroyed five trucks per sortie, compared to two trucks per sortie for the AC-119 and 0.29 trucks per sortie for McDonnell Douglas F-4 Phantoms strike jets.

Crucial to its success was the ability of the AC-130 to loiter for extended periods over Ho Chi Minh Trail and use its night-vision systems to find communist trucks.

The North Vietnamese came to fear the AC-130 and put considerable effort into trying to shoot them down. Six AC-130s were lost to enemy fire, including one to an SA-7 shoulder-launched man-portable surface to air missile (SAM) and one to a radar-guided SA-2 SAM.

The AC-130 was a revolutionary aircraft. It incorporated an impressive array of weapons but perhaps more

BELOW: AC-130A, serial number 54-1625, at Elmendorf Air Force Base in Alaska, in October 1969 en route to Southeast Asia. (USAF)

LOCKHEED MARTIN AC-130 GUNSHIPS OF THE VIETNAM WAR				
Serial	**Name**	**Configuration**	**Loss**	**Notes**
53-3129	*First Lady*	Plain Jane, then Pave Pronto		First production C-130A, preserved USAF Armament Museum, Eglin AFB
54-1623	*Ghost Rider*	Plain Jane, then Pave Pronto		Preserved Aviation History and Technology Center, Marietta, Georgia
54-1625	*War Lord*	Plain Jane, then Pave Pronto	Shot down over Laos April 22, 1970, 10 KIA	
54-1626	*Vulcan Express, Super Spooky*	Gunboat/Gunship II/Pave Spectre Prototype		Preserved National Museum of USAF, Dayton, Ohio
54-1627	*Gomer Grinder*	Plain Jane, then Pave Pronto		
54-1628	*The Exterminator*	Plain Jane, then Pave Pronto		
54-1629	*The Arbitrator*	Plain Jane, then Pave Pronto	Crash landed at Ubon Airbase in Thailand, May 24, 1969, 2 KIA	
54-1630	*Mor's De Caelis, Azreal - Angel of Death*	Plain Jane, then Pave Pronto		Preserved National Museum of USAF, Dayton, Ohio
55-0011	*Night Stalker*	Surprise Package Prototype, Pave Pronto		
55-0014	*Jaws of Death*	Pave Pronto		Preserved Museum of Aviation, Warner Robins AFB, Georgia
55-0029	*Midnight Express*	Pave Pronto		
55-0040	*Orion the Hunter*	Pave Pronto		
55-0043	*Odin*	Pave Pronto	Shot down by SA-7 SAM over the Ashau Valley, South Vietnam on June 18, 1972, 12 KIA	
55-0044	*Prometheus*	Pave Pronto	Shot down by SA-2 SAM over Tchepone, Laos, March 28, 1972, 14 KIA	
55-0046	*Proud Warrior*	Pave Pronto		
56-0469	*Grim Reaper*	Pave Pronto		
56-0471	*Blind Bat*	Pave Pronto		
56-0490	*Thor*	Pave Pronto	Shot down near Pakse, Laos, December 21, 1972, 14 KIA	
56-0509	*Raids Kill um Dead*, then *Ultimate End*	Pave Pronto		On display Hurlburt Field Memorial Air Park , Florida

ABOVE: Pave Pronto variants of the AC-130A featured the Black Crow magnetic anomaly detector which could detect the electrical signals from the ignitions of North Vietnamese trucks under the canopy of the Laotian jungle. (USAF)

ABOVE: Spectre gunners re-load the 105mm howitzer of an AC-130 during a mission over Laos. (USAF)

RIGHT: The USAF acquired 105mm howitzers from the US Army to equip its AC-130s with the ultimate aerial stand-off weapon. (USAF)

importantly it pushed the envelope in terms of fielding advanced night-vision equipment. The image intensifying and thermal imaging sensors used on the AC-130 were far in advance of those used on any other aircraft of the era. Today, this technology is in widespread use on military aircraft and helicopters.

Over the course of the Vietnam War, the AC-130 underwent a process of rapid technological evolution. Often in a matter of months, new weapons and sensors were installed and then deployed back to Southeast

BELOW: Colonel Ron Terry headed up the USAF's AC-130 project office to bring the gunship into service. He flew many of the aircraft's first missions in Southeast Asia and had previously played a key role in the development of the AC-47. (USAF)

LEFT: The 16th Special Operations Squadron remained in Thailand after the ending of US combat operations in August 1973 and helped cover the US withdrawals from Cambodia and South Vietnam in April 1975. (USAF)

Asia to go into action. Today this is known as 'spiral development'. A cadre of USAF gunship experts drove the development of the AC-130. By 1971, Ron Terry, who played such an important part in the development of AC-47, was a colonel and head of the USAF's AC-130 programme office.

By the time the US combat operations in Vietnam formally ended in 1973, the USAF hierarchy decided that the AC-130 had earned its spurs and should remain part of its 'peacetime' order of battle. The then US Air Force Chief of Staff General John Ryan declared: "We intend to keep this capability to deliver a tremendous volume of sustained accurate firepower in the tactical force."

BELOW: USAF AC-130s sported black underside colour schemes throughout the Vietnam conflict to help protect them from detection during night missions. (USAF)

Gunships go to War

USAF Gunships over Southeast Asia 1964 to 1975

ABOVE: An AC-47D Spooky lights up the sky over Saigon during a night mission in 1968. (USAF)

With communist insurgents escalating their attacks across South Vietnam in 1961, US President John F Kennedy ordered the Pentagon to respond. US Army 'Green Beret' special forces soon headed out across the Pacific to begin training and advising the South Vietnamese army or ARVN. By November 1961, the first Air Commandos had arrived at Bien Hoa Airbase outside Saigon to begin supporting the Green Berets and training the South Vietnamese air force.

The initial contingent of 140 Air Commandos took four C-47 Dakotas,

RIGHT: A US Air Force A-1 Sky Raider drops napalm on a Vietcong position, under the direction of O-1 Bird Dog observation aircraft during the early days of the war in South Vietnam. (USAF)

LEFT: In the space of only four years US gunship technology developed rapidly from the basic AC-47D through to the AC-130, which boasted stand-off firepower and advanced night-vision sensors. This AC-130A is seen at Da Nang Airbase in South Vietnam in 1972. (USAF)

eight North American T-28 strike aircraft, and four Douglas B-26B Invader bombers with them to officially launch Operation Farm Gate. The unit was formally titled the 440th Combat Crew Training Squadron to hide its true purpose from the numerous journalists in Saigon covering the escalating war.

Operation Farm Gate crews were officially in South Vietnam to train up their allies but as the whole country was a war zone, they always flew training missions in fully armed aircraft. The USAF personnel were officially just instructors, but invariably when they took off, they ended up dropping bombs or strafing Vietcong-held territory.

This was very much 'on-the-job' training for the South Vietnamese pilots. On many occasions when Green Beret teams were trapped and under threat of being overrun, the Air Commandos would just scramble their T-28s or B-26s to fly to rescue without even waiting for their 'students'. This was typical of the Air Commando ethos, of

BELOW: Air Commando C-47 Goony Birds flew many different missions over South Vietnam, including dropping leaflets to win over the population to the anti-communist cause. (USAF)

finding unconventional solutions to unexpected events.

The next two years saw a continued growth in Air Commando operations across South Vietnam as more US advisors fanned out across the country to try to bolster ARVN resistance to Vietcong infiltration from North Vietnam, via Laos and Cambodia.

More Air Commando squadrons deployed with new aircraft and helicopters to support Green Beret attachments. New roles emerged with C-47s being fitted loudspeakers to broadcast propaganda to civilians and Vietcong insurgents. A squadron of C-123 Provider transport aircraft were dispatched in 1962 to lead Operation Ranch Hand, which was a top-secret mission to spray the jungles of South Vietnam with chemicals to kill the vegetation and deny the Vietcong a hiding place.

The arrival of the first US combat troops in South Vietnam in March 1965 fundamentally changed the nature of the conflict. It was now a conventional war, with the Air Commandos relegated to a supporting role.

ABOVE: Gunship crews adorned their aircraft with nose art and nicknames to highlight their nocturnal role. (USAF)

RIGHT: Gunship crews had to work hard re-loading the thousands of rounds of ammunition required during missions. (USAF)

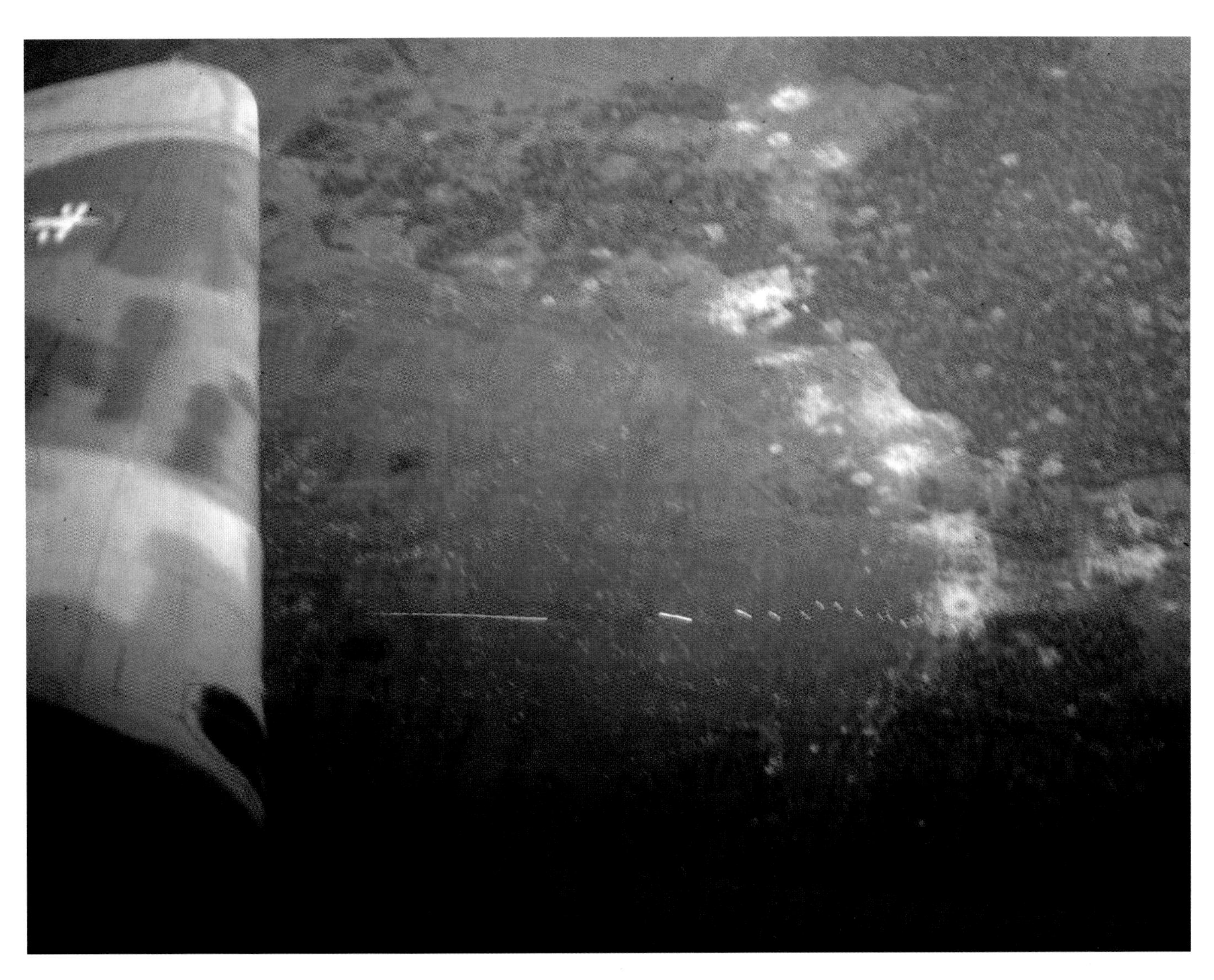

US unconventional warfare forces had to adjust their role and new equipment started to flow to the Air Commando units in Southeast Asia, leading to the formation of wing-sized units in Vietnam and Thailand. These units were eventually renamed as Special Operations wings and squadrons in 1968, along with the remainder of the Air Commando units worldwide.

Genesis

The genesis of the gunship lies in the early days of the Air Commando deployment to South Vietnam in 1962. US Green Berets were fanning out around the country to advise South Vietnamese units in isolated jungle bases. Night after night Vietcong guerrillas would probe the perimeters of these bases, trying to find weaknesses in the defences.

Air Commando officers came up with the idea of putting up one of their C-47 or C-123 transports to circle over the threatened bases to drop a steady stream of flares to illuminate the night. With the shield of darkness removed, the Vietcong invariably withdrew into the jungle. These 'flare ships' dropped some 7,000 flares in 1963 alone.

USAF weapons experts were soon called upon by the Air Commandos to give them more aerial firepower. One idea was to mount sideways-firing mini guns into transport aircraft, which would then circle around an aim point creating a devastating 'cone of fire' to eliminate ground targets. From an altitude of 3,000ft a circling AC-47 could fire hundreds of rounds a second from its three mini guns and put high explosive or incendiary bullets into every square yard of a US football pitch-sized piece of ground. The aircraft's endurance meant they could stay on duty for several hours providing armed overwatch for isolated US and ARVN bases.

The first experimental AC-47s arrived in South Vietnam in December 1964 were in action every night across the country

"Spooky" AC-47 Dragonship

RVN'S #1 Fly By Night Outfit

We Defend: Outposts Hamlets Special Forces Camps Ambush Patrols and any Other TIC

Our 762 Devastates: Rubber Trees Monkeys Sampans Ground Makers Campfires Water Buffalo

4th SPECIAL OPERATIONS SQUADRON

#1 Call Nhatrang EXT 2994 Daily: 1800 - 0600

When You Hurt Enough to Want the Very Best

#2 Don't call second best. Shadow don't know, call Spooky.

ABOVE: A rare daytime fire mission from an AC-47 over South Vietnam is caught on camera. Tracer rounds were used to help crews identify their point of impact. (USAF)

LEFT: AC-47D crews printed calling cards to give to US and allied ground units to big up their capabilities and gently put down their AC-119 rivals. (USAF)

RIGHT: An AC-47 crewmember prepares to throw a flare out of an open fuselage door. These flares helped expose Vietcong night attacks. (USAF)

putting down devastating fire to blunt Vietcong offensives. In one incident in February 1965 a gunship fired 20,500 rounds during a single engagement and reportedly killed 300 Vietcong fighters.

Despite objections from the USAF 'Fighter Mafia', the service's senior leadership gave the gunship project the go ahead and by November, 1965 a squadron of 20 AC-47s was ready to deploy to South Vietnam. The AC-47's firepower proved decisive in numerous battles and soon the USAF was looking at bringing more gunships online. US commanders in Southeast Asia wanted gunships with more firepower and the ability to stand off better from targets so they could strike at enemy positions defended by anti-aircraft artillery or surface-to-air missiles. They wanted to transition the gunship from a defensive weapon into an offensive platform that could take the fight to the main North Vietnamese supply route into the south via Laos, known as the Ho Chi Minh Trail after the North's communist leader.

US military chiefs were convinced that if they could cut off the flow of supplies down the Ho Chi Minh Trail, then communist forces in South Vietnam would be denied the ability to fight.

Laos became the most bombed country on the planet between 1969 and 1972, as US airpower was unleashed against the Ho Chi Minh Trail. The country was divided in

BELOW: US gunship operations were carried out predominately at night to reduce their vulnerability to enemy anti-aircraft fire. (USAF)

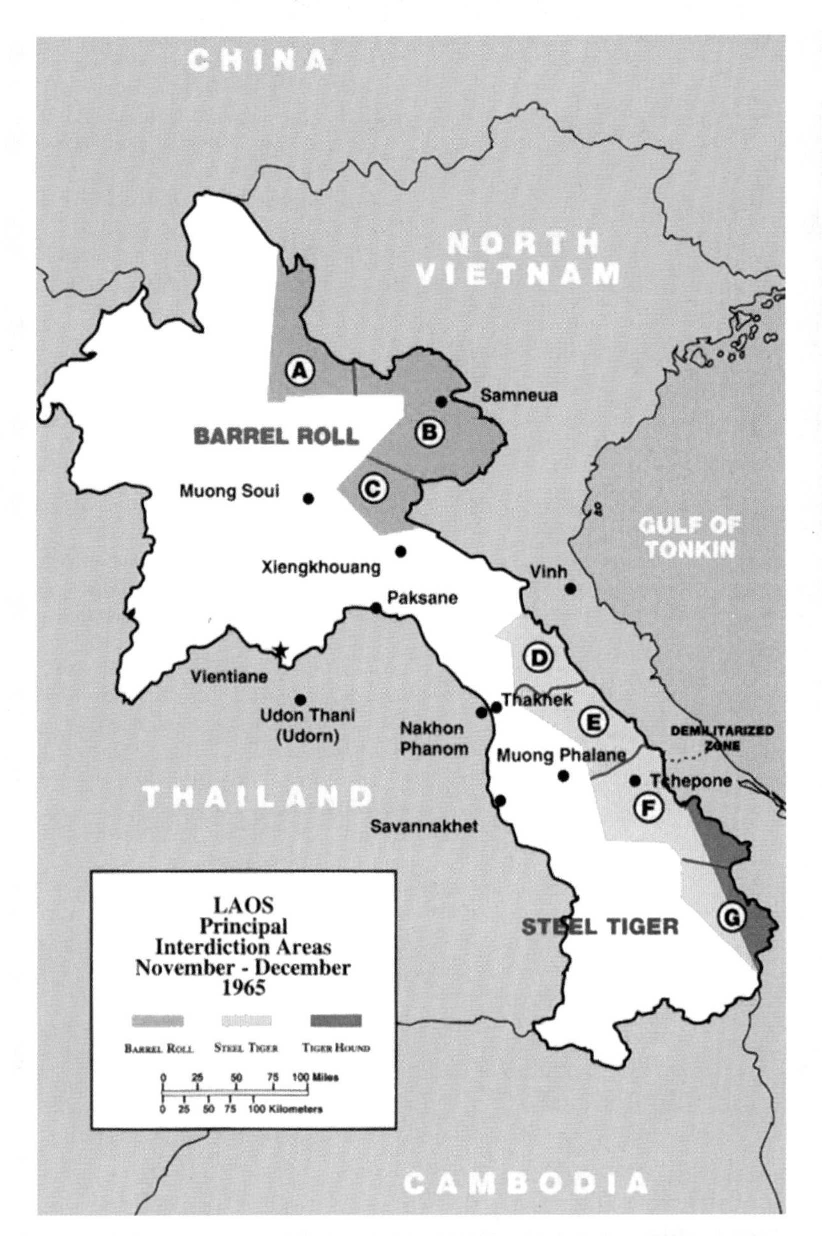

two operational zones, Barrel Roll in the north along the border with North Vietnam, and Steel Tiger in the south of Laos, where its border linked to South Vietnam and Cambodia.

Photographic reconnaissance aircraft would criss-cross Laos in daylight looking for North Vietnamese truck convoys. Fields of acoustic sensors were sewn long the Ho Chi Minh Trail to allow US intelligence operatives in Thailand to monitor the movement of vehicles. US special forces teams were also inserted to watch key stretches of the trail. However, the communists became expert at hiding their trucks from view during daylight, in camouflaged staging areas. Only at night did they begin to move, confident that the Americans would not be able track them in the darkness.

ABOVE: Each day, thousands of North Vietnamese soldiers and porters moved supplies down the Ho Chi Minh Trail on trucks, bicycles, and hand carts. (CENTER OF MILITARY HISTORY, US ARMY)

LEFT: The USAF divided Laos into two main operational zones and tasked gunships to strike at North Vietnamese supply convoys moving through the country. (CENTER OF MILITARY HISTORY, US ARMY)

BELOW: AC-130s of the 16th Special Operations Squadron operated nearly exclusively from US air bases in Thailand against targets along the Ho Chi Minh Trail in Laos. (USAF)

ABOVE: AC-130E, serial number, 69-6573, of the 16th SOS showing the results of a near hit from a man-portable SA-7 surface-to-air missile in May, 1972. The warhead sprayed fragments through the back of this AC-130 and seriously wounded Staff Sergeant Ken Felty, who subsequently took this photo. (USAF)

Boxcar Interim

USAF commanders were convinced that gunships were the answer to closing the Ho Chi Minh Trail. The ambition was to create the ultimate gunship by arming a Lockheed C-130 Hercules transport aircraft, but the project was delayed so, as an interim, the USAF turned to the Fairchild C-119G Flying Boxcar. In a crash programme, four mini guns and early generation night-vision systems were fitted and the Shadow, as they were codenamed, deployed to South Vietnam in December 1968. A year later they were joined by the AC-119K Stinger, which boasted four mini guns and two 20mm cannon. The more powerful AC-119K had the stand-off firepower to be able to begin hunting supply trucks moving down the Ho Chi Minh Trail.

The next generation gunship, the AC-130 took longer to get into the fight in significant numbers. It boasted even more firepower – four mini guns and four 20mm cannon. Prototype AC-130s visited South Vietnam in 1967 and 1968. By the end of 1968, AC-130s were permanently deployed to Ubon Royal Thai Air Force Base in Thailand to participate in the US interdiction campaign to cut the Ho Chi Minh trail in Laos. This became the main effort of the AC-130 gunship force and a sizable part of the AC-119K force, with the remaining AC-47Ds and AC-119G being focused on operations within South Vietnam.

The Barrel Roll and Steel Tiger zones were divided into engagement boxes by the USAF, which covered the main communist supply routes through the mountainous valleys of Laos. In daytime, USAF strike jets were directed to targets by observation aircraft that patrolled over the engagement boxes.

Night after night, the USAF gunships would head out over Laos to stalk communist trucks. This was the iconic mission of the AC-130 and the AC-119K during the Southeast Asia conflict. Their long endurance meant gunship crews could patrol the same engagement box for up to seven or eight hours at a time, enabling their sensor operators to get to know their target area. If the communist truck drivers made mistakes, switching on their engines, or failing to camouflage them properly, then the gunships would strike.

In January 1969 alone, the four AC-130As in Thailand accounted for 28% of all truck kill claims in Laos. By the time the US air combat mission in Southeast Asia was concluded in August 1973, the AC-130 was credited as the top truck killer in the theatre, with more than 10,600 claimed destroyed.

Phantom Cover

As the gunships wrought havoc on the Ho Chi Minh Trail the communists bolstered their air defences by an estimated 400%, positioning anti-aircraft guns and then surface-to-air missiles to defend the vital supply route from

RIGHT: Soviet supplied SA-7 surface-to-air missiles provided a major threat to gunships after 1972, bringing down one USAF AC-130A and several South Vietnamese gunships. (USAF)

ABOVE: The AC-130H variant entered service with 16th Special Operations Squadron at Ubon Royal Thai Air Force Base in the spring of 1973. (USAF)

BELOW LEFT: US AC-130H gunships patrolled over the Cambodian capital Phnom Penh in April 1975 during the evacuation of the US embassy before the fall of the city to the Khmer Rouge. (USAF)

BELOW RIGHT: The AC-130 was credited with being the most effective 'truck killing' aircraft of the war in Southeast Asia. (CENTER OF MILITARY HISTORY, US ARMY)

1969. One of the AC-130s was badly damaged by enemy fire and crashed while attempting to land at its home base. To counter the communist air defences, the gunships were teamed with F-4 Phantom strike jets which flew ahead of the AC-130s to neutralise the enemy flak guns or missile launchers. The North Vietnamese responded by fielding SA-2 radar guided missiles, which claimed an AC-130 in May 1972.

In February 1972, the first AC-130A armed with a 105mm artillery piece appeared as the communists launched a major offensive against the South. This was a rare conventional assault involving the deployment of tanks, heavy artillery and other heavy weapons. US President Richard Nixon ordered US airpower to be massed to defeat the communist invasion. This saw the remaining AC-130 and AC-119K gunships in Southeast Asia to be re-directed from the Ho Chi Minh Trail to hit the North Vietnamese army division advancing in the south. Scores of tanks, guns, and other weapons were knocked out. communist air defences remained strong and one AC-130A was shot down by an SA-7 missile with the loss of 12 crew members.

By now, President Nixon was moving to end the US presence in South Vietnam to put a line under what had become America's most unpopular war. The 16th SOS remained in Thailand during this period flying some of final offensive operations of the conflict. The US and North Vietnamese did a deal

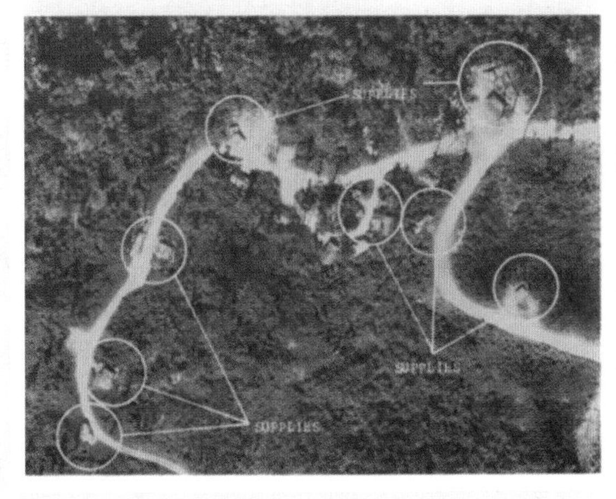

Gunship Medal of Honor

On February 24, 1969, a 3rd Special Operation Squadron AC-47D, call sign 'Spooky 71', serial 43-48770, was in action over South Vietnam when it was hit by enemy mortar fire. The aircraft was later found to have more than 3,500 holes in its wings and fuselage. As the pilots struggled to control the stricken aircraft Airman First Class John Levitow made a decisive intervention. He was awarded the Medal of Honor for his bravery, becoming the the first enlisted serviceman in the US Air Force to receive the American military's highest honour. To date, he is the only gunship crewman to be recognised for this level of bravery in combat. His citation says it all:

"For conspicuous gallantry and intrepidity in action at the risk of his life above and beyond the call of duty. Sergeant John Levitow (then Airman First Class), US Air Force, distinguished himself by exceptional heroism while assigned as a loadmaster aboard an AC-47 aircraft flying a night mission in support of Long Binh army post.

Levitow's aircraft was struck by a hostile mortar round. The resulting explosion ripped a hole two feet in diameter through the wing and fragments made over 3,500 holes in the fuselage. All occupants of the cargo compartment were wounded and helplessly slammed against the floor and fuselage. The explosion tore an activated flare from the grasp of a crew member who had been launching flares to provide illumination for army ground troops engaged in combat. Levitow, though stunned by the concussion of the blast and suffering from over 40 fragment wounds in his back and legs, staggered to his feet and turned to assist the man nearest to him who had been knocked down and was bleeding heavily.

As he was moving his wounded comrade forward and away from the opened cargo compartment door, he saw the smoking flare ahead of him in the aisle. Realizing the danger involved and completely disregarding his own wounds, Levitow started toward the burning flare. The aircraft was partially out of control and the flare was rolling wildly from side to side. Levitow struggled forward despite the loss of blood from his many wounds and the partial loss of feeling in his right leg. Unable to grasp the rolling flare with his hands, he threw himself bodily upon the burning flare.

Hugging the deadly device to his body, he dragged himself back to the rear of the aircraft and hurled the flare through the open cargo door. At that instant, the flare separated and ignited in the air, but clear of the aircraft. Levitow, by his selfless and heroic actions, saved the aircraft and its entire crew from certain death and destruction. Levitow's gallantry, his profound concern for his fellow men, at the risk of his life above and beyond the call of duty, are in keeping with the highest traditions of the US Air Force and reflect great credit upon himself and the armed forces of his country."

to end their conflict in January 1973 but fighting continued in Laos and Cambodia. AC-130 strikes continued in Laos up to April 1973 when the final US air missions were flown.

US air support for the anti-communist regime in Cambodia continued for many more months and the AC-130s were in the forefront of these missions, flying close air support for government troops under attack from Khmer Rouge forces. The US Congress finally pulled the plug on American military support in August 1973, but the gunship crews of 16th SOS remained on standby at Korat Royal Thai Air Force Base in Thailand.

A strong contingent of USAF remained in Thailand, ready to

RIGHT: AC-47D gunship, serial number 43-49770, flying under the callsign 'Spooky 71', at Bien Hoa Air Base, in South Vietnam on February 24, 1969. After the mission John Levitow was awarded the Medal of Honor. (USAF)

BELOW: Gunships at Bien Hoa Air Base were protected from Vietcong mortar and rocket attacks by revetments. (USAF)

LEFT: Airman First Class John Levitow before the famous mission in February 1969 on which he won the Medal of Honor, America's highest award for gallantry. (USAF)

intervene across Southeast Asia if the communists breached the peace agreements that ended the conflict. However, this veiled threat lost its impact in August 1974 when President Nixon resigned under threat of impeachment by Congress after the Watergate scandal.

In the spring of 1975, communist forces launched all out assaults in Cambodia and South Vietnam. The US Congress vetoed attempts by the new US President Gerald Ford to provide more military aid to both countries. It was now a matter of time before Phnom Penh and Saigon fell. During April, the US military launched operations to evacuate US citizens and local people associated with Americans from the two cities. USAF airpower in Thailand flew air cover for these operations and in the run up to the withdrawal from Saigon, AC-130s patrolled over the city.

The Thai-based USAF aviators had one last mission on May 14, 1975, to rescue the crew of a US freighter that had strayed into Cambodian waters. Sikorsky HH-53C 'Jolly Green Giants' and CH-53 Sea Stallion helicopters landed a rescue force while AC-130s provided overwatch and fire support. They met furious resistance. Fifteen US troops were killed, four helicopters were lost to enemy fire, and nine were damaged.

This was the final gunship action of America's war in Southeast Asia and within months the 16th SOS moved back to the continental United States and took up home at Hulburt Field in Florida.

BELOW: 'Spooky 71' was peppered with multiple shrapnel hits including this one in a wing, which was more than two feet across. (USAF)

STOL Gunships

Project Credible Chase

ABOVE: The AU-23 Peacemaker gunship was meant to be a low-cost, low-tech solution to interdiction communist supply routes into South Vietnam. (SAN DIEGO AIR AND SPACE MUSEUM ARCHIVE)

RIGHT: A rival solution based on the AU-24A Helio Stallion was tested during live trials in South Vietnam. (SAN DIEGO AIR AND SPACE MUSEUM ARCHIVE)

As the US withdrawal from South Vietnam gathered momentum, the Pentagon began looking at ways to boost Saigon's airpower to hold the communists at bay. A key requirement was to find a way to strike at North Vietnamese supply routes in border regions to prevent a buildup of communist forces in the South.

One idea was to set up small detachments of short take-off and landing (STOL) gunships that could be based in remote jungle air strips to rapidly strike at any communist truck convoys that were spotted. These would take the place of the big USAF gunships based at airbases in Thailand.

Project Credible Chase was launched in May 1971 by the USAF, and it was aimed at providing the Republic of Vietnam Air Force (RVNAF) with a new family of gunships. Two commercial aircraft were selected for testing: the Fairchild PC-6 Porter and the Helio HST-550 Stallion.

The Porter gunship, designated AU-23 Peacemaker by the USAF, was fitted with a side-firing 20mm M197 electric cannon, four wing pylons and a centre fuselage station for external ordnance. The Helio Stallion gunship, designated the AU-24 by the USAF, was equipped with an M197 cannon mounted in the left cargo door. It also had five underwing and fuselage hardpoints for bombs and rockets.

A combat evaluation, dubbed Pave Coin, was carried out in South Vietnam in June and July 1971, using a leased aircraft. USAF crews flew 94 sorties and RVNAF crews flew a further 85. More than 8,000 rounds of 20mm ammunition were fired. This led to 15 AU-23A and 18 AU-24s being ordered. A further operational evaluation was carried in February 1972. Despite the aircraft being in production, the USAF and RVNAF did not think they were very effective, and the South Vietnamese wanted to order more Northrop F-5 Freedom Fighter strike jets. The project was cancelled, and the aircraft were sent to the famous 'boneyard' storage site at Davis-Monthan AFB in Arizona.

AU-23 PEACEMAKER
Powerplant: Single Garrett TPE-331-1-101F turboprop engine
Wingspan: 49ft 8in (15.14m)
Length: 36ft 10in (11.23m)
Height: 14ft 4in (4.37m)
Gross weight: 6,100lb (2,767kg)
Max speed: 274kph (170 mph)
Combat Range: 323km (175nm)
Crew: Three (pilot, co-pilot, gunner)
Capacity: Six passengers
Armament:
Single XM197 20mm cannon, door-mounted
XM93 7.62mm mini gun
Five underwing plyons for assorted guns and rockets

The AU-23s were eventually sold to the Thai air force, who went on to order 20 more of them for operations in the country's remote border regions. Fifteen of the AU-24s were delivered to the Khmer Air Force (KAF) in Cambodia by November 1972, under Project Fly Catcher. Over the next two and half years they saw action against Khmer Rouge forces.

Communist guerrillas dominated the countryside and Cambodian government forces used their AU-24 and Douglas AC-47D Spooky gunships to escort road convoys and supply flotillas on the Mekong River. The aircraft reportedly proved effective, but US support was starting to dry up and their operations were limited by a lack of ammunition. US advisers dubbed the AU-24As the 'Mean Green Fighting Machine'.

In the final months of the Cambodian war, the KAF employed their AU-24A mini-gunships in night bombing operations against entrenched Khmer Rouge 107mm rocket launcher positions that ringed the capital city. It was only a matter of time until the city fell. US helicopters evacuated the American embassy staff on April 12, 1975.

Four days later the Khmer Rouge surged into the city and the remains of the KAF fled to Thailand in their surviving operational aircraft, including three AU-24As. Nine of the gunships were abandoned. The Khmer Rouge got a couple of them in flying condition, and they were taken over by the country's new government in 1979 after the defeat of the brutal communist regime. At least one aircraft served on until 1993.

AU-24 STALLION
Powerplant: Single Pratt & Whitney Canada PT6A-27 turboprop engine
Wingspan: 12.50m (41ft)
Length: 12.07m (39ft 7in)
Height: 2.82m (9ft 3in)
Max take-off weight: 2,313kg (5,100lb)
Max speed: 348kph (216mph)
Range: 1,032km (557nm)
Crew: One
Capacity: Nine passengers
Armament:
Single M197 three-barrel 20 × 102mm rotary cannon mounted in the left cargo door
Five underwing plyons for assorted guns and rockets

LEFT: The AU-23 sported door mounted XM197 20mm cannons from its rear cabin. (SAN DIEGO AIR AND SPACE MUSEUM ARCHIVE)

BELOW: Eventually, Thailand bought several of the unwanted AU-23s from the USAF and operated them from remote jungle airstrips. (Z3144228)

Allied Gunships

South Vietnamese, Laotian and Khmer Gunship operations

ABOVE: The last ever South Vietnamese AC-119K mission was flown on the morning of April 29, 1975, in a doomed bid to protect Than Son Nhut Airbase from the final communist assault on Saigon. The aircraft was shot down by a surface-to-air missile. (USAF)

By 1969 America was tired of its war in Southeast Asia and wanted to bring its troops home. US President Richard Nixon promised 'peace with honour' and opened negotiations with the North Vietnamese to end the war.

A key part of his policy was dubbed 'Vietnamization. This involved handing over the fight to America's South Vietnamese allies and withdrawing US combat forces. The US taxpayer would fund the war, as well as providing specialist support, but American GIs would not be fighting and dying.

As the US troop withdrawal gathered momentum, the USAF gunship force in South Vietnam took a leading role in helping the Republic of Vietnam Air Force

RIGHT: Most of the remaining AC-47Ds were handed over to the South Vietnamese, Cambodian and Laotian air forces as the US retreated from Southeast Asia from 1969 to 1975. (USAF)

LEFT: South Vietnamese AC-47D gunship crews proved highly skilled and determined. The aircraft's rugged design and simple construction made it ideal for US allies to operate. (USAF)

(RVNAF), sometimes referred to as the Vietnam Air Force or VNAF, expand its fighting power. Eventually almost all the surviving USAF Douglas AC-47Ds Spooky and Fairchild AC-119G/K Shadow/Stinger gunships would be transferred to the South Vietnamese under what was dubbed the Military Assistance Program, or MAP.

USAF crew ran conversion courses to allow their allies to fly their new aircraft and the long-term logistic support was looked after by the Pentagon, either by attached USAF advisors or civilian contractors.

The first gunships to be transferred were the AC-47Ds and by the end of 1969 all had been handed over to the RVNAF. The AC-119Gs followed in August 1971 and then the AC-119Ks were transferred in late 1972.

In the final years of the conflict, the South Vietnamese gunship crews proved very effective, but the war was changing and soon their gunships found themselves outclassed. By the time of the final communist offensive in the spring of 1975, the RVNAF gunships were grouped in three main units. The 817th Attack Squadron at Nha Trang Air Base operated the remaining AC-47Ds, while the 819th and 821st Attack Squadrons at Tan Son Nhut Air Base operated the AC-119G/Ks.

At the same time, the USAF handed 13 AC-47s to the Royal Laotian Air Force and 14 eventually found their way to the Khmer Air Force in Cambodia, via Laos. They saw action until their countries fell to the communists in the spring of 1975.

As North Vietnamese troops surged towards Saigon in April 1975, the

BELOW: Udon airbase in northern Thailand was the hub of covert US air operations in support of anti-communist forces in Laos. (USAF)

ABOVE: Than Son Nhut Airbase outside Saigon was ravaged by North Vietnamese rocket fire on the morning of April 29, 1975, prompting what was left of the South Vietnamese air force and its remaining gunships to flee to Thailand. (SAN DIEGO AIR AND SPACE MUSEUM ARCHIVE)

RIGHT: The US government transferred the unused AU-23 Stallion gunships to the Khmer air force in 1973 and they saw action against the Khmer Rouge insurgents until the fall of Phnom Penh in April 1975. (USAF)

RVNAF's gunships found themselves having to face highly effective air defences. It was just too dangerous for them to operate in their old way. The days of the RVNAF gunships and their country were numbered.

In the early hours of April 29, communist divisions were on the outskirts of Saigon and spearhead troops were on the perimeter wire of Tan Son Nhut Air Base, home of the last operational RVNAF gunships.

At least one AC-119 was aloft most of the night expending flares and ordnance on the advancing enemy. It landed, refuelled, rearmed, and took off again at about daybreak to resume the fight to protect their base.

US military personnel running the evacuation operation at the air base recalled watching the single AC-119 as it continued to fire on the North Vietnamese troops just off the east end of Tan Son Nhut's runway. At about 0700, the gunship was also hit by an SA-7 man-portable surface-to-air missile. It broke up and plummeted to earth in flames.

"The pilot was orbiting in an AC-119 gunship over the base at 7,000 feet, desperately trying to locate the source of the rocket fire [against the airbase]," recalled a former RVNAF officer. "He requested permission to drop to 4,000 feet to get a better fix on the enemy location. I could hear the roar of the AC-119 but could not see the aircraft because the pilot was operating without lights. As dawn turned the sky grey, the AC-119, a bulky, black transport with guns mounted along the port side of the fuselage, swept into view, and laid down a sheet of 7.62mm fire on the enemy position. It was the final act of bravery I saw in the battle to save my country."

The officer watched as an SA-7 shoulder-fired missile sailed wide of the attacking gunship. "Then a second missile appeared, its exhaust tracing a crooked line as the SA-7 adjusted its course to follow its target," he said. "It struck the airplane's right engine. As the airplane dove, the right wing

caught fire. A crewman baled out, but his chute got tangled in the tail as the aircraft started to break apart. Flames billowed behind the gunship. It rolled inverted and made three-quarters of a turn before slamming into the ground."

Exodus

The game was up and the remaining RVNAF crews at Tan Son Nhut and other airbases decided it was time to save themselves and their families. Around Saigon and the Mekong Delta, aircraft and helicopters took off for safety. The helicopters headed out to sea to find refuge with the US Navy fleet in the South China Sea and the fixed wing aircraft headed east to Thailand.

By the end of April 29, 165 RVNAF aircraft including three AC-119s had landed at the giant USAF air base at U-Tapao.

The victorious North Vietnamese claimed to have captured 877 RVNAF aircraft and helicopters, including 36 fixed wing gunships.

A similar fate befell the gunships operated by the Laotian and Cambodian air forces. When the Cambodian capital Phenom Penh fell to the Khmer Rouge on April 12, the surviving 97 Khmer air force aircraft took to the skies and headed to safety in Thailand.

The pro-US regime in Laos held out for another month before communist Pathet Lao entered the capital, Vientiane. With hours to spare the remaining Laotian air force aircraft also headed to Thailand.

US and Thai air force commanders now had to ponder what to do with this collection of assorted aircraft, including several gunships, which had sought sanctuary on their air bases. Both countries claimed ownership. The US said MAP aircraft belonged to US taxpayer and the Thais claimed them as well. In the end, it was decided that the Royal Thai Air Force would take over some of the AC-47s and AU-23s. The Americans collected the rest. Several gunships eventually ended up in the United States and some ended up in frontline service in the Philippines air force.

Today there are no original AC-47s and AC-119s in museums in the United States. Fittingly, the last surviving AC-119 is in Ho Chi Minh City, as Saigon is now called by its communist rulers.

ABOVE: A South Vietnamese F-5 Freedom Fighter arrives at U-Tapao air base in Thailand on the morning of April 29, 1975, as part of the escape from Saigon. (USAF)

LEFT: 165 RVNAF aircraft had landed at the giant USAF air base at U-Tapao in Thailand on the morning of April 29, 1975, as part of the escape from Saigon. (USAF)

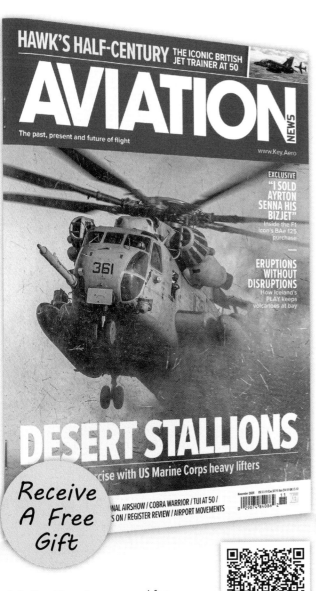

AC-130H Spectre

The Classic Gunship

ABOVE: The AC-130H Spectre was the workhorse of the USAF gunship force during the 1980s and 1990s as American troops fought bushfire wars around Central America, the Middle East, and Africa. They were provided with chaff and flare dispensers to decoy away surface-to-air missiles. (USAF)

In the final months of 1975, the United States Air Force withdrew its remaining aircraft and units from Thailand. America was turning its back on the war in Southeast Asia.

At the height of the Vietnam conflict, the Lockheed AC-130 Spectre gunship established a fearsome reputation for bringing devastating firepower to bear with pinpoint accuracy. Consequently, the USAF leadership wanted to keep the AC-130 in its order of battle, but it was not sure where it sat in its plans for future air warfare.

USAF special operations forces, including the active duty gunship units, were concentrated under the control of Tactical Air Command (TAC).

The 1st Special Operations Wing (SOW) had moved from South Vietnam to Hurlburt Field in the northwest of Florida, and it took the 10 remaining AC-130H gunships of the 16th Special Operations Squadron (SOS) under its command. Nearby at Duke Field, the 711th SOS, of the 919th Special Operations Group, was formed out of a USAF Reserve C-130 transport unit to begin operating the surviving 10 AC-130A. This unit was initially bolstered with

RIGHT: AC-130H crews continued the traditions started in the Southeast Asia conflict of painting nose art on their aircraft and giving them supernaturally themed names. (JIM YOUNG)

many veterans from the Southeast Asia war who wanted to remain involved in gunship operations, via reserve service. Although the AC-130A was not as capable as its H model cousin, the 711th SOS personnel brought a great deal of experience to the fight. This was the structure of the gunship force for the next 20 years, when the new AC-130U variants were brought into service in a new active duty squadron.

During the late 1970s and early 1980s, the USAF's fleet of special operations aircraft received few upgrades and improvements. The aircraft were not considered central to USAF war plans in Europe to defend NATO against the huge Soviet tank threat. Thick Soviet air defences in Central Europe made it very difficult to image that the 'slow and high flying' AC-130 would be able to operate safely. Instability in the Middle East and Central America looked like more permissive theatres for the AC-130 to operate in.

In 1979, US President Jimmy Carter announced the formation of the Rapid Deployment Force (RDF) to spearhead any US intervention in the Middle East in response to Soviet interference. The need to rapidly move US forces into the region saw the 1st SOW move to the fore. Its leaders were ahead of the curve and were already thinking how they could be relevant to the new strategic environment.

When the AC-130s returned from Southeast Asia, plans were put in place to make them ready for global employment. The initial enhancement was the installation of in-flight refuelling so the gunships could deploy from their home bases in Florida, direct to operational theatres without having to land to refuel. This was a potential game changer, allowing aerial firepower to be provided for small teams of special forces or paratroopers delivered at short notice into war zones around the world. AC-130s could fly alongside transport aircraft carrying air assault forces. Air-to-air refuelling also allowed AC-130s to 'top up their tanks' during combat missions, extending their time on station considerably. Mission times of 10 to 15 hours now became routine in AC-130 operations.

This modification involved installing a receptacle just behind the cockpit, on the roof of the forward fuselage, which was able to take on fuel from the flying boom of the USAF Boeing KC-135 Stratotanker and McDonnell Douglas KC-10 Extender tanker aircraft. As well as the receptacle, additional piping needed to be installed to move the fuel down into the AC-130's fuel tanks.

After the first aircraft were modified, a demonstration mission was planned and flown from Hurlburt Field, nonstop, to conduct a two-hour live-fire mission over Empire Firing Range in the Republic of Panama, then return home. This 13-hour mission, with two in-flight refuelling linkups from KC-135 tankers proved the validity of flying long-range missions outside the

AC-130H SPECTRE
Powerplant: Four Allison T56-A-15 turboprop engines
Wingspan: 40.4m (132ft 7in)
Length: 29.8m (97ft 9in)
Height: 11.7m (38ft 6in)
Max take-off weight: 69,750kg (155,000lb)
Speed: 482kph (300mph)
Range: 2,407km (1,300nm); unlimited with air refuelling
Crew: 13
Armament:
Two × 7.62mm MXU-470/A mini guns, two × 20mm M61A cannon and two × 40mm M2A1 cannon or single M102 105mm howitzer

LEFT: TheAC-130H's twin 7.62mm mini guns were positioned just ahead of the starboard undercarriage bay. (GREG GOEBELS)

BELOW: The 16th Special Operations Squadron operated all versions of AC-130 Spectre family from 1968 to 2015, when its last H model was retired. (USAF)

RIGHT: The AC-130H was armed with a 105mm howitzer to give the gunship devastating stand-off firepower. (CLEMENS VASTERS)

continental United States to attack targets then return to home base without intermediate stops.

New time aloft and nonstop distance records were subsequently set by a 16th SOS when a two-ship AC-130H formation flight departed Hurlburt Field on November 13, 1979, and landed on November 15, at Andersen Air Force Base on Guam, 13,300km, and 29 hours 43 minutes nonstop, refuelling four times in-flight. Tanker support for the Guam deployment was provided by KC-135 crews from the 305th Air Refueling Wing from Grissom AFB in Indiana.

As a result of combat experience during the Iran hostage rescue mission in 1980 and Grenada in 1983, a major reorganisation of the US special forces was ordered. In 1985 US Special Operations Command (USSOCOM) was stood up and it had its own air component, which controlled all special operations aircraft and aviation support units. This was at first dubbed the 23rd Air Force but in 1990 it was retitled Air Force Special Operations Command or AFSOC.

BELOW: To keep up its rate of fire, an AC-130H's cargo cabin was full of ammunition racks. (USAF)

One of the first moves to bolster the gunship fleet was a major upgrade to the AC-130H force. As a result of this effort, in December 1986 Lockheed was awarded a contract to modify the aircraft under the Special Operations Force Improvements (SOFI) package. This was subsequently expanded to include a wide range of new capabilities that would make the AC-130 a very potent weapon system for another 15 years.

At the heart of the SOFI upgrade was the complete replacement of many of the AC-130H's 1960s-era electrical and avionics components to improve reliability and maintainability. These included new core avionics, computers, navigation systems, air surveillance/weather radar, and cockpit displays.

ABOVE: A Spectre on patrol. By the 1980s, USAF AC-130s sported grey colour schemes to replace the Vietnam-era black under surface colour schemes. (USAF)

LEFT: A maintenance engineer preps an AC-130H for a mission. The aircraft was very much an analogue machine with switches and dials, rather than electronic displays. (USAF)

ABOVE: In the 21st century, the AC-130H underwent improvements to its defensive systems and communications to enable it to continue to be relevant in the 'Global War on Terror'. (USAF)

By the late 1980s, the AC-130 fleet was plagued by unreliability and major components needed to be changed after around 100 hours of flight. After SOFI, components only had to be changed after between 1,500 and 2,000 hours of flight. Overall availability rose by 90%, according to USAF data.

Fighter Input

A second round of SOFI upgrades included a new head-up display (HUD) from the F-16 fighter, video display systems, enhanced gun sights, new secure communications, new electronic warfare systems, GPS navigation, new forward looking infra-red (FLIR) and targeting systems. Few of the improvements could be seen from outside the aircraft, except for the new high resolution FLIR, which was moved to a turret under the aircraft's nose from the port undercarriage sponson. There were also numerous additional radio antenna on the aircraft.

Progress on this upgrade was initially very slow and the first aircraft were still undergoing flight testing in 1989. The first example, 69-6568, was only delivered in July 1990 after being partially converted to the new configuration, but it was lost in action over Kuwait in January 1991. It took another two and a half years for all the remaining nine AC-130s to be converted fully to the new configuration.

A senior USAF gunship commander described the progress on the SOFI upgrade at the turn of the 1990s.

RIGHT: Gunners bring an AC-130H's 105mm howitzer to bear during a night mission. (USAF)

LOCKHEED AC-130E/H SPECTRE GUNSHIPS				
Serial	**Name**	**Configuration**	**Loss**	**Notes**
69-6567	*Ghostrider*			
69-6568	*Nightstalker*	first SOFI conversion, 1987-89	Callsign Spirit 03 lost to a SAM, Khafji, Kuwait, January 31, 1991. 14 KIA	
69-6569	*Excalibur, Fatal Attraction*			Last AC-130H to be retired May 27, 2015
69-6570	*The Hussy*	3rd Pave Spectre, May 72		
69-6571	*Destroyer,* then *Bad Company*	2nd Pave Spectre, May 72	Shot down over Laos, March 30, 1972. All crew rescued	
69-6572	*Grave Digger*	Pave Spectre Prototype, December 1971		On display at Cannon AFB, New Mexico
69-6573	*Heavy Metal*			
69-6574	*Iron Maiden*			
69-6575	*Wicked Wanda*			On display Hurlburt Field Memorial Air Park , Florida
69-6576	*Predator, Bad Company, Widow Maker,* then *Hellraiser*		Callsign Jockey 14, lost on March 15, 1994 over the Indian Ocean off the coast of Kenya. 8 KIA	
69-6577	*Death Angel*			

"While planning Operation Just Cause, we had also been flying test missions on the Special Operations Forces Improvement (SOFI) modification to the AC-130H," he said. "With an F-16 HUD, digital fire control, ring-laser gyros, GPS, advanced navigation algorithms, and better sensors, the AC-130H was becoming a modern weapon system. Although it was fielded too late for Operation Desert Storm, the SOFI mod would prove crucial for all contingencies to follow."

"Defensive improvements were also long overdue," he said. "The antiquated flare system carried by [the AC-130 lost in the 1991 Gulf War] Spirit 03 was useless against later-generation, man-portable surface-to-air missiles (SAMs)". In the years following Desert Storm, modifications included modern chaff and flare dispensers, infrared missile-launch warning, and modern electronic countermeasures."

Survivability of the aircraft was now a top priority because of the proliferation of heat seeking man-portable surface-to-air missiles, known as 'manpads', as well as longer range radar guided surface-to-air missiles. This resulted in the Spectres being one of the first USAF C-130s to field AAR-44 radar and warning receivers to alert the crew to threats. Automated chaff and flare dispensers were positioned around the aircraft's hull. An improved APR-36 and ALT-32 jamming system was also installed to defeat radar guided missiles and anti-aircraft guns.

In 1996, a further upgrade of the AC-130H's electronic warfare system was launched with the installation of AN/ALQ-172(V)3 jammers. This was a fuselage mounted system, which replaced the old wing

BELOW: After over three decades with Hurlburt Field as its home station, the AC-130Hs of the 16th Special Operations Squadron relocated to Cannon Air Force Base, New Mexico in 2009. (USAF)

ABOVE: In the years before the retirement of the last AC-130H in 2015, the type received many upgrades to its defences and communications fit. (USAF)

mounted AN/ALQ-131 jamming pods. The system's distinctive antenna pods were positioned just behind the cockpit.

The AC-130H continued to serve into the 21st century with 16th SOS but the pace of upgrade activity slowed as investment was directed toward a new generation of gunships. One major upgrade during the 'Global War on Terror' after 2001 was the installation of remote viewing devices so crews could stream 'live' video to special forces teams on the ground. These remote viewing devices were soon known as Rover terminals, and they transformed how AC-130s operated.

During the 1980s, the newly formed USSOCOM began to look at how to modernise its aging fleet of gunships. The development of the aircraft that eventually became the AC-130U was launched in 1985 and Rockwell was contracted to build 11 new aircraft two years later.

This started the clock ticking on the aging AC-130As flown by the reservists of the 711th SOS. They were some of the last A model C-130 airframes in USAF service, so it was not a surprise that they needed replacing. The first four AC-130As were retired in 1994 and the rest were used for training for another year. The last of the AC-130As were retired in September 1995. This marked the ending of 711th SOS as a gunship unit and the ending of the gunship role for the USAF reserve for 20 years.

The 16th SOS remained the sole operator of the AC-130H through until the aircraft was retired by the USAF in 2015. It moved from its long-standing home at Hurlburt Field in Florida to Cannon AFB in New Mexico in 2009, as part of AFSOC's expansion of its gunship force with the introduction of the AC-130W Stinger.

During the aircraft's time in the service, AC-130H operations were overseen until October 1993 by the 1st SOW, when it was controversially renamed the 16th SOW. Thirteen years later the 1st SOW was resurrected. After 16th SOS moved to Cannon AFB, the AC-130Hs came under the control of the newly formed 27th SOW.

AC-130H Retirement

In the second decade of the 21st century, the AC-130H was counting down towards its retirement. The 16th SOS kept AC-130Hs in

BELOW: The twin 40mm Bofors guns of the AC-130H were sourced from the US Navy and to the right is the APG-150 beacon tracking radar, which helped crews identify friendly forces during confused battles. (GREG GOEBELS)

Kuwait to cover the withdrawal of the last US ground troops from Iraq in December 2011 and these aircraft returned to Cannon AFB in January 2013.

AC-130Hs remained on duty in Afghanistan for another year and the final aircraft returned from the Central Command area of responsibility in January 2014.

Up to May 2015, one AC-130H was retired each month until the final aircraft, serial 69-6569 *Excalibur* was sent off to the Davis-Monthan AFB 'boneyard'. This marked the end of 46 years of dedicated service by the AC-130E/H.

"Over the last 12 years, the 16th SOS has flown over 6,500 combat sorties, 26,000 combat hours and has been responsible for over 4,600 enemies killed in action, along with over 5,200 enemy captures," said Captain Aaron Magger, 16th SOS navigator at the AC-130H retirement ceremony. "As the AC-130H chapter of gunship evolution comes to a close, the AC-130H is the single deadliest aircraft and flying squadron in the war on terrorism."

To help celebrate the illustrious accomplishments of the decorated aircraft, Lieutenant Colonel Andrew Koegl, then 16th SOS commander, praised the AC-130H and its crews.

"Being a part of Spectre is more than what model gunship you fly; it is a culture," Koegl said. "It is about training hard to become systems and tactics experts. It is about leadership and doing the right thing by knowing when to hang it all out there to protect your teammates on the ground.

"How can you not develop pride in yourself and your unit when you hear these stories, and you talk with fellow Air Commandos who have served before you?" he continued. "Tomorrow, we are sending off the legacy of the AC-130H and what it has done over the last 46 years. I am honoured to be here today; it has been a privilege to have flown this aircraft."

LEFT: Cannon AFB in New Mexico became home to the 16th Special Operations Squadron in 2009 and its AC-130Hs were replaced by AC-130Ws and then AC-130Js. (USAF)

BELOW: AC-130H, serial number 69-6572, has been preserved and is on display at Cannon AFB in New Mexico. (USAF)

Bush Fire Wars

Gunships over Iran, Grenada, El Salvador, and Panama 1980 to 1989

RIGHT: In the 1980s the AC-130Hs of the 16th Special Operations Squadron found themselves on operations in Central America and the Middle East. (USAF)

The images of abandoned helicopters and a burned-out C-130 epitomised the failure of the April, 1980 US attempt to rescue its hostages held in Iran. Six months earlier, Iranian militants had stormed the US Embassy in Tehran and captured 52 diplomats.

US President Jimmy Carter's administration was thrown into turmoil by the brazen act of hostage taking, and planning began for a rescue mission immediately. The ground element was to be provided by the US Army's newly formed 1st Special Operations Detachment Delta - or as it more popularly known, Delta Force.

To get them to Tehran a complex plan was drawn up involving USAF Lockheed C-130 Hercules and US Navy Sikorsky RH-53D Sea Stallion mine sweeping helicopters crewed by US Marine aviators. The helicopters were to launch from the USS *Nimitz* in the North Arabian Sea and fly to a rendezvous point in central Iran, known as Desert One, where the assault force would arrive on six C-130s and then transfer into the helicopters for the rescue mission in downtown Tehran. EC-130E tankers would refuel the RH-53Ds on the ground at the desert airstrip. US Navy fighter jets from the USS *Coral Sea* and USS *Nimitz,* were to provide air support during the rescue. Once the hostages were freed, the force would be lifted by helicopters to a nearby airfield, which was to be captured by US Army Rangers to allow Lockheed C-141 Starlifters to evacuate all the Americans.

A key role in the plan was given to four gunships of the 16th Special Operations Squadron, which had

BELOW: The ill-fated US attempt to rescue hostages held in the Iranian capital Tehran heavily involved the support of AC-130H Spectre gunships. (USAF)

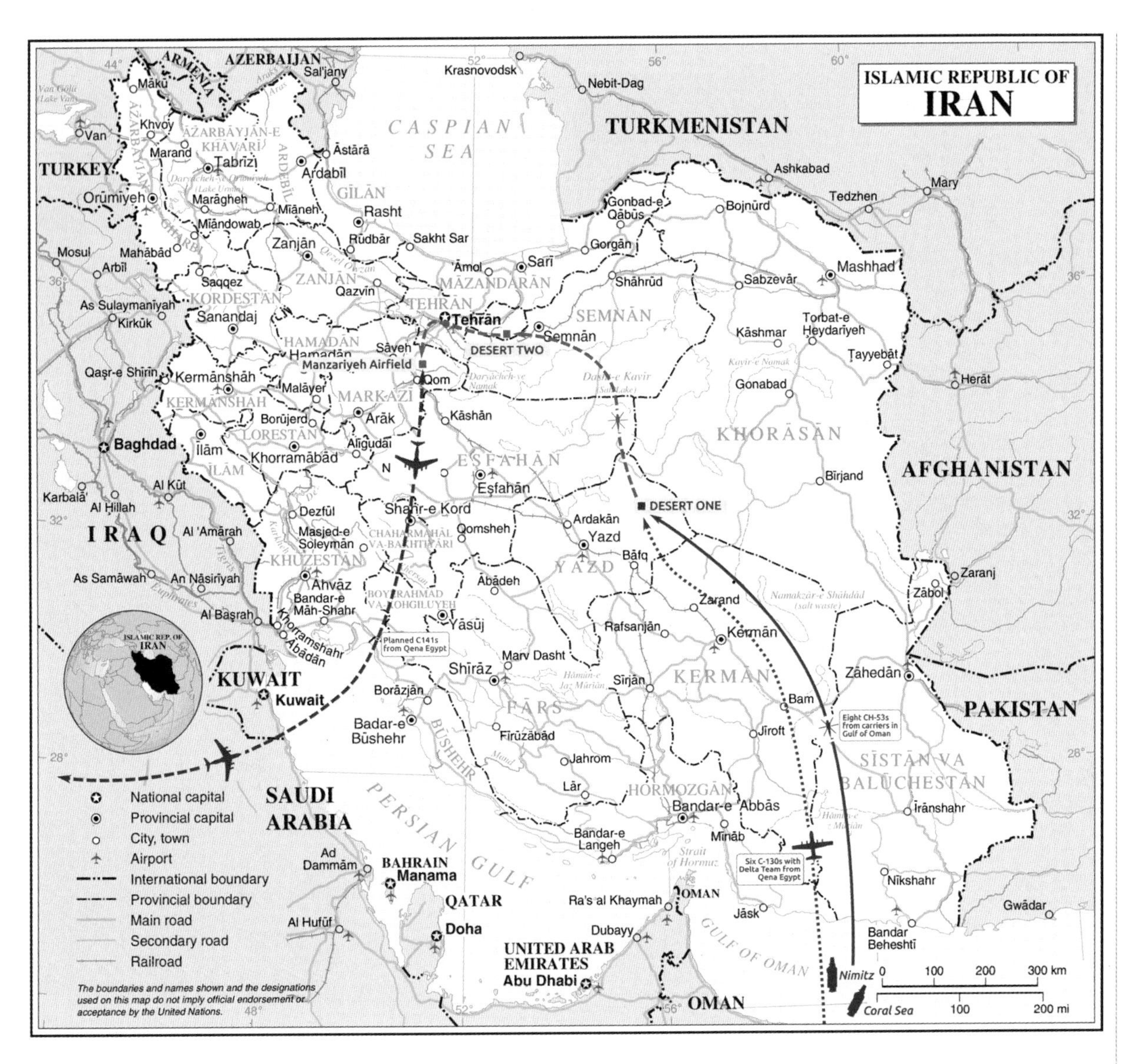

LEFT: Operation Eagle Claw was a highly complex plan, and it ultimately failed after US helicopters crashed into a Hercules transport aircraft at the Desert One air strip. (FARAWAYMAN)

forward deployed to Wadi Qena air base in Egypt. At each stage of operations, AC-130Hs were to be overhead providing surveillance and fire support for the Delta assault teams. One aircraft was to be circling over the US Embassy as the main hostage rescue force attacked. Another Spectre was to patrol over Mehrabad airfield outside Tehran to stop Iranian fighter jets intervening. A third gunship was to escort the rescue force and the released hostages to an airfield at Manzariyeh, where they would be recovered by US aircraft. The gunships would then destroy the US helicopters and vehicles left behind to deny them to the Iranians. A fourth AC-130H was to act as an airborne reserve.

After negotiations failed to free the hostages, President Carter gave the go ahead for the operation, with April 24-25 set for the mission to be executed. At first preparations went smoothly but the Desert One landing zone was soon hit by disaster as one of the RH-53D helicopters crashed into an MC-130, starting a fire that left eight Americans dead. The operation was called off even before the AC-130Hs had launched from the base in Egypt.

Grenada

When the government of the Caribbean Island of Grenada was overthrown by a pro-communist coup in October 1983, US President Ronald Reagan saw an opportunity to strike back at what he saw as a Moscow-backed revolution in America's backyard. The presence of several hundred American students on the island was a useful pretext for US intervention.

Operation Urgent Fury would give several new US Special Operations units - formed after the Desert One debacle - a chance to show what they could do. US Air Force MC-130E Combat Talons had a starring role in the first phase of the operation by parachute dropping a battalion

BELOW: Reservists of the 711st Special Operations Squadron supported their active duty colleagues in many theatres throughout the 1980s. (MIKE FREER)

RIGHT: Point Salines airport in Grenada was the scene of a US parachute landing, backed by AC-130H gunships, in October 1983. (USAF)

of US Army Rangers to seize the island's main airport at Port Salinas, which was controlled by Cuban engineers. This was to be the first US combat parachute drop since the Vietnam conflict and the most daring battalion-sized US parachute assault since World War Two. During the early hours of October 25, the 1st and 2nd Battalions of the 75th Ranger Regiment loaded on board two MC-130Es and ten C-130s at Hunter Airfield in Georgia. The initial plan envisaged that one company of Rangers would jump onto the airfield to secure the airport's runway and allow the rest of the aircraft carrying the force to land on the runway.

Flying ahead of the transports was an AC-130H Spectre gunship of the 16th SOS. This heavily armed aircraft was also equipped with advanced night-vision systems, so they were given the mission of overflying the runway to check out if it was blocked to prevent the MC-130Es and C-130s landings. The main formation was staggered with two MC-130E and five C-130s carrying the first wave of Rangers. They were followed by two more AC-130s and a final cell of five more C-130s carried the second wave of paratroopers.

A few minutes after arriving on station it was obvious to the first Spectre's crew that no Hercules would be landing on the runway as it was blocked by construction equipment and piles of building material. In the following wave of transport aircraft, Ranger commanders told their troops that the air landing operation was

RIGHT: Night-time fire support from AC-130Hs was instrumental in the success of the parachute assault by US Army Rangers on Grenada in the opening hours of Operation Urgent Fury. (USAF)

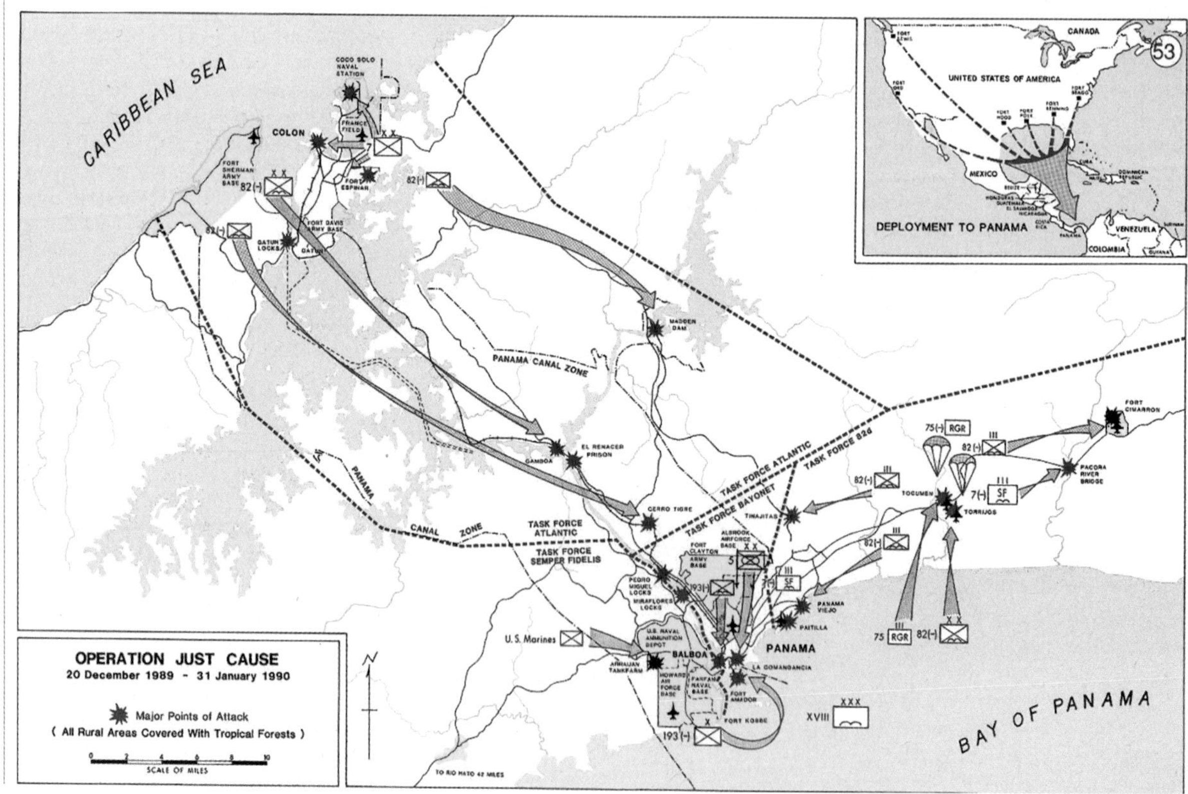

RIGHT: Activity duty and reserve gunship crews played a key role in the US invasion of Panama in December 1989 to topple the regime of General Manuel Noreiga. (USAF)

cancelled, and they had to rig for a combat parachute jump.

As the first cell of US aircraft approached the airfield the defenders opened fire with their anti-aircraft guns. The jump was temporarily aborted with minutes to go to allow the two AC-130Hs to fly forward and put the enemy anti-aircraft guns out of action.

The remainder of the US aircraft circled and then returned once the AC-130Hs had finished taking out the anti-aircraft defences. As this was underway, Ranger companies began to take on groups of Cubans and local revolutionaries in the airport's buildings and compounds on hills overlooking the runway. The defenders made only a token effort to resist after the Rangers called in more AC-130H strikes. The Cubans started to surrender, and the revolutionaries began to withdraw.

By the afternoon, the revolutionaries had recovered from the shock of the US invasion and staged a counterattack. Three Soviet-made BTR-60 wheeled armoured personnel carriers led the attack on the US defences at the eastern edge of the airport. Rangers knocked out two APCs with handheld Light Anti-tank Weapon (LAW) rockets and an AC-130 finished off the third vehicle. By the end of the day Grenada had been secured.

President Reagan remained concerned that Moscow-backed insurgents were threatening US interests in central America, particularly in El Salvador, where the country's right-wing junta was under attack from revolutionaries based in neighbouring Nicaragua. To monitor cross border insurgent activity, the 16th SOS was given a top-secret mission to fly surveillance using their night-vision sensors. Operations Bield Kirk/Blinking Light lasted from March 1983 to October 1987. The nightly gunship missions required air-to-air refuelling to allow them to reach El Salvador from their forward base in Panama. One Boeing KC-135A Stratotanker was lost with all its crew in 1986 during the operation.

LEFT: **US Rangers opened Operation Just Cause with a series of parachute drops at key points around Panama, supported closely by AC-130 strikes on pro-Noriega bases and units.** (US DOD)

Panama

The Panama Canal had long been considered a strategic asset by the United States so when the country's de facto leader Manuel Noriega, refused to accept the results of an election in May 1989, relations with Washington rapidly deteriorated.

By early December 1989, US forces were being massed in the Panama Canal Zone ready to strike to overthrow Noriega's regime. US Southern Command had developed a complex plan that envisaged some 27,000 US troops simultaneously assaulting multiple targets across Panama, in the early hours of December 20. The idea was to overwhelm Noriega's outnumbered forces in a matter of hours.

The gunships of the 16th and 711th SOS played a key role in the opening minutes of Operation Just Cause, providing fire and surveillance support to the assault troops. The involvement of both active and reserve gunship squadrons was testament to the scale of the task they were given. In the face of overwhelming US firepower, Noriega's troops put up minimal resistance and the renegade leader was soon in US custody.

LEFT: **Advanced night-vision systems gave US forces a key advantage during the opening hours of Operation Just Cause.** (USAF)

AC-130U Spooky II

Arrival of the U-Boat

RIGHT: The AC-130U bristled with weapons, defensive systems, and communications antenna to make it the most sophisticated gunship in the US arsenal when it entered service in 1994. (USAF)

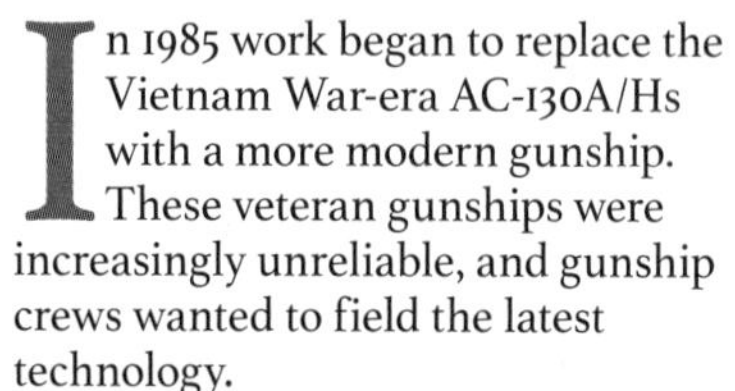

In 1985 work began to replace the Vietnam War-era AC-130A/Hs with a more modern gunship. These veteran gunships were increasingly unreliable, and gunship crews wanted to field the latest technology.

It was also decided that more gunships were needed because of unrelenting demand from US special forces commanders operating in combat zones around the world. The AC-130U programme officially got underway in August 1985 when the Pentagon launched a competition to select a contractor to provide the new aircraft.

Two years later, Rockwell International (now part of Boeing) of El Segundo in California won the competition and began work to convert a brand-new production C-130H airframe into the prototype of the new gunship. This was a controversial decision, because almost at the same time Lockheed – the original manufacturer of the Hercules – was working on the AC-130H SOFI upgrade programme. Two parallel programmes were underway to field new models of gunships for the USAF and soon both hit technical problems and delays. The technology was highly complex and getting all the new sensors and electronic equipment to work together threw up unexpected problems.

As well as boasting many of the advanced features already being installed on the AC-130H SOFI, including the high resolution ALQ-117 forward looking infra-red (FLIR) sensor mounted in a turret under the nose, GPS navigation, advanced ALQ-172 fuselage mounted jammers, and self-defence systems to protect against heat seeking missiles, the AC-130U incorporated a new weapons configuration. In place of the AC-130H's twin 20mm single barrel cannons, mounted on the port forward fuselage, the AC-130U now had a single trainable GAU-12U Equalizer five-barrelled 25mm Gatling gun. A 40mm M2A1 Bofors cannon and a 105 mm M102 howitzer were installed in the rear weapon compartment. The trainable 25mm meant the AC-130U had the capability to track and engage two targets simultaneously with its various weapons - a first for a gunship.

BELOW: Officially the AC-130U was named the Spooky II and its had its own a distinctive logo. (USAF)

New Sensor Technology

In a major advance in gunship sensor technology, the aircraft was fitted with the ALQ-180 nose mounted radar. This was a first-generation synthetic aperture radar that was able to generate three-dimensional radar images of large metal objects, such as tanks and trucks. Consequently, it allowed AC-130U crews to detect enemy vehicles in bad weather or when hidden under jungle canopies. It allowed targeting airmen see the impact point of their rounds and adjust fire without requiring a ground observer in bad weather.

The aim of all the AC-130U capability improvements was to allow the gunship to engage targets from greater distances, even at night or in bad weather. By allowing the AC-130U to attack targets from slant ranges of more than 10,000ft it moved the aircraft out of the engagement envelopes of many anti-aircraft weapons.

Gunship commanders were enthusiastic about the improved capability and in 1987 Rockwell received an initial contract to build 12 AC-130Us. The first prototype was to fly in 1989, and all the aircraft were to be delivered by late 1991.

Very quickly the programme ran into technical difficulties and the delivery schedule slipped. The first aircraft were not delivered to Hurlburt Field until July 1, 1994. The order having been increased to 13 aircraft to compensate for the loss of an AC-130H in action in the 1991 Gulf War.

Increased demand for gunships to police what was dubbed the 'new world disorder' during the 1990s resulted in the USAF forming

AC-130U SPOOKY II
Powerplant: four Allison T56-A-15 turboprop engines
Wingspan: 40.4m (132ft 7in)
Length: 29.8m (97ft 9in)
Height: 11.7m (38ft 6in)
Max take-off weight: 69,750kg (155,000lb)
Speed: 482kph (300mph)
Range: 2,407km (1,300 nm), unlimited by air refuelling
Crew: 13
Armament:
One M2A1 40mm cannon, one 105mm M102 howitzer and one 25mm GAU-12 Gatling gun

LEFT: The AC-130U featured a 'steerable' 25mm Gatling gun, so for the first time a USAF gunship could engage two separate targets simultaneously. (USAF)

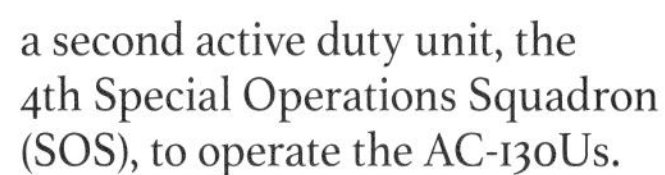

a second active duty unit, the 4th Special Operations Squadron (SOS), to operate the AC-130Us.

The unit, which stood up on May 5, 1995, traced its heritage back to Vietnam when it was the first Air Command squadron to operate the new Douglas AC-45D gunship. As a result, the USAF formally designated the AC-130U as the 'Spooky II' after the Vietnam era callsign of the AC-47Ds. Many crews of the new gunship, however, quickly started calling the AC-130U the 'U-Boat' after the German World War Two submarines. "No matter what the name, they are still Spectres and

BELOW: Two distinctive electro-optical sensor turrets allowed the AC-130U crews to monitor multiple targets on the ground. (USAF)

LOCKHEED AC-130U SPOOKY II GUNSHIPS			
Serial	**Name**	**Configuration**	**Notes**
87-0128	*Big Daddy*	Prototype, first flew December 20, 1990	On display Hurlburt Field Memorial Air Park, Florida
89-0509	*Total Carnage*		
89-0510	*Gunslinger/Armageddon*		
89-0511	*Predator/Lost Boys*		
89-0512	*Dead On*		
89-0513	*Killer Instincts*		
89-0514	*Maximum Carnage*		
89-1052		Plus 4	
89-1053		Plus 4	
89-1054		Plus 4	
89-1056	*Hondo*	Plus 4	
90-0163	*Bad Omen*		
90-0164	*Bad Intentions*		
90-0165	*Thumper* (previously *Midnight Medussa/ Widow Maker/Death before Dawn*)		
90-0166	*Hell Raiser*		
90-0167	*Azrael*, then *Terminator II*, *Intimidator*		
92-0253	*Eight Ball*		

RIGHT: The AC-130U continued to sport a 105mm howitzer to provide stand-off firepower. (USAF)

are AC-130 gunships," commented one gunship veteran.

The AC-130U first saw action in the 1999 Kosovo war, where it used its ALQ-180 radar to find and engage a target purely using a radar sensor. This was a first for a USAF gunship.

War on Terror

The 2001 9/11 attacks and the subsequent 'Global War on Terror' saw the AC-130U and AC-130H squadrons sustaining a heavy operational tempo in Afghanistan, Iraq, and elsewhere.

In 2006, the Pentagon approved a $1.3bn project to buy four extra AC-130Us to augment the gunship force and allow to it to sustain its heavy rotation of foreign deployments. These were referred to as AC-130U Plus 4 or AC-130U+4 aircraft. This saw the conversion of four C-130H2 airframes into AC-130U. The initial plans envisaged that the 25mm GAU-12/U and 40mm Bofors cannon would be replaced with two 30mm Mk 44 Bushmaster II cannons. However, the new weapon fit did not prove a success during flight tests because the Bushmaster cannons did not deliver the required level of accuracy. Consequently, the aircraft were stripped of their new weapons and 25mm Gatling guns and 40mm cannons were installed to bring them into line with the configuration of the core AC-130U. This bought the AC-130U fleet up to 17 aircraft.

With the AC-130H fleet starting to show its age and being ultimately retired between 2013 and 2015, the AC-130U force stepped up and took

RIGHT: A trial to install 30mm Bushmaster cannons into an AC-130 was not a success and the prototype reverted to baseline configuration after a series of test firings. (USAF)

LEFT: Sensor operators on the AC-130U were able to monitor hostile battlefields on multiple computer screens. The new aircraft avionics brought the USAF gunship community into the digital era. (USAF)

on the bulk of deployments to the Middle East and Africa during the 2010s.

By this point, the USAF was moving quickly to retire all its E and H model C-130s in favour of the more modern C-130J variant, which featured glass cockpits and new six bladed propellers. When the USAF decided to create a J variant gunship, the days of AC-130U were numbered. The 4th SOS received its first AC-130J Ghostrider and the last AC-130U was flown to the boneyard at Davis-Monthan AFB in Arizona to begin long term storage on June 26, 2020.

"The men and women of the 4th SOS have been executing the close air support and air interdiction mission with one of the most feared gunships, the AC-130U, for 20 years," said Colonel Michael Conley, 1st Special Operations Wing commander at a ceremony to mark the arrival of the first AC-130J with the 4th SOS in March 2019. "The technology in this fifth generation gunship will ensure our combat relevance in the skies above today's battlefields and the battlefields of the future."

"The 4th SOS will start receiving J-qualified crew members in the coming months," said Lieutenant Colonel Pete Ventres, 4th SOS commander, at the same event. "The vast majority of U-model aircrews and maintainers will retrain into the AC-130J to ensure we retain already-developed talent.

"This is a significant milestone in our heritage and the gunship nation," Ventres continued. "The AC-130J represents a leap into the future without abandoning the lessons of the past. The protection of special operations forces on the ground remains paramount. The 'C' in CAS stands for 'Close', and when we're needed, that's where you'll find us."

BELOW: The 4th Special Operations Squadron operated the AC-130U from Hurlbert Field from 1995 to 2019. (USAF)

Gulf War to Kosovo

Gunships police 'new world disorder' 1990 to 1999

ABOVE: The AC-130U Spooky II made its debut in the USAF gunship fleet in 1994, augmenting the veteran AC-130H. (USAF)

RIGHT: US Army General Norman Schwarzkopf masterminded the US victory in the 1991 Gulf War, and he was keen to use the firepower of the AC-130 Spectres to devastate Iraqi troop positions. (US DOD/ COMBAT CAMERA)

When Iraqi troops surged across the border with Kuwait in the early hours of August 2, 1990, it set off a chain of events that culminated in the largest US military deployment since Vietnam.

US President George HW Bush ordered more than 500,000 US troops to the Middle East to protect the oil rich Gulf States from further Iraqi advances, under the banner of Operation Desert Shield. After the Iraqi President, Saddam Hussein, refused to withdraw his troops from Kuwait, President Bush ordered Operation Desert Storm to drive them out of the kingdom in January 1991.

The USAF's two gunship units, the 16th and 711th Special Operations Squadrons (SOS), were heavily involved in Operations Desert Shield and Desert Storm.

In the weeks after the Iraqi invasion of Kuwait, US and British special forces commanders were tasked with developing plans to rescue coalition diplomats blocked inside their embassies in Kuwait City. To support this mission, six AC-130H Spectres of the 16th SOS took up residence at King Fahd Airport, outside the city of Dammam on Saudi Arabia's east coast. It was envisaged that they would provide fire support for special forces rescue teams as they tried to bring the diplomats out of Kuwait. Fortunately, a diplomatic solution was found, and the diplomats were evacuated safely in December 1990.

As US commanders started to plan their invasion, they assigned an important mission to their special operations forces. Their main task was to help allied armies from Arab coalition partners operate as a coherent force. Arab troops of 'Joint Forces Command – North' were assigned to defend the border between Kuwait and Saudi Arabia, while the main US Army land force assembled out to the west in the Saudi desert to strike behind the Iraqi occupation army.

US Army 'Green Beret' special forces advisor teams and US Marine Corps forward air control teams were assigned to each Arab army unit, to stiffen their morale by providing the ability to rapidly call in US airpower and artillery fire. The 16th SOS was assigned to help these teams neutralise Iraqi artillery and tanks firing into Saudi Arabia after coalition aircraft launched their air offensive in the early hours of January 17, 1991.

The Iraqi air defences contained hundreds of large, radar guided, surface-to-air missiles (SAMs) and thousands of small, man-portable heating SAMs, known as manpads, so USAF gunship commanders had to take care to keep them at a safe distance until USAF 'Wild Weasel'

ABOVE: **The old AC-130As saw action for the last time in the 1991 Gulf War before the Vietnam-era aircraft were finally retired in 1994.** (USAF)

LEFT: **A huge Iraqi convoy was caught on the infamous 'Highway of Death' outside Kuwait airport and devastated by US airpower, including an AC-130A.** (US DOD/JOINT COMBAT CAMERA)

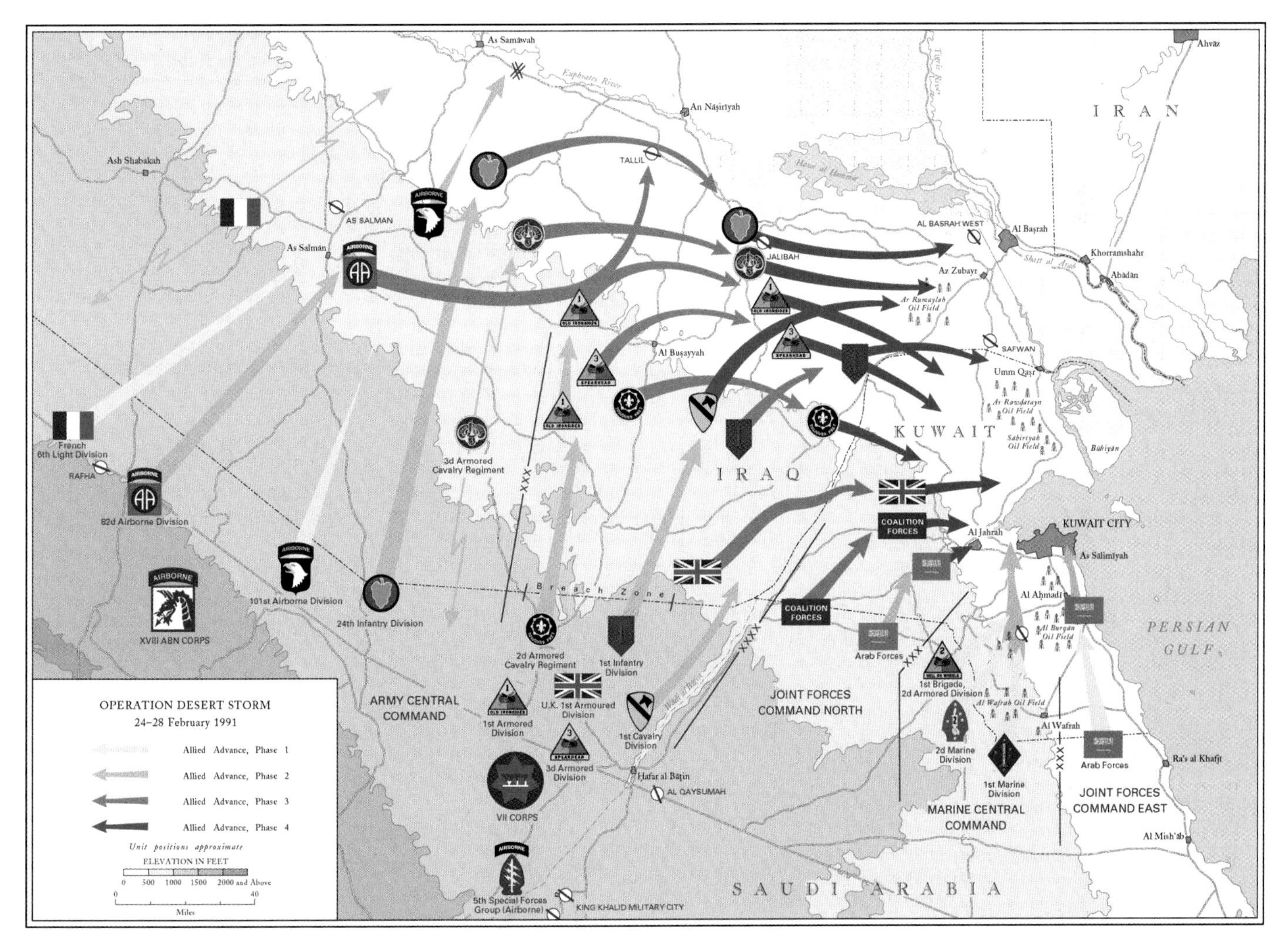

BELOW: **Operation Desert Storm land offensive, February 1991.** (US DOD)

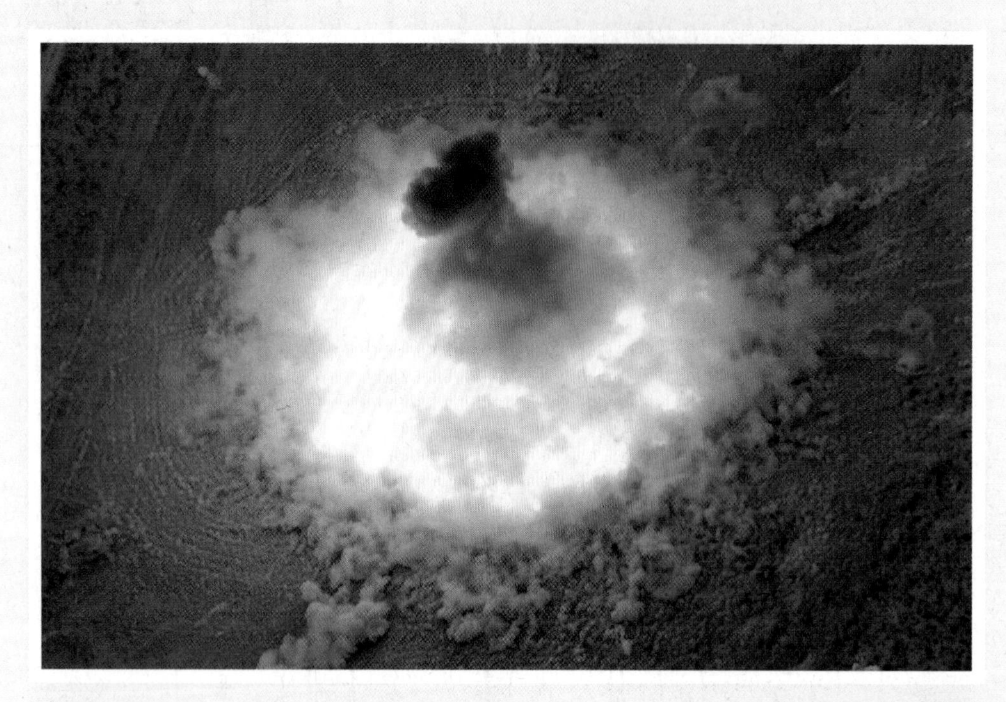

Spirit 03

The aircraft, callsign 'Spirit 03', had spent the early hours of January 31, engaging Iraqi targets astride the Iraq-Kuwait border when it responded to a call for help from US Marines to find a missile launcher firing on them. Dawn was rising and rather than break off to head south and out of range of Iraqi air defences, the gunship remained on station engaging the target. At first light, the Iraqi heat seeking missile found its target and 'Spirit 03' tumbled into the Northern Arabian Gulf, killing all the 14 crew onboard. The incident highlighted the limited effectiveness of the defensive systems then fitted to the AC-130H and the danger of operating slow-moving gunships close to enemy air defence weapons in daylight.

As well as the active duty gunships of the 16th SOS, the reservists of

ABOVE: Iraqi morale was crushed under the weight of B-52 bomber and AC-130 strikes, as well as attacks with massive BLU-82 Daisy Cutter fuel explosive bombs dropped from US Air Force Special Operation Command MC-130 Combat Shadow transports. (USAF)

RIGHT: AC-130H callsign 'Spirit 03' lingered too long over Khafji on January 31, 1991, and fell victim to an Iraqi surface-to-air missile. (USAF)

BELOW: AC-130A, nicknamed *Azreal - Angel of Death*, played an important part in the devastating US air strikes on the infamous 'Highway of Death' outside of Kuwait in the final days of the Gulf War. (USAF)

aircraft could put the Iraqi air defences out of action.

On January 30, Iraqi tank units in Kuwait launched five surprise thrusts over the border into Saudi Arabia aimed at capturing the town of Khafji. Arabs units and their USMC fire controllers held the Iraqis at bay until reinforcements arrived to stabilise the situation. The Iraqi tanks columns breaking cover to advance represented the ideal opportunity to unleash the AC-130Hs.

In a series of night strikes to help the hard-pressed US Marines defending the line around Khafji, the gunships started to hit Iraqi troop columns moving into Saudi Arabia. Unfortunately, the Iraqi air defences had not been fully suppressed and an SA-7 manpad team was able to detect and then shot down an AC-130H.

ABOVE: Brindisi airport in southern Italy was home to the USAF Combat Search and Rescue Task Force, including a contingent of AC-130H gunships, throughout the Bosnian and Kosovo conflicts. (PAUL BEAVER)

the 711th SOS were mobilised for Operation Desert Storm. They deployed six of their veteran AC-130s to Incirlik and Batman airbases in Turkey as part of the US Europe Command's Combined Task Force Proven Force. It launched air strikes across Northern Iraq and the gunships were part of combat search and rescue forces that stood ready to rescue downed US aviators.

On February 24, 1991, US and coalition ground forces began their long-awaited land offensive to surround and defeat the Iraqi occupation army in Kuwait. Two days later the Iraqis realised they would be trapped in Kuwait unless they made a rapid escape. During the evening of February 25/26, USAF Northrop Grumman E-8 Joint STARS radar aircraft spotted a convoy of thousands of Iraqi army vehicles driving 'nose to tail' up the main road out of Kuwait City. US commanders ordered a series of air strikes to stop and then destroy the convoy on what soon became known as the 'Highway of Death'. US fast jets first bombed the front and end of the convoy to trap it on the two-lane highway and then more aircraft were called into finish off the surviving Iraqis before they could flee on foot.

In this wave of aircraft were two 711st SOS AC-130A gunships, which were diverted from other missions to join the assault. One of the gunships was low on fuel and turned for its home base before engaging targets. The remaining AC-130A successfully decoyed an Iraqi manpad with flares before arriving on station and beginning its attack run.

In the course of the night, the gunship destroyed at least 20 enemy trucks and four armoured personnel carriers. President Bush ordered the air attacks to be called off when the level of destruction became apparent. When US troops reached the highway the following day, the remains of between 1,400 and 2,000 vehicles were found, along with the bodies of hundreds of Iraqi soldiers. As a result of the engagement, the crew of the gunship, renamed it *Azrael*, who in the Koran, is the angel of death who severs the soul from the body.

Bosnia

In the summer of 1992, as Bosnia descended into a bloody civil war, the capital of the former Yugoslav republic, Sarajevo, was surrounded by Serb forces. As the city's residents

LEFT: The besieged capital of Bosnia, Sarajevo, was the focus of a United Nations airlift between 1992 and 1995 before NATO aircraft, including USAF AC-130Hs, struck at Serbian artillery positions around the city to lift the siege. (TIM RIPLEY)

ABOVE: The AC-130U entered service in 1994 and allowed the Vietnam-era AC-130As to be retired. (USAF)

RIGHT: AC-130U gunships hunted for Serb tanks hiding in forests along the Albanian-Kosovo border during Operation Allied Force in 1999. (USAF)

started to run out of food and medical supplies the United Nations launched an airlift into Sarajevo airport. Early in 1993, the USAF started to parachute food and humanitarian aid to besieged enclaves in the east of the war-torn country.

The UK-based USAF 352nd Special Operations Wing was soon deployed to Italy to provide sustained combat search and rescue (CSAR) coverage for US and allied aircraft flying the airdrop missions. The US CSAR Task Force stood up at Brindisi airbase in southern Italy in February 1993 in time to provide coverage for the first airdrop missions. Whenever the airdrop C-130s were making their runs over Bosnia, the Sikorsky MH-53Js Pave Low helicopters, and Lockheed HC-130Ps Combat Shadow tankers,

RIGHT: AC-130U gunships received their baptism of fire during the 1999 Kosovo war when they flew night strikes along the Albanian-Kosovo border. (USAF)

backed by AC-130Hs, would stand alert ready to launch if the USAF airlifters ran into trouble.

In September 1995 after NATO launched a bombing campaign to lift the siege, the 352nd Wing were scrambled from Brindisi to look for the crew of a downed French Mirage jet. NATO intelligence had spotted what they thought was an 'SOS' emergency signal from the crew on the ground but it turned out to be a trap and Serb gunners were waiting for the helicopters. One Pave Low took fire, with two crew being slightly wounded. The escorting AC-130H returned fire to neutralise the threat.

The AC-130Hs were also involved in the UN operation to lift the siege, flying missions to hit Serb gun positions around the city. On the first night of the NATO bombing campaign, AC-130H 'Ghost 31', struck an artillery/mortar position southeast of Sarajevo, thus marking the first time this particular aircraft had ever fired in combat. During the operation, which lasted until September 15, the 16th SOS expended 268 rounds of 105mm and 125 rounds of 40mm against Serb gun positions, early warning radar sites and command and control facilities.

When NATO peacekeepers deployed in December 1995 to enforce the Dayton peace treaty, the AC-130Hs remained on duty in Italy. In March 1997, Albania was engulfed in civil war, and the AC-130Hs in Italy were scrambled to provide top cover as US Marines evacuated US and allied citizens.

Africa

Throughout the 1990s, the gunships remained in high demand to support US special operations forces around the world. Between 1993 and 1994, the 16th SOS was regularly deployed to East Africa to support US and UN peacekeepers delivering humanitarian aid to the famine-stricken country of Somalia. They carried out several strikes on militia fighters in the capital Mogadishu but had been withdrawn by the time of the infamous 'Black Hawk Down' battle that left 18 US soldiers dead. In March 1994, an AC-130H, callsign Jockey-14, crashed off the coast of Kenya after a weapon system malfunction, leading to the death of eight crew members.

In March 1999, USAF gunships were back in action in the Balkans after NATO began launching air strikes in the Serb-controlled province of Kosovo. Yugoslav air defences were too strong to risk sending the gunships over Kosovo itself and they were heavily involved in hitting Serb troop positions along the Kosovo-Albanian border. This gave the new AC-130U Spooky of the 4th SOS the chance to see action for the first time including using their APG-80 synthetic aperture radar to find and control the engagement of targets hidden in forests.

The 1990s saw the AC-130 gunship force heavily committed across several operational theatres, sometimes simultaneously. It was a busy time for gunship crews but the 'ops tempo' would surge to a new level after the 9/11 attacks of September, 2001.

ABOVE: An impressive array of defensive systems was installed on the AC-130U to allow it to operate close to enemy air defence systems. (USAF)

Into Afghanistan

Gunships strike against al-Qaeda, 2001 to 2002

RIGHT: USAF gunships had to make the long transit from bases in Oman and Uzbekistan, using air-to-air refuelling, to provide fire support for US Special Operation Forces teams inside Afghanistan. (USAF)

After the terrorist attacks on New York and Washington DC on September 11, 2001, US President George W Bush ordered the Pentagon to strike back at al-Qaeda and its Taliban allies in Afghanistan. US military planners eventually developed a multi-pronged strategy with special operations forces being inserted into Afghanistan from the north – via Uzbekistan and Tajikistan – and the south – via Oman and Pakistani airspace. US special operations aviators, including gunship crews from the 4th and 16th Special Operation Squadrons, would be central to these plans. Over the next five months they led America's strike back.

Within days of the terror attacks, the US State Department reached an agreement with the Uzbek government to allow US troops to begin using Karshi-Khanabad, or K2, airbase, 200km from the border with Afghanistan. Within a week, more than 1,000 US personnel had turned K-2 into a major military base. Colonel John Mulholland, the commander of the 5th Special Forces Group, was designated head of the newly established Joint Special Operations Task Force-North. This would soon be renamed Task Force Dagger. It did not immediately have its own dedicated gunship unit but three AC-130H of the 16th SOS were eventually cleared to deploy in November 2001.

To strike into southern Afghanistan, the Pentagon turned to the Arab state of Oman to open

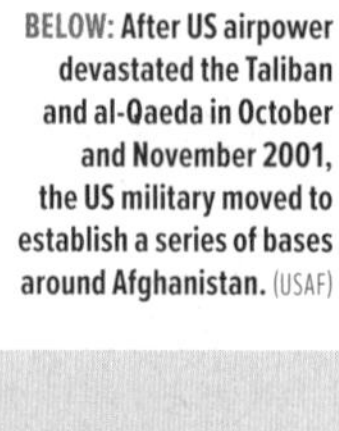

BELOW: After US airpower devastated the Taliban and al-Qaeda in October and November 2001, the US military moved to establish a series of bases around Afghanistan. (USAF)

the air base on Masirah Island to US forces, allowing them to activate pre-positioned tents, command posts, and aircraft ground-handling equipment stored on the Indian Ocean island. Masirah became the forward headquarters of Task Force Sword, or as it was later known Task Force 11, which controlled the US special operations forces destined to operate in southern Afghanistan. This was led by Major General Dell Dailey and included a strong contingent of highly secret Joint Special Operations Command (JSOC) direct action units, including Delta Force and SEAL Team 6. The focus of Dailey's operation was the Taliban and al-Qaeda leadership around the southern city of Kandahar.

USAF AC-130U Spectre gunships of the 4th SOS, MC-130 Combat Talon deep penetration transports, and MC-130 Combat Shadow tankers, as well as MH-53 Pave Low helicopters, soon arrived to give Dailey's forces the reach and firepower they needed to strike into Afghanistan.

On the morning of October 6, 2001, the US President had given up on the Taliban ever handing over Osama bin Laden. He issued the formal orders for the launching of Operation Enduring Freedom, as the Afghan campaign would be code-named. The following evening several packages of strike aircraft and Tomahawk Land Attack Missiles (TALM) started hitting some 31 separate targets, involving 275 individual weapon aim points, around Afghanistan.

The first phase of offensive land operations in southern Afghanistan got under way in the early hours of October 20 with a raid by US Army Rangers on a suspected Taliban-held compound and airstrip, dubbed Objective Rhino, in the deserts of Helmand province, to the southwest of Kandahar city.

Some 200 Rangers parachuted into the desert and then assaulted the compound, with fire support from a B-2 Spirit stealth bomber and AC-130U gunships before securing the airstrip to allow two MC-130 Combat Talons to land and recover them back to Masirah. The operation went well, with 11 enemy fighters being killed and a haul of intelligence documents being captured.

Heavy fighting was now underway in northern Afghanistan between US-backed rebel forces and Taliban units. The 16th SOS finally got to K2 on November 11 and within a day the unit was attacking Taliban and al-Qaeda forces near the city of Konduz in support of Northern Alliance forces and was directly responsible for the city's surrender the next day. During the first mission, after few hours on task the AC-130H had attacked so many targets that it called 'Winchester' the signal that it had run out of ammunition.

Qala-i-Jangi

On November 26, the squadron was called on to help suppress a rebellion at the prison fort of Qala-i-Jangi, near the city of Mazar-i-Sharif. While supporting the beleaguered US Central Intelligence Agency operatives and British special forces troops, two AC-130Hs put down withering 40mm and 105mm fire which succeeded in ending the rebellion of Taliban and al-Qaeda prisoners.

LEFT: The ruins of the Twin Towers. US Special Operations Forces were dispatched to Afghanistan to hunt down the perpetrators of the attack. (US DOD/ COMBAT CAMERA)

LEFT: 'Wanted Dead or Alive'. US President George W Bush declared the al-Qaeda leader Osama bin Laden to be an outlaw and sent the US military to Afghanistan to hunt him down. (US DOD/ COMBAT CAMERA)

TOP AND ABOVE: MC-130 Combat Talons made night-time forays over Afghanistan, supported by air-to-air refuelling, to parachute supplies to US Army special forces teams and anti-Taliban fighters. They were accompanied by AC-130s to protect US forces on the ground. (US DOD/COMBAT CAMERA)

As pro-US rebels surged across Afghanistan, the AC-130Hs began to expand their zones of operations. On a famous occasion, the 16th SOS provided on-call close air support and armed reconnaissance near Kandahar after an assassination attempt against Afghanistan's future president, Hamid Karzai.

By the end of 2001, the Taliban had been driven from power in Afghanistan and the al-Qaeda chief, Osama bin Laden, was on the run.

In early 2002, US intelligence analysts became convinced that there was a large concentration of several hundred al-Qaeda fighters, including many senior commanders, in the Shah-i-Kot Valley in Paktia province, near the mountainous border with Pakistan. US Central Command (CENTCOM) chief General Tommy Franks decided that a large-scale offensive was needed to trap and destroy the enemy fighters. To avoid a repeat of the problems that had bedevilled a drive to trap Osama bin Laden at Tora Bora in December 2001, the US military wanted US Army infantry troops to be involved in strength, but JSOC units were first to 'prepare the battlefield'.

Covert observation teams were first inserted onto three mountain peaks dominating the Shah-i-Kot Valley to try to locate the al-Qaeda positions. Then an Afghan militia force, led by US Army special forces teams, was to launch a direct attack to drive the enemy fighters towards a cordon of US soldiers from the 101st Airborne and 10th Mountain Division who were to be simultaneously dropped by Chinook helicopters in the hills on the eastern side of the valley.

The whole operation would be supported throughout by AC-130Hs of the 16th SOS, now flying from Masirah Island. Gunship operations over Afghanistan had been consolidated at the Omani airbase, to allow the 4th SOS to return home to reconstitute itself for the coming invasion of Iraq. The 16th SOS provided on-call firepower and overwatch to detect threats to the small US and allied force on the ground.

The operation kicked off in the early hours of March 2, 2002, with the advance up the valley by the Afghan militia force. Things started to go wrong almost immediately. Disaster struck when a technical fault in the AC-130H's navigation system led it to attack the Afghan militia convoy by mistake. Two militia fighters were killed, and more than a dozen injured. Several of their US advisors were also wounded.

Just as the 'friendly fire' incident was unfolding, US Army CH-47Ds were arriving at their landing zones to drop off hundreds of American soldiers. As they ran off the giant helicopter's ramps they came under intense fire from AK-47s, heavy machine guns, rocket-propelled grenades (RPGs), mortars, and light artillery.

By dawn, the Shah-i-Kot was the scene of the most intense battle involving US forces since the infamous *Black Hawk Down* incident in Somalia in 1993. Hundreds of American troops were pinned down and frantic calls for close air support were filling US radio networks.

ABOVE: CIA and US Army special forces teams fought alongside anti-Taliban fighters in Afghanistan and repeatedly called down fire from AC-130s. (US DOD/COMBAT CAMERA)

Rescue Mission

Senior JSOC officers on Masirah Island ordered that the personnel manning three observation posts monitoring the battle be replaced by US Navy SEAL commandos. They insisted that this happen during the coming night and the only way this could be achieved was by helicopter. A pair of MH-47Es from the 160th Special Aviation Operations Regiment (Airborne) were loaded with one of the teams destined to occupy Takur Ghar peak, which dominated the Shah-i-Kot Valley. As they approached the objective an AC-130H flew ahead to check out the landing zone and reported it clear of enemy fighters.

However, the MH-47E approached the landing zone and was raked with enemy machine gun and RPG fire. It shuddered under the weight of fire and one of the SEAL operatives, Petty Officer Neil Roberts, who was standing on the rear ramp waiting to disembark, was thrown off the helicopter. The pilot immediately aborted the landing and flew away to safety. When it was realised that one of the SEAL team was missing a rescue mission was ordered.

The rescue helicopter approached the same landing zone and this time managed to land its troops but was hit several times and was forced

BELOW: To break the back of Taliban resistance in northern Afghanistan, MC-130s dropped several BLU-82 Daisy Cutter fuel air explosive weapons on their positions. (US DOD/COMBAT CAMERA)

ABOVE: AC-130Us based on Masirah Island in the Indian Ocean supported the insertion of US forces into southern Afghanistan during the final three months of 2001. (USAF)

to make an emergency landing after limping away from the battlefield.

A third helicopter carrying additional rescue troops approached the battlefield, but the changing of the radio frequencies meant it could not be alerted to the enemy positions overlooking the landing zone. This third Chinook was severely damaged by enemy fire and could not escape from the killing zone and crashed close to the al-Qaeda positions. The survivors linked up with the first rescue force, who formed a desperate defensive perimeter.

An AC-130H had provided protection for the beleaguered Americans during the night but as dawn approached it had to turn for its base after three man-portable surface-to-air missiles were fired at it. The gunship circled over the battle and repeatedly engaged any Taliban fighters who

RIGHT: Heavy resistance was soon encountered during Operation Anaconda and reinforcements had to be mobilised at Bagram airbase to relieve isolated US units. (US DOD)

tried to rush the surrounded US troops. Evacuation was not possible during daylight and the US SEALs and Rangers on the Takur Ghar peak had to rely on a constant stream of McDonnell Douglas F-15E Strike Eagles and Lockheed F-16C Fighting Falcons making bombing and gun strafing runs to keep al-Qaeda fighters at bay until the night. Under cover of darkness, the trapped Americans found a route to safety further down the mountainside. Eight Americans died during the confused battle on Takur Ghar peak, which had now been re-named Roberts Ridge in honour of the SEAL who was killed in the battle. The fighting in the Shah-i-Kot valley continued for almost another week as US troops fought their way through the al-Qaeda positions, which were found to be deserted. The enemy made their escape back to safety in Pakistan.

In March 2002, the 16th SOS flew 39 combat missions in support of Operation Anaconda. It had only three aircraft and three crews, but the squadron amassed 322 combat hours over 12 days, resulting in 45 enemies killed in action, nine vehicles destroyed, 11 damaged vehicles, and 12 destroyed and 25 damaged buildings. During the intense fighting, its aircraft expended more than 1,300 40mm and 1,200 105mm rounds. Their actions earned them the 2002 Mackay Trophy, and 2002 Air Force Aviator Valor awards.

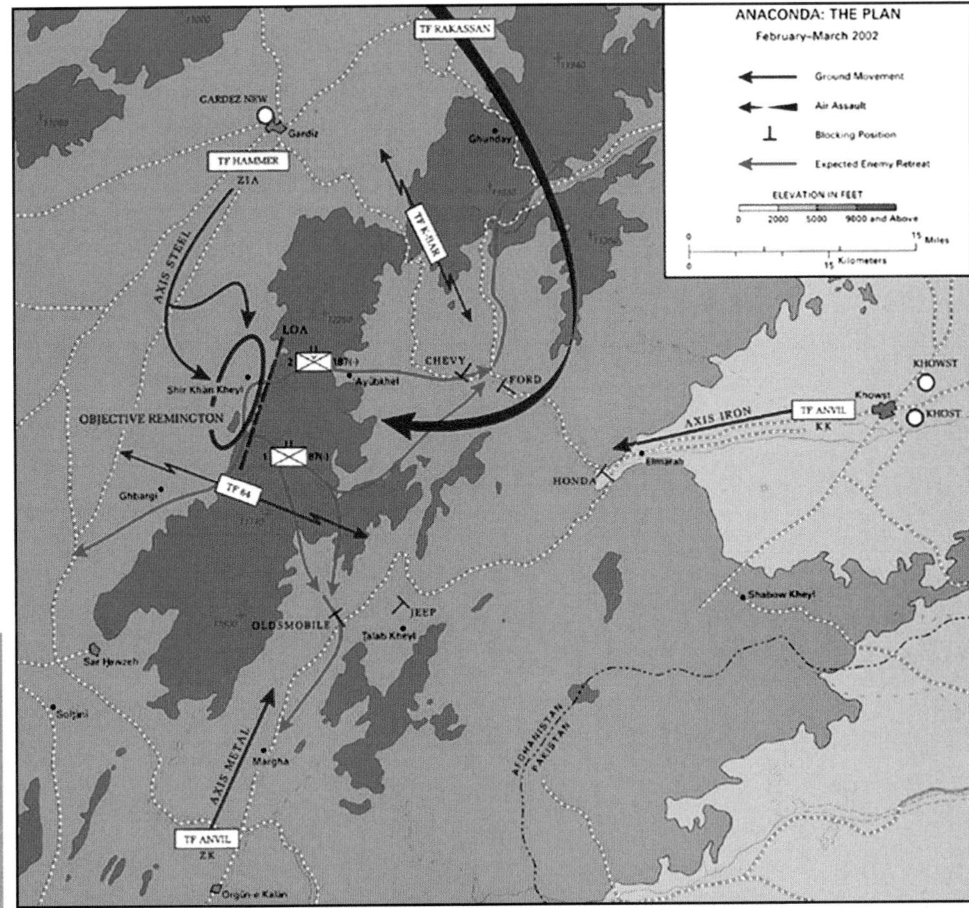

ABOVE: Operation Anaconda February-March 2002. (US ARMY)

LEFT: Beleaguered US Navy SEALs gathered around a crashed MH-47E Chinook on a hilltop during the opening hours of Operation Anaconda. Precision fire from an AC-130H, call sign 'Grim 32', kept the enemy at bay to allow the SEALs to escape. Eight special operations forces personnel were killed in the battle. The hill was renamed Roberts Ridge in honour of SEAL Petty Office First Class Neil C. Roberts who was killed during the battle. (US DOD)

LEFT: AC-130s operated only at night over Afghanistan to stay out of the sights of enemy man-portable surface-to-missiles. (USAF)

Invading Iraq

Gunship action in Middle East 2003 to 2011

ABOVE: Gunners load 105mm rounds into an AC-130U's main armament during a mission over Iraq. (USAF)

In 2002, US President George W Bush resolved to depose the Iraqi President Saddam Hussein and set about mobilising an invasion force around the Middle East country's borders. His defence secretary, Donald Rumsfeld crafted a plan based on 'shock and awe' attacks using air power and special forces to shatter the Iraqi will to fight.

He wanted to repeat the success of the Afghanistan campaign, which had up to then avoided the deployment of a large occupation army. Rumsfeld wanted rapidly moving special forces teams to spearhead the invasion of Iraq, rather than massed tank columns.

The US Central Command began planning for the invasion in the spring of 2002 and by the autumn the first troops were beginning to deploy to Jordan, Kuwait, Qatar, and other countries in the Gulf region. A complex special operations plan was developed to insert raiding teams into Iraq ahead of the main invasion force to try to persuade Iraqi troops to desert or surrender. A key target for the special operations forces was the location and destruction of Iraq's weapons of mass destruction, which was officially the White House justification for the invasion.

The USAF's AC-130U Spooky II unit, the 4th Special Operations Squadron, was given an important role in this operation, providing fire and surveillance support for assault units. In January 2003, it deployed to Ali Al Salem Airbase in Kuwait with eight gunships and was assigned to support the highly secret Task Force 20 (TF 20) which included elements of the Delta Force commando unit, US Navy SEALs, and Central Intelligence Agency paramilitary teams.

RIGHT: Eight AC-130Us of the 4th Special Operations Squadron deployed to the Middle East for the US-led invasion of Iraq in early 2003. (USAF)

TF 20 reported directly to General Franks at the US Central Command forward headquarters in Qatar and was only used for strategic missions, such as locating weapons of mass destruction and regime leadership targets. The first mission of TF 20 was the securing of Iraqi oil installations around Basra to prevent their sabotage. Reconnaissance teams were inserted inside Iraq in the days before the invasion to scout out Iraqi units that might want to defect or surrender.

Al Faw Oil Refinery

The AC-130Us were given a central role supporting the US and British operation to seize key oil facilities on the Al Faw peninsula during the early hours of March 21. A reconnaissance team of US Navy SEALs was landed to monitor the Iraqi garrison and as waves of British Royal Marines landed by helicopter, a gunship engaged the defenders. The shell-shocked Iraqi troops were unable to put up much resistance and the British secured all their objectives before any sabotage could take place.

As this operation was underway, AC-130Us patrolled over the northern Arabian Gulf to make sure no Iraqi reinforcements were sent by boat to the peninsula. During this mission, one of the gunships had the honour, according to the USAF, of being "the first US Air Force aircrew and aircraft to sink a maritime combat surface vessel during a war effort since World War Two."

The AC-130U crew engaged and destroyed an Iraqi fast-attack patrol boat after the vessel had been spotted and tracked by a US Navy Lockheed P-3 Orion patrol aircraft. The boat's crew fired on the AC-130U, and in dry official language, a US Navy officer noted that the US Navy aircraft's crew "coordinated with the AC-130 to have the boat destroyed."

ABOVE: British Royal Marines received fire support from AC-130Us during the first hours of their assault on the Al Faw Peninsula on March 21, 2003. (MOD/CROWN COPYRIGHT)

Once Iraq's integrated air defence system was suitably degraded by allied air strikes, the AC-130Hs were able to operate further into the country without fear of being shot down. Rumsfeld was disappointed that the Iraqi army was not surrendering en masse to US troops but was starting to put up determined resistance in towns along the Euphrates valley. US Marines and US Army columns were ambushed, prompting a request for the AC-130s to be diverted to fly close air support missions. Gunship strikes were instrumental in breaking Iraqi resistance around As Samawah on March 30 and 31. The most high-profile gunship mission was

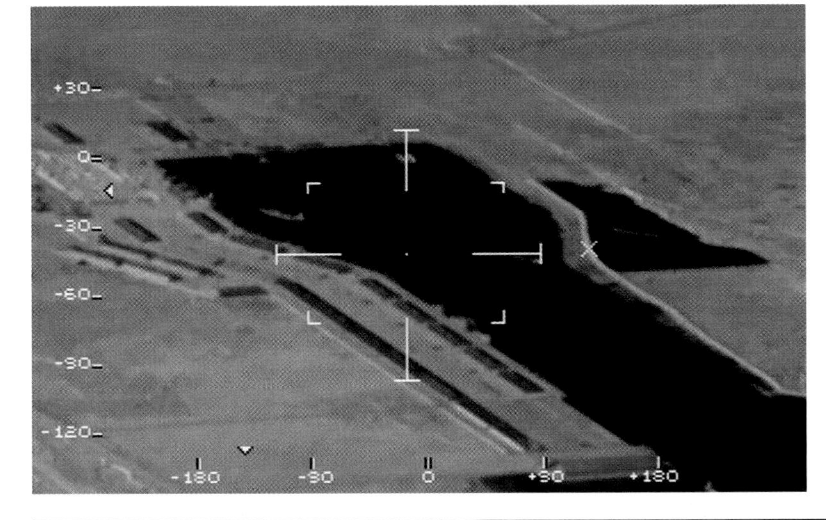

LEFT: Coalition special forces operations to seize Umm Qasr port in southern Iraq on the first day of the invasion received top cover from USAF AC-130U gunships. (ROYAL AUSTRALIAN AIR FORCE)

LEFT: AC-130H Spectre of the 16th Special Operations Squadron took their turn to deploy to Iraq during the US occupation of the Middle East country from 2003 to 2011. (US DOD)

ABOVE: A British C-130J Hercules fires flares to decoy away hostile missile threats during its landing at Baghdad airport in the summer of 2003. Soon after the official US 'defeat' of the Iraqi armed force in April 2003, insurgents started to strike against coalition troops and aircraft across the country. (USAF)

to support a TF 20 recovery mission to Nasiriyah civilian hospital on April 1 to secure a US Army prisoner of war, Private Jessica Lynch.

By the middle of April, US tank columns had battled their way to Baghdad, prompting Saddam Hussein and his loyalists to melt away. Many of the Iraqi army troops just went home, rather than surrender. AC-130Us of the 4th SOS played a pivotal role during Operation Iraqi Freedom by firing some of the first shots of the conflict. During the initial two months of action, it flew more than 1,000 combat hours from three separate forward operating locations.

The rapid occupation of Baghdad proved deceptive. Within weeks of the US Army capturing the city, it was in turmoil as a wave of looting engulfed the Iraqi capital and most basic services – water, electricity, sanitation, telephones, and garbage collections – collapsed. Very soon afterwards, US troops started to come under attack by well-armed and organised insurgents. This was the start of a seven-year long occupation that would cost the lives of 4,431 US soldiers and leave nearly 40,000 wounded. More than 100,000 Iraqi civilians would be killed in the insurgency that raged across Iraq.

The 4th and 16th SOS were soon pulling back-to-back rotations to deploy their gunships to Ali al Salem and flying missions in support of the US occupation army. In early 2004, the insurgency morphed into a major uprising by the Iraqi majority Shia population. For several months, US and coalition troops in Baghdad and the south of the country were besieged in their compounds. Gunships proved highly effective at finding and neutralising insurgent sniper and mortar teams attacking coalition bases. At the same time, Sunni insurgents in central Iraqi seized control of the city of Fallujah for most of the summer of 2004. In October 2004, a divisional sized force of US Marines assaulted the

city with strong gunship support and much of Fallujah was devastated in the fighting.

JSOC Overwatch

With open resistance crushed, the US occupation forces moved to confronting small groups of insurgents across the cities of Iraq. The elite Joint Special Operations Command (JSOC), made up of the US Army Delta Force and US Navy SEALs, launched a campaign of intelligence-led raids to kill or capture individual insurgents in their homes or hideouts. AC-130 gunships were drafted in to provide overwatch for the JSOC assault teams during their unrelenting series of night raids.

Between 2006 and 2008, JSOC staged raids on a nightly basis, across the length and breadth of Iraq. Assault teams were inserted rapidly by helicopters, while gunships or drones circled overhead monitoring the reaction of the target and standing ready to provide fire support if they put up resistance.

A 4th SOS mission in September 2007 was typical of how the gunships supported JSOC raids. It resulted in three AC-130U crew members being awarded the Distinguished Flying Cross for their endeavours. The medal is awarded to any officer or enlisted member of the US armed forces who distinguishes themself in combat in support of operations

BELOW: EC-130J Commando Solo aircraft flew in support of AC-130U missions to broadcast propaganda messages to undermine Iraqi morale and will to fight. (USAF)

RIGHT: The 4th Special Operations Squadron's AC-130Us bore the brunt of Iraq missions during the invasion phase in March and April 2003. USAF gunships also were committed to other fronts of the 'Global War on Terror' on missions to Libya, Somalia, and Yemen. (USAF)

by heroism or extraordinary achievement while participating in an aerial flight.

Major David Torraca, Captain Timothy Hood, and Staff Sergeant JH Smith each received the honour for a high-priority mission providing cover and situational awareness to a Navy SEAL team infiltrating enemy territory.

While conducting the mission, the gunship crew noticed a group of suspicious individuals moving away from the village in a nearby field and notified the SEAL team. The SEALs sent an eight-person team to investigate, and the insurgents unexpectedly opened fire, wounding three of the team members. Before the SEAL's forward air controller called for fire support, the gunship crew was already preparing to engage the enemy, and within 23 seconds from receiving the call, rounds were on the ground.

The gunship provided a protective wall of fire that allowed the SEALs to move their wounded to a medical evacuation helicopter. The rain of fire power eventually eliminated the threat, and the gunship crew continued their originally tasked mission.

Lieutenant Don Nichols, one of the eight SEALs on the ground during the mission attended the medal ceremony for the gunship crew in June 2008 and said: "Without your guys, our guys would have been killed. They saved three of my comrades."

"For any given night, that crew could have been any of the 4th SOS crews," said Colonel Brad Webb, 1st Special

BELOW: Gunners onboard an AC-130U Spooky of the 4th Special Operations Squadron load the 40mm Bofors gun (rear) and 105mm howitzer in the aircraft's cargo compartment. (USAF)

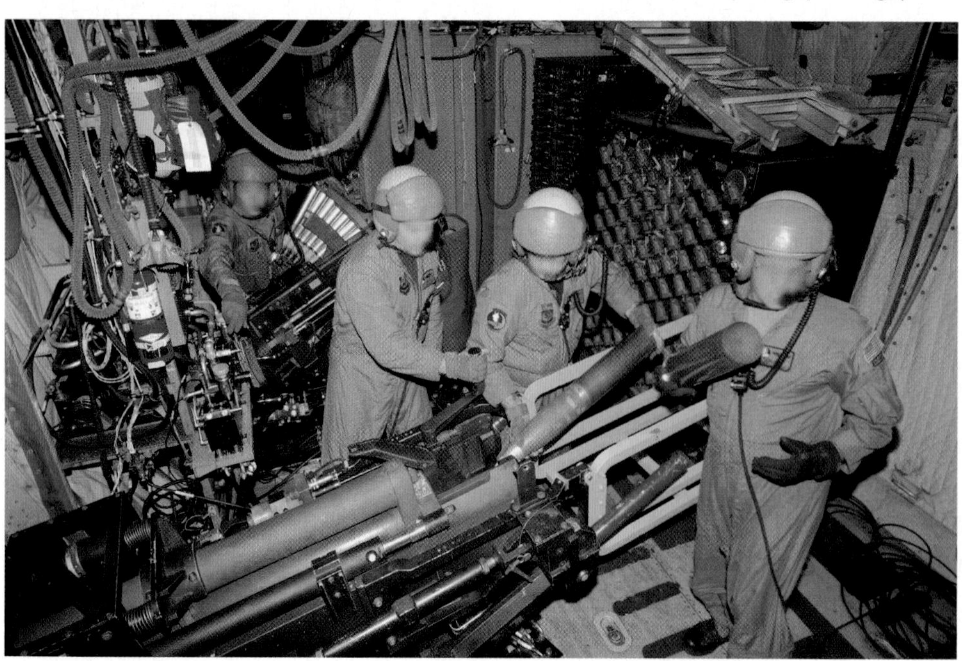

LEFT: AC-130H of the 16th Special Operations Squadron took the lead in Afghanistan in early 2002 to allow the AC-130Us to prepare for the invasion of Iraq. Eventually both units took turns to operate over Iraq until December 2011 when US troops finally withdrew from the country. (USAF)

Operations Wing Commander. "It speaks volumes of the professionalism of this squadron that it happened to be this crew. They did a fantastic job. This is business as usual for the 4th SOS."

By 2009, the back of the insurgence was broken but US troops remained on duty in Iraq for another two years helping to rebuild the country's security forces. Fittingly, as the last US troops drove into Kuwait from Iraq on December 18, 2011, an AC-130H of the 16th SOS was on patrol overhead to ensure the symbolic event passed off peacefully.

BELOW: Insurgents in Iraq were heavily armed with anti-aircraft guns and missiles, so AC-130Us had to regularly deploy their self defence systems. (USAF)

AC-130W Stinger II

The Precision Strike Gunship

ABOVE: The 73rd Special Operations Squadron brought the MC-130W Combat Spear/ AC-130W into service in 2006. (USAF)

In May 2009, US Air Force Special Operations Command (AFSCOC) declared the need to grow the gunship fleet and expand its firepower. It decided to replace its older H and U model gunships with a more powerful variant based on the more modern C-130J airframe, which featured a glass cockpit and distinctive six bladed propellers.

There was initially talk of using the Italian-built Alenia C-27J Spartan as the basis of the USAF next generation gunships, but eventually it was decided to stick with the C-130J. However, this would not be ready until the mid-2010s at the earliest. In the meantime, more gunships were needed to fight the 'Global War on Terror' in Iraq and Afghanistan.

To fill this gap, four more AC-130U Spooky gunships were ordered and it was also decided to arm Lockheed

RIGHT: The AC-130W Stinger II saw the introduction of major technological developments, including the fielding of precision guided missiles on a gunship for the first time. (USAF)

MC-130W Combat Spear covert insertion aircraft. The idea was to fit them with a 'Precision Strike Package' of advanced night sensors, guided missiles, and a limited gun armament. This was to be a 'gunship-lite' capability, but nowhere near the full firepower of the AC-130U. The MC-130W already had many of the sensors, communications and defensive systems installed in the AC-130U so the conversion work was considered straightforward.

All the sensors and weapons systems to be carried in the AC-130W's cargo cabin were mounted on roll-on-roll-off installation kits. So, unlike, earlier models of AC-130 gunships, no major structural engineering changes were required to install weapons. This dramatically speeded up the progress of the programme and reduced costs. L3 Communications was awarded a $61m contract in September 2010 to convert eight aircraft into a configuration which was initially dubbed 'Dragon Spear'.

Fast Track Deployment

The original MC-130Ws were delivered to the 73rd Special Operations Squadron (SOS) at Hurlburt Field in Florida in 2006 and in December it relocated to Cannon AFB in New Mexico. After being initially used for the covert insertion role, the conversion into gunships began in 2009. The MC-130W Dragon Spear went from concept to flying with a minimum capability in less than 90 days, and from concept to deployment in 18 months. A month after arriving in Afghanistan, the first aircraft fired its first weapons in combat. This success won the programme the William J. Perry Award for excellence in military procurement.

AC-130W STINGER II
Powerplant: Four Allison T56-A-15 turboprop engines
Wingspan: 40.4m (132 ft 7in)
Length: 29.8m (97 ft 9in)
Height: 11.7m (38 ft 6in)
Max take-off weight: 69,750kg (155,000lb)
Speed: 482kph (300mph)
Range: 4,630km (2,500 nm); limited by crew duty day with air refuelling
Crew: Seven
Armament:
Precision Strike Package with one × GAU-23/A 30mm cannon and one × M102 105mm cannon
GBU-44/B Viper Strke missile, GBU-39/B Small Diameter Bombs and AGM-176 Griffin missile

ABOVE: AC-130W serial 90-1058 was nicknamed *The Fourth Horseman*. (TOMAS DEL CORO)

The new aircraft were to be armed with a Bushmaster II GAU-23/A 30mm cannon, and a Gunslinger precision-guided munitions system: a launch tube designed to fire up to 10 GBU-44/B Viper Strike missiles or AGM-176 Griffin small stand-off munitions in quick succession.

Once the programme was underway the USAF upped its requirements and a 105mm

LEFT: The cockpit of the AC-130W was a mix of the old and new, combining 1950s vintage dials with 21st century multi-function displays. This aircraft from the 73rd Special Operations Squadron was carrying out a live-fire mission in support of Exercise Emerald Warrior in Florida in April 2015. (USAF)

LEFT: An AC-130W employs its main armament during gunnery training exercises in 2016. (USAF)

LOCKHEED MARTIN AC-130W STINGER II GUNSHIPS			
Type	Serial	Names	Notes
	87-9286		
	87-9288		
	88-1301		
	88-1302		
	88-1303		
	88-1304		
	88-1305		
	88-1306		
	88-1307		
	88-1308		On Display Cannon AFB, New Mexico
	89-1051		
	90-1058	*Fourth Horseman*	

howitzer was installed. Later, GBU- 39 SDB and GBU-69B Small Glide Munitions, as well as AGM-114P-2 Hellfire missiles, were added to the aircraft weapons fit. Other upgrades included Enhanced Situational Awareness (ESA) for near real-time intelligence and data fusion including threat detection, avoidance, geolocation, and adversary-emitter identification and infra-red suppression.

In 2012, the aircraft was renamed the AC-130W Stinger II to tap into the Vietnam heritage of the USAF's gunship community. Its crews tended to call it the 'Whiskey Gunship', after its 'W' designation. More aircraft were ordered to take the inventory up to 12 by September 2013. The 16th SOS took over the AC-130Ws in 2015 after they had retired their last H model gunships.

The AC-130W saw extensive service in Afghanistan and Iraq but when the AC-130Js started to arrive the Stinger II's time was up. In October 2020, the first aircraft was retired, and the last

Harvest Hawk

In the wake of the USAF's rapid conversion of the MC-130W into the Stinger II using roll-on-roll off weapon pallets, the United States Marine Corps was keen to follow their example and arm their own Hercules.

In 2009 it launched Project Harvest HAWK (Hercules Airborne Weapons Kit), to arm its Lockheed Martin KC-130J Hercules tanker/transporter aircraft. This rapid acquisition project involved fitting a AN/AAQ-30 targeting sight system in a turret mounted under the left wing's external fuel tank. Wing pylons were installed to allow the aircraft to carry AGM-114 Hellfire guided missiles. AGM-176 Griffin small stand-off munitions were installed on the aircraft's rear cargo ramp.

The USMC at first planned to acquire three kits per active-duty KC-130J squadron for a total of nine kits, each costing up to $22m. Ten KC-130Js were modified to accept them so the weapon kits could be rapidly installed when they were needed to fly combat missions.

Harvest HAWK was first test flown in August 2009 by the US Navy test squadron, VX-20, and first deployed to Afghanistan in October 2010 with USMAC transport/tanker squadron, VMGR-352. It first saw action at Sangin in Afghanistan on November 4, 2010, while supporting 5th Regiment Marines, killing five Taliban insurgents with a Hellfire missile.

In 2016, the Marines formulated a major upgrade called Harvest Hawk+ and announced plans to introduce HAWK-compatibility on its remaining 69 un-upgraded KC-130Js. The new format swaps out the AAQ-30 bolted on the left wing for a higher-quality L3 Wescam MX-20 sensor turret mounted under the nose. A long-promised but long delayed 30mm side-firing cannon could eventually follow to convert the aircraft into a true gunship.

The AC-130W and KC-130J Harvest Hawk conversions showed the potential for rapid low-cost gunship conversions. As a result, Lockheed Martin has launched a marketing campaign to export customers.

BELOW: The AC-130W was the last gunship based on the C-130H model Hercules and can be identified by its four bladed propellers. (USAF)

one was withdrawn from service in June 2022.

In just over 10 years of service the Stinger II flew a combined 2,170 combat sorties, totalling over 15,000 hours. In this time, they expended 300,000 rounds of 30mm and 105mm ammunition and over 2,000 precision guided munitions in close air support, direct fire, and air interdiction missions.

During the ceremony to mark the installation of the last AC-130W, *Excalibur II*, serial 88-1308, in a permanent display at Cannon AFB, Colonel Kaveri Crum, deputy commander of the 1st Special Operations Wing highlighted the historical importance of the aircraft "Thirteen-o-eight is the last of the whiskeys," said Crum. "Her 11 friends have long left her to carry on the legacy, but today this aircraft gets a well-deserved retirement and a fitting resting place. From her ramp, we launched the first PGMs (Precision Guided Munitions), from her wings we launched the first SDBs, and from her sides we fired the first 30mm," said Crum. "Every shot was another drumbeat pushing us further. This beautiful machine represents something much greater than a combination of nuts and bolts," said Crum. "It represents intangibles, like people, courage, and service."

ABOVE: The US Marine Corps armed its KC-130J tanker/airlifters with precision guided munitions under the Harvest Hawk programme. Although not a true gunship, their crews borrowed many tactics and procedures from the USAF gunship community. (USMC)

LEFT: Packs of four AGM-114 Hellfire missiles were mounted on racks under each wing of Harvest Hawk KC-130Js. (USMC)

AC-130J Ghostrider

The Gunship for the 21st century

ABOVE: The distinctive six-bladed propellers of the AC-130J Ghostrider make it easy to differentiate from earlier gunship variants based on the C-130E/H model of the Hercules. (USAF)

The Lockheed Martin AC-130J Ghostrider is the USAF's current gunship, with 31 aircraft in service in four active duty squadrons. A reserve unit provides individual personnel and crews to augment the active duty units.

The USAF gunship fleet has never been this big and for the first time a single variant is in use. These aircraft look set to remain in use for at least two more decades and could still be flying into the second half of the 21st century.

US Air Force Special Operations Command (AFSOC) senior leaders had been looking at a long-term programme to introduce a new gunship based on the C-130J variant. In the mid-1990s the United States eventually signed up to buy this variant progressively replacing its older E and H model C-130s, which were showing their age and becoming more expensive to maintain. Since the Hercules first flew in 1954, the aircraft had been progressively updated to incorporate new technology and improve reliability.

In the 1990s Lockheed had been working to develop its new C-130J variant, which features glass cockpits, advanced avionics, and new Rolls-Royce AE 2100D3 turboprop engines. As the older models went out of production, the USAF had to look to migrate their units to the new airframe. It is easy to differentiate the E and H models from the J model because of the new aircraft's six distinctive shaped propeller blades. The older aircraft had four 'flat' bladed propellers.

RIGHT: AC-130Js continue to sport aircraft nose art in the tradition of the Air Commandos dating back to the Vietnam era. (USAF)

Enhanced Performance

The J model's performance was enhanced over the E and H models, allowing it to carry more cargo, over longer ranges, as well as being more agile. The move to glass cockpit technology brought the Hercules into the era of 'software drive' aircraft. This revolutionised the Hercules, allowing pilots and crew to view flight and mission information on computer screens and rapidly share combat data. This turned the Hercules from a 1950s-era aircraft into a 21st century aircraft. Special operations aviators were keen to take advantage of this technology leap and exploit the capabilities of the latest variant of the Hercules.

Consequently, a programme to replace its legacy Hercules airframes with newer J variants was worked up by AFSOC but this at first did not include a gunship variant.

In the first decade of the 21st century the USAF focused on developing a gunship variant of the two-engine Alenia C-27J. This was a modernised version of the Italian G.222 light transport aircraft that had been fitted with the same glass cockpit, avionics, and engines used in the AC-130J. Lockheed and the Italian company co-operated to work up the design of the new gunship, which was tentatively designated AC-XX. Funding was allocated by the Pentagon in 2008 to develop the design of the AC-27J. By using proven systems from the C-130J and the MC-130J Dragon Spear gunship, it was hoped to save money and remove risk from the project.

The weapon fit was intended to be modular, involving either 30mm or 40mm guns or precision-guided munitions such as the Viper Strike bomb. At the Air Force Association's 2008 conference, it was even named 'Stinger II' after the Vietnam-era AC-119K Stinger.

AC-130J GHOSTRIDER
Powerplant: Four Rolls-Royce AE 2100D3 turboprop engines
Wingspan: 39.7m (132ft 7in)
Length: 29.3m (97ft 9in)
Height: 11.9m (39ft 2in)
Max take-off weight: 74,389kg (164,000lbs)
Speed: 670 km/h (316mph)
Range: 5,556km (3,000nm); unlimited with air refuelling
Crew: Nine
Armament:
Precision Strike Package with one × GAU-23 30mm cannon and one × M137 105mm howitzer
GBU-39 Small Diameter Bombs, GBU-69 Small Glide Munitions
AGM-114 Hellfire missile and AGM-176 Griffin missile

LEFT AND BELOW: Crews of AC-130Js keep up their skills in regular gunnery exercises at ranges across the USA and in allied countries. Here tank hulks on the Melrose bombing range in New Mexico are engaged with 105mm howitzer fire. (USAF)

RIGHT: An AC-130J Ghostrider makes its first official sortie from Eglin Air Force Base in Florida in January 2014. The MC-130J arrived at Eglin in January 2013 to begin the modification process into the AC-130J. (USAF)

A C-27A, serial 90-0170, was removed from storage at AMARC in October 2008 and delivered to Eglin AFB in Florida, for use by the Air Force Research Laboratory to assess the feasibility of mounting 30mm and 40mm guns. In May 2009, the programme was put on hold because the US Army pulled its financial contribution to the project. The AFSOC now decided to switch its attention to the C-130J to ensure commonality with the other specialist aircraft in its portfolio.

Work was already underway to create J variants of the MC-130 Combat Talon covert insertion aircraft and HC-130 air-to-air refuelling tankers. There was a great deal of commonality between these variants and the requirements for a future gunship, in particular its advanced sensors, communications and defensive systems.

By 2011 the project was ready to move forward, and the USAF sought to acquire 16 new AC-130J gunships, based on new built MC-130J Commando II special operations aircraft. It was proposed to outfit them with a 'precision strike package'

BELOW: Hurlburt Field in Florida is the home of two AC-130J squadrons and the first unit, the 73rd Special Operations Squadron, converted to the aircraft in 2018. (USAF)

to give them an attack capability. The initial budget was set at $1.6bn to be run from 2011 through to 2015. This project was aimed at following the path of the Dragon Spear programme that had transformed the MC-130W into a gunship. It was named Ghostrider in May 2012 after the supernatural avenger.

Weapons Fit

The AC-130J is fitted with a similar weapons fit to the AC-130W, including a trainable 30mm GAU-23/A cannon and a M102 105mm cannon, which are mounted on pallets for rapid insertion and removal. Up to eight wing pylon-mounted GBU-39 SDB or AGM-114 Hellfire can be carried. Aft-firing GBU69B Small Glide Munition or AGM-176 Griffin can be deployed from 10 Common Launch Tubes integrated into the aircraft's ramp/door.

Two MX-20 electro-optical/infrared sensor/laser designator pods and multiple video, data, and communication links allow the Ghostrider's crew to find targets themselves as well as receive intelligence from external sources.

The AC-130J is operated by nine aircrew. The new glass cockpit allows the flight deck crew to be reduced to two pilots. Its weapons are operated by one combat system officer, one weapons system operator, and five special mission aviators, which include a sensor operator, a loadmaster, and three gunners. A dual-console mission operator pallet in the cargo bay

ABOVE: In 2023 USAF commanders hinted that the 105mm howitzer might be removed from AC-130Js to allow more stand-off weapons to be carried, but to date, the devastating weapons have remained in the aircraft. (USAF)

LEFT: The AC-130J boasts the ability to launch AGM-114 Hellfire missiles for stand-off attack missions. (USAF)

BELOW: To allow for a full spectrum of responses, the AC-130J routinely carries a full war load of 105mm shells for their howitzers. (USAF)

ABOVE: The development programme for the AC-130J saw a gradual releases of blocks of capabilities and the early aircraft did not have the 105mm howitzers. All the fleet now have this weapon. (USAF)

controls all weapon systems and sensors, and links them to remote displays and control panels on the flight deck.

The entry to service of the AC-130J involved a progressive introduction of new capabilities, via a series of software releases and installation of new hardware. Initial aircraft were in the Block 10 configuration, which included an internal, pallet-mounted 30mm side-firing chain gun, wing-mounted GPS-guided Small Diameter Bombs (SBD) and Griffin laser-guided missiles mounted internally and launched through the rear cargo door.

Block 20 added a 105mm gun, laser-guided SDB, side-facing pilot tactical HUD, and Large Aircraft Infrared Countermeasures (LAIRCM). Block 20+/30 improved gun accuracy, hardened GPS, and added Hellfire missile and Small Glide Munition capability.

The first Block 30 aircraft was delivered for testing in 2019 and featured more mature software and avionics. These features were retrofitted across the fleet and by 2024 they were all configured to the same standard.

On January 9, 2013, Lockheed Martin began converting the first MC-130J into an AC-130J, at its Gunship Modification Facility in Crestview in Florida, but the project suffered a major setback when the initial aircraft was overstressed beyond repair when it departed controlled flight during a test sortie on April 21, 2015. However, Pentagon assessors declared they were happy with the test programme and in July 2015 opened the way for deliveries to commence to the AFSOC, with initial operating capability being achieved in 2017.

RIGHT: Despite its high technology, gunners still have to manually load shells and clear spent cases from the AC-130J's 105mm howitzer. (USAF)

The USAF had originally planned to buy 37 AC-130Js but it eventually reduced its order to 31 airframes. Plans were also scrapped to assess an Airborne High Energy Laser (AHEL) weapon on the aircraft.

The deliveries of the AC-130J resulted in major changes to the structure of the USAF gunship force.

73rd SOS

The first operational AC-130J squadron, the 73rd Special Operations Squadron (SOS), was reactivated at Hurlburt Field in Florida in February 2018. It had previously flown the AC-130W up to 2015. Sixteen months later the squadron undertook its first deployment to Afghanistan to relieve the AC-130U Spooky IIs that had been supporting US, coalition, and Afghan special forces. This allowed the Spooky IIs to return to the United

States, marking the last scheduled combat deployment for that version of the AC-130. In March 2019, the 4th SOS began to receive its first AC-130J to replace its old AC-130Us, becoming the second operational gunship squadron to fly the new variant from Hurlburt Field.

AC-130Js started to be delivered to Cannon AFB in New Mexico in July 2020 to allow the 17th SOS to begin converting from the MC-130J to the new gunship.

The final active duty unit to convert to the AC-130J was the original Spectre unit, the 16th SOS, which officially received its new aircraft in April 2022 and retired its last AC-130W.

As well as fielding aircraft for four active duty gunship squadrons, the AC-130J roll-out resulted in complete US Air Force Reserve crews flying gunships for the first time since 1995, when the 711th SOS stood down. The Duke Field-based 5th SOS achieved the landmark on June 5, 2020; by flying the first all reserve crewed AC-130 mission in 25 years to augment its active duty counterparts.

The delivery of the 31st and final AC-30J to Cannon AFB on November 3, 2022, completed AFSOC's

ABOVE: An AC-130J Ghostrider over interior Wisconsin during the EAA AirVenture Oshkosh 2021 event. The aircraft was part of a gunship legacy flight which paid tribute to Air Force Special Operations Command's heritage and displayed its newest gunship to the American public. (USAF)

BELOW: The first AC-130J takes to the skies over Eglin Air Force Base in Florida on January 31, 2014. (USAF)

RIGHT: The 'glass' cockpit of the AC-130J allows flight crew to access massive amounts of data on multi-function displays. (USAF)

BELOW RIGHT: The distinctive six bladed Dowty's R391 propellers power the C-130J aircraft in conjunction with the Rolls-Royce AE 2100 turboprop engines. (USAF)

LOCKHEED MARTIN AC-130J GHOSTRIDER GUNSHIPS		
Serial	**Name**	**Loss**
09 -5710		April 2015, written off after aircraft being over stressd
11-5735		
12-5753		
12-5772	*Hell's Belle*	
13-5783		
14-5787		
14-5789		
14-5797		
14-5802		
14-5803		
14-5809	*Azrael*	
15-5811		
16-8525		
16-5835		
16-5837		
16-5844		
16-5846		
16-5852		
16-5861		
17-5869		
17-5872		
17-5877		
17-5882		
18-5886		
18-5888		
18-5891		
18-5905		
18-5913		
18-5916		
18-5920		
19-5922		
19-5926		
19-5926	*Slugge*	

transition from the legacy AC-130W, AC-130U, and AC-130H fleets.

During the AC-130J Ghostrider dedication and delivery ceremony at Lockheed Martin's Crestview site on November 2, 2022, Lieutenant Colonel Joe Allen, the USAF's Gunship Program manager explained that the final aircraft had been named after one engineer who designed the Precision Strike Package used on the MC-130W and AC-130J. He said this was following the tradition of naming aircraft, started in World War Two and resurrected by the gunship force in Southeast Asia.

"Aircraft #31 is being named in honour of Mr. Stan 'Sluggo' Siefke who was instrumental in the developments of the precision strike package prior to cutting first metal on the MC-130W," said Allen. "Sluggo's impacts on Whiskey and Ghostrider have been nothing short of outstanding and we are honoured to have him in attendance today."

During the ceremony, Lieutenant General Jim Slife, AFSOC commander, recalled that it had been only a few years earlier when he was working at the Pentagon for the Office of Secretary of Defense. He began the messaging and formative language that initiated the Ghostrider programme that he was seeing come full circle.

"In the fall of 2009, the secretary of defence decided to recapitalise

[the AC-130] with C-130Js to build the platforms we see behind us today," Slife said.

"The airplane and its predecessors have exceeded all our expectations and kept more Americans alive than any other airplane on the battlefield. The future is going to be different than what we have experienced for the last 20 years, but one thing I'm certain of is this airplane will be relevant to whatever the future operating environment brings, so thank you all for delivering such a magnificent capability to today's warfighters."

ABOVE, LEFT AND BELOW: Changing threats have prompted the USAF to use its AC-130Js in new environments so in April 2024 a gunship of 27th Special Operations Wing, practiced engaging vessels during a maritime littoral strike exercise near Lubang in the Philippines. (USMC)

The Long War

Gunships over Afghanistan 2003 to 2021

RIGHT: A gunner reloads 40mm rounds during a mission over Afghanistan in 2020. (USAF)

BELOW: Bagram Airbase was the home of USAF gunship detachments in Afghanistan up until a few weeks before the US withdrawal from the country in 2021. Mountain ranges surrounded the valley where the air base was located. (US NAVY)

In early 2002, US and NATO troops started to fan out across Afghanistan to help establish the country's new government and then start to rebuild the war-torn country.

It was the start of the longest commitment of USAF gunship units to an overseas combat zone, with AC-130s operating over Afghanistan until August 2021 when the US and coalition troops finally withdrew from the country.

There were few big battles, but a series of small engagements, raids, or ambushes, which required gunships to intervene to protect US and coalition troops. During mid-2002 and early-2003, the USAF started to establish Bagram Airbase outside Kabul as its main hub in the country and it soon had gunship units in permanent residence. From this massive base, gunship units mounted nightly patrols over the countryside to stand ready to protect coalition troops under attack or to monitor raids by US and allied special forces. Every US gunship unit took its turn to pull duty in Bagram at some point over the two-decade long US presence in Afghanistan.

The long endurance of the AC-130, its high effective sensors and precision firepower, meant the aircraft was ideal for flying long overwatch patrols across Afghanistan. Increasingly the USAF introduced

the General Atomics MQ-1 Predator and MQ-9 Reaper armed unmanned aerial vehicles to Afghanistan to fly similar missions, which reduced the burden on the small AC-130 force.

However, these drones could not totally replace the AC-130, which had more firepower, and its guns could deliver sustained fire to neutralise big groups of insurgents dispersed over large areas. The day of the gunship was not over.

Lite Footprint

The then US Defense Secretary Donald Rumsfeld called the initial American presence in Afghanistan a 'Lite Footprint' and the country's size meant that air power was the main means to help isolated US contingents that came under attack.

Between 2009 and 2014, the US surged more than 100,000 troops into Afghanistan and during this period US fast jets and attack helicopters had borne the biggest burden of providing close air support in the country. The withdrawal of NATO combat troops meant a return to a 'Lite Footprint' approach, with small teams of US advisors operating across the country attached to Afghan combat units. From 2014 to 2021, the AC-130 came back into its element to protect these small teams of advisors.

The US military had fielded new communications and sensor technology to help improve the provision of close air support, with remote viewing terminals known as ROVERS being introduced from 2003. These were computer tablets that allowed video imagery to be downloaded from AC-130s to ground controllers in the midst of battle, helping them identify targets for the gunship crews to attack.

Despite the withdrawal of US and NATO combat troops from Afghanistan in 2014, the Taliban were trying to step up their attacks across the country to overthrow the Kabul-based government. Their focus was initially to isolate and then overrun provincial capitals and military outposts.

In November 2016, the Taliban launched a surprise offensive aimed at capturing the northern city of Kunduz. On November 2, 2016, AC-130U call sign 'Spooky 43' provided close air support to a US special forces team and 43 Afghan soldiers, near the city. As the ground force advanced on a compound, they were caught in an ambush. Surrounded by a large enemy force armed with small arms, heavy machine guns, and grenades fighting from multiple defensive fighting positions, friendly forces sustained 16 casualties in the opening moments of battle.

As the enemy rapidly converged on the beleaguered US-led force, a US

ABOVE: Ground crew clean the barrel of an AC-130H's 105mm howitzer at Bagram Airbase between missions over Afghanistan. (USAF)

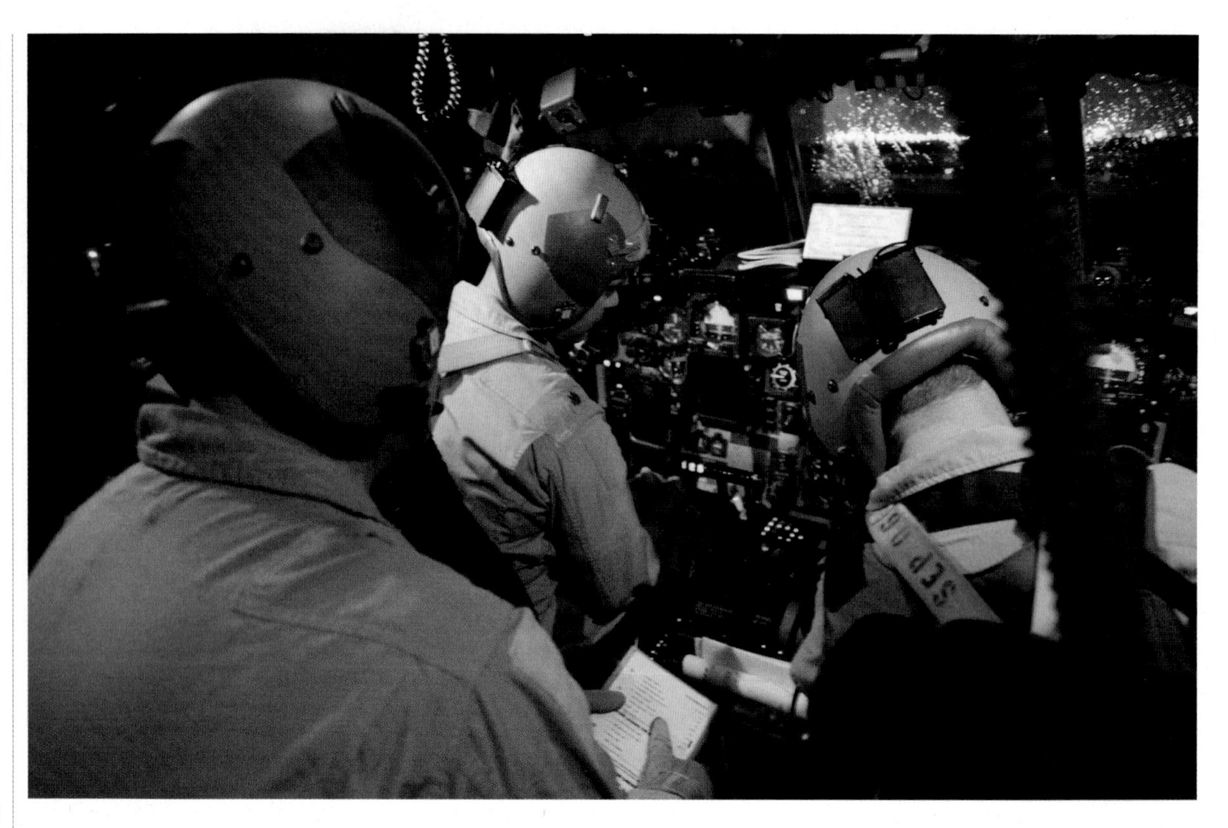

RIGHT: Pilots aboard an AC-130 gunship conduct final systems checks prior to take-off from Bagram Airbase in Afghanistan in March 2010. (US ARMY)

combat controller with the ground troops rapidly cleared the gunship crew to engage targets within ten metres of injured friendly forces, attacking massing insurgents and structures. As a result, the US team was able to clear their wounded from the immediate kill zone.

The ambush persisted as friendly forces attempted withdrawal. The aircrew conducted 19 'danger-close' attacks, consistently placing lethal fire to within ten metres of the severely wounded and outgunned friendly force. The firepower necessary to deter the enemy required the crew to exceed cooling requirements of the aircraft's 105mm howitzer, risking potential detonation inside the aircraft. The crew managed the temperature of the howitzer while continuing the firefight with the 40mm cannon, despite multiple weapon malfunctions. Expert co-ordination enabled the crew to manually fire rounds to defeat the enemy.

SPOOKY 43
AC-130U CREW
MAJOR ALEXANDER HILL
AIRCRAFT COMMANDER
MAJOR AARON HALL
FIRE CONTROL OFFICER
CAPTAIN GARRETT ROBINSON
AC-130U PILOT
1ST LT. ZACHARY HANLEY
NAVIGATOR
1ST LT. MARSHALL SHEFLER
ELECTRONIC WARFARE OFFICER
STAFF SGT. WILLIAM CODY
FLIGHT ENGINEER
STAFF SGT. FREDDIE COFFEE
SENSOR OPERATOR
STAFF SGT. CODY FLORA
SPECIAL MISSIONS AVIATOR
STAFF SGT. DAVID KERNS JR.
DIRECT SUPPORT OPERATOR
STAFF SGT. TIMOTHY LEWIS
SPECIAL MISSIONS AVIATOR
STAFF SGT. ALEXANDER SKIDGEL
SPECIAL MISSIONS AVIATOR
SENIOR AIRMAN KELLEN LLOYD
SPECIAL MISSIONS AVIATOR
SENIOR AIRMAN JONATHAN RUSSELL
SENSOR OPERATOR
AIRMAN 1ST CLASS RAYMOND BOURNE
SPECIAL MISSIONS AVIATOR

BELOW: The crew of AC-130U 'Spooky 43' received the prestigious MacKay Trophy for their efforts to provide close air support to US and coalition troops during the 2016 Battle of Kunduz in Afghanistan. (USAF)

Mackay Trophy

The AC-130U expended all their point-detonate fused 105mm rounds, and only eight airburst fused rounds remained at the end of the mission. This munition is designed to be employed on personnel in open areas, hundreds of metres from friendly forces. With enemy fighters closing fast, the crew stabilised the aircraft and fired the airburst round an unprecedented 12 metres from the friendly forces, annihilating the insurgents with a solitary shot.

During the battle, the gunship crew facilitated additional fire support from US Army Boeing AH-64D Apache helicopters, prepared medical helicopters to evacuate casualties, and helped co-ordinate a quick reaction force to help evacuate the coalition ground force from the city. Then, with minimal ammunition and fuel, the team led a dissimilar formation engagement between AC-130U and AH-64Ds to complete the defeat of the Taliban.

The AC-130U gunship crew's persistent fire support, presence of mind, and courage during two hours of intense combat saved 50 US and allied lives. The crew was awarded the MacKay Trophy for the most meritorious flight of the year by an USAF aircrew. In addition, five crew members were nominated for a Distinguished Flying Cross with Valor while the remaining crew members were submitted for Air Medals with Valor.

Taliban offensives continued across Afghanistan and in March 2017 a gunship crew was decorated for providing close air support for 35 American and Afghan special operations forces during a high-risk daylight armed reconnaissance mission in Kot Valley, near Nangahar Province in eastern Afghanistan. The official report of the engagement read: "Overwhelming hostile fire erupted, pinning the ground force inside hostile territory with a heavily armed and concealed force of more than 65 insurgents impeding their path to secure territory.

"The gunship crew immediately dropped to a lower altitude to increase weapons accuracy, putting them at risk from effective anti-aircraft artillery and man-portable air defence systems.

"Over the next 90 minutes, the gunship conducted 25 fire missions, 21 of those within danger-close range with the closest strike 35 metres away from friendly forces. Its crew battled gun malfunctions, low fuel, and man-portable surface-to-air-missile launch indications, to enable the friendly force to repel the enemy attack and return to their forward base without a single casualty."

Afghanistan Abandoned

By late 2020, the then US President Donald Trump had struck a peace deal with the Taliban that would allow Washington to remove all its troops from Afghanistan by the end of the summer of the following year. In the first days of July 2021, Bagram Airbase, outside Kabul, was abandoned and only a few hundred US troops remained in Kabul to cover the evacuation of the US embassy and secure the capital's airport. The AC-130J gunship contingent from the 73rd SOS had relocated from Bagram to Al Dhafra Airbase in the United Arab Emirates to allow them to continue to provide overwatch for the last US outpost in Kabul.

In the first days of August 2021, Taliban forces were surging towards Kabul and the US deployed an additional security force to secure the airport for the final evacuation. The situation went critical in

ABOVE: AC-130J Ghostrider gunships deployed to Afghanistan for the first time in June 2019. (USAF)

LEFT: USAF Chief of Staff General Norton Schwartz presents Captain Chad Bubanas with the Cheney Award on October 6, 2008, for his actions as the aircraft commander of an AC-130H Spectre gunship providing close-air support to troops on the ground in Afghanistan in May 2007. The Cheney Award is presented each year to aviators who demonstrate an act of valour, extreme fortitude, or self-sacrifice in a humanitarian venture. (USAF)

RIGHT: The last AC-130U Spooky II was retired in 2020 after seeing extended service in Afghanistan, Iraq, and elsewhere. (USAF)

the early hours of August 15, when Taliban fighters penetrated Kabul. The US ambassador decided to activate plans to evacuate the American embassy and helicopter shuttles started to move the last staffers to the airport. This prompted the Afghan president to flee his palace and fly out of the city for safety in Tajikistan. Tens of thousands of civilians followed him to the airport to seek seats on the US and allied evacuation flights. During the evening, they swarmed through the airport's gates and onto its runways.

Two AC-130Js, callsigns 'Shadow 77' and 'Shadow 78', were circling over the airport as this chaos unfolded. "There were just cars and people everywhere trying to get on to the airfield," recalled 1st Lieutenant William Bachmann, copilot on board Shadow 78.

BELOW: AC-130s flew almost all of their missions over Afghanistan at night from Bagram Airbase until the US force left the site in July 2021. (USAF)

LEFT: Twenty-one Distinguished Flying Crosses lay on a table before a ceremony at Hurlburt Field in May 2018. Lieutenant General Brad Webb, commander of Air Force Special Operations Command, presented the medals to four AC-130U crews of the 4th Special Operations Squadron for their heroic actions in Afghanistan. (USAF)

For the crews of two gunships, the mission to support the US withdrawal from Afghanistan would go on to last nearly 30 hours combined - resulting in the evacuation of roughly 2,000 Americans.

"[We knew the withdrawal] was going to happen at some point and that we were definitely going to be part of it," said Bachmann. "It was surreal."

On the morning of August 15, the crew to Shadow 77 were woken up to a notification telling them to report earlier than planned to begin their mission. Captain Lawrence Bria, aircraft commander of Shadow 77, said his crew had just enough time to quickly grab food, before heading to the gunship to get ready for take-off.

"We didn't know how long the night was going to go," Bria said. "But, as we flew toward Afghanistan, we talked about how we were going to be there as long as we needed to be and as long as leadership would allow us to be there."

As the gunship approached Kabul, they could see celebratory gunfire from the Taliban, as well as fireworks in the distance. On arrival, Shadow 77's initial mission was to provide overhead support as helicopter crews worked to evacuate the embassy and transport Americans to Kabul's Hamid Karzai International Airport.

Shortly afterwards, Shadow 78 arrived on scene to assist in the evacuation efforts. The crews on board Shadow 77 and Shadow 78 served as "eyes in the sky [for US ground forces]," Bria explained. "We were there in case things went even worse and a threat came to the Americans, either at the embassy or on the airfield, we would be there, ready for it," he said.

As well as its 105mm and 30mm cannons, the AC-130J is equipped with non-lethal, overt lasers markers or spotlights that can be used for crowd control and to deter violence. This feature became helpful as chaos broke out on the airfield, Bria noted. "During the rush toward the airfield, we were able to use the spotlight to help friendly forces on the ground," he explained. "If we saw anyone try to jump the fence or make a break for it on the runway, we used it to help ground forces to stop them."

Crowd Control

Their crowd dispersion efforts allowed eight US Air Force C-17 Globemaster III aircraft to land and take-off from Hamid Karzai International - carrying 2,000 Americans and Afghan refugees to safety.

In total, Shadow 77 and 78 executed a 29.8-hour mission - with Shadow 77 flying the longest AC-130J operations flight to date at 15.7 hours.

BELOW: Bagram Airbase was east of the Afghan capital Kabul and for a time it was the busiest US military airfield in the world. By the summer of 2021 it was abandoned without a shot being fired as US forces withdrew from Afghanistan. (USAF)

RIGHT: On August 30, 2021, the last US soldiers flew out of Kabul to end America's longest foreign war. Fittingly, an AC-130W flew 'top cover' for the last C-17 Globemaster to take off from Kabul. (USAF)

And while the mission lasted longer than some may have expected, Bria said the crews simply fell back on their training to push through.

"At that point, your instincts just kick in to make sure the Americans on the ground are safe, and you push your exhaustion and your stress and your worries to the side to get the mission done," Bria said.

Shadow 77 and 78 were not done yet with missions over Kabul. Every night until the evacuation was complete on August 30, AC-130Js were airborne over Kabul ready to support the beleaguered US and coalition security force at the airport if it came under attack. AC-130Ws of the 16th SOS also shifted theatres from Iraq to Afghanistan one last time, joining the nightly overwatch missions, logging as many flight hours as they were legally allowed to defend the remaining US personnel in the city.

RIGHT: US and British paratroopers held the perimeter around Kabul's Hamid Karzai International Airport for almost two weeks to cover the evacuation of more than 100,000 civilians seeking sanctuary from the victorious Taliban. (USAF)

BELOW: An AC-130W of the 16th SOS covered the final US flight out of Kabul. (USAF)

On August 30, 2021, an AC-130W flew the final gunship mission of the Afghan campaign as the last American forces departed Kabul. The presence of the gunships and other US aircraft proved a powerful deterrent and the AC-130Js and Ws did not fire a single shot during the evacuation operation.

Those members of the 73rd SOS were honoured for their efforts during the withdrawal from Kabul as recipients of the 2021 MacKay Trophy during a ceremony at the National Museum of the US Air Force at

Wright-Patterson Air Force Base in Ohio, December 7, 2022.

The trophy, which is administered by the Air Force and the National Aeronautic Association (NAA) for the 'most meritorious flight' of the year by a US Air Force person or organisation, was presented to the crews by US Air Force vice chief of staff of the air force, General. David Allvin, alongside Greg Principato, NAA President.

"Shadow 77 and Shadow 78 - you own, now, a special place," said Allvin. "Your name is on the same board with the greats...there's not many that can say that. You earned your way onto that by being the best airmen that you could when the nation called upon you."

Each of the 18 crew members received a medallion to commemorate their selection for the prestigious award.

During the ceremony, Air Force Special Operations' deputy commander, Major General Matthew Davidson lauded the crews for their "relentless" commitment to the mission's success.

"Shadow 77 and Shadow 78 have earned their spot on an incredible list of Airmen that are historic in our Air Force," said Davidson. "America's competitive advantages are these airmen and those hundreds of thousands [of] others that are out there. No adversary will ever compete with the airmen that the United States Air Force will put on the battlefield."

ABOVE: The crews of Shadow 77 and 78, received the Mackay Trophy for their role during the evacuation of the embassy in Kabul, Afghanistan, in August 2021. The awards ceremony took place in the National Museum of the US Air Force at Wright-Patterson Air Force Base on December 12, 2022. (USAF)

LEFT: The security ring around Kabul airport by US and allied ground troops, backed by AC-130s in the skies overhead, allowed more than 100,000 civilians to be safely evacuated from the city. (USAF)

Gunships Against ISIS

Operation Inherent Resolve, Iraq, and Syria 2014 to 2024

ABOVE: Air-to-air refuelling was an essential enabler of all AC-130 gunship missions over Iraq and Syria during Operation Inherent Resolve. (USAF)

In June 2014 reports started emerging from Iraq that a fanatical Islamic group had launched an offensive across the west and north of the country. Town after town appeared to fall with ease, as the US-trained and equipped Iraqi army just melted away when the black-dressed Jihadi fighters approached. The group's leader declared a 'caliphate', or Islamic State, in a sermon in the newly captured Iraqi city of Mosul. Nothing was able to stop this relentless advance.

By the first week of August 2014, so-called Islamic State (ISIS) columns were pushing into Kurdish held regions of Iraq and their spearheads were a few hours' drive away from its capital city, Erbil. Kurdish leaders made frantic calls to the US government asking for help. On August 8, US President Barak Obama answered the call by authorising US air strikes against the threat. US Navy strike jets from the USS *George HW Bush* were soon in action, bombing the ISIS columns.

The immediate crisis had passed but no one in the Pentagon or US Central Command had any doubts that more forces would be needed to fully defeat the threat. President Obama soon approved a war plan to deploy US advisors to boost the training of the Iraqi and Kurdish forces, as well as ramping up air strikes against ISIS. US, British, French, and Canadian special forces teams headed to Iraq to guide the air strikes onto their targets.

Across the Middle East, US and allied aircraft were arriving to join the air campaign to defeat the insurgency. It was no surprise when USAF gunship squadrons got the call to return to their old haunt at Ali Al Salem Airbase in Kuwait. The AC-130Us of the 4th Special Operations Squadron (SOS) and AC-130W of 16th and 73rd SOS were

RIGHT: Nighttime air-to-air refuelling from USAG KC-135 Stratotankers became second nature to gunship crews during the first 10 years of Operation Inherent Resolve. (USAF)

soon fully committed to Operation Inherent Resolve, as the new mission was code-named. Over the next decade the units took their turns to deploy and were joined by AC-130J units after the Ghostrider had entered service.

2014

Within days of the gunships arriving in August 2014, they were in action along the front, hitting ISIS positions under the direction of US and allied forward air controllers. It was a chaotic time, with shaken Iraqi troops retreating towards Baghdad. The arrival of the allied special forces teams to call down gunship and other air support was instrumental in stabilising the situation.

As the war continued into 2015, the US commanders and special operation forces became better organised at directing airpower against ISIS fighters. A joint strike centre was set up in Baghdad to filter requests for air support and then rapidly direct strike aircraft to their targets.

AC-130s were usually assigned nightly patrol boxes over critical sectors of the frontline, so could be well positioned to respond to requests for close air support.

US military planners then began to organise air strikes against ISIS positions in Syria, which were being used to assist their forces in Iraq. In November 2015, US special forces teams arrived in Syria to begin helping Kurdish fighters open a second front against ISIS. US airpower began sustained operations to protect these teams, with AC-130s flying nighttime defensive patrols over their positions.

US air strikes along the Euphrates valley close to Iraq were stepped up, with almost nightly AC-130 patrols looking for the ISIS supply columns. On November 16, 2015, the US launched Operation Tidal Wave II to destroy 116 ISIS fuel tankers clustered near Abu Kamal, a city on the Syrian border with Iraq. Four Fairchild A-10A Warthog strike jets and two AC-130 Spectre gunships participated in the raid. The aircraft devastated the vulnerable convoy, resulting in the Pentagon releasing video footage of several tankers exploding.

In 2016, the Iraqi army was ready to begin a series of offensive to take back several cities, including Mosul, from ISIS. By May, Iraqi troops were on the verge of capturing the city of Fallujah in central Iraq thanks to the support of more than 100 US and coalition air strikes.

Hundreds of ISIS fighters - recognising that their defeat was imminent - tried to flee the city. Two large convoys of vehicles were spotted by US drones as they departed Fallujah, with the first leaving in the morning and heading south and the second leaving in the evening and heading north. The first convoy took US commanders by surprise, and the Baghdad strike cell could not positively identify the vehicles as valid targets before they rapidly dispersed. By the end of the day, however, the strike cell had used drones to find and destroy the vehicles from the first convoy. In contrast, US air commanders were prepared for the evening convoy and waited until the caravan of vehicles had entered channelised terrain before interdicting the lead two vehicles, thus trapping the rest of the convoy. Passengers were allowed to flee before the US and Iraqi aircraft destroyed the remaining 150 vehicles. A-10s were assigned to engage the front third of the convoy, AC-130s were responsible for the middle section, and Iraqi Army helicopters were tasked with destroying the final third.

2017-2018

During 2017, Kurdish forces backed by coalition airpower drove the ISIS forces from the capital of their caliphate in the Syrian city of Raqqa, dispersing its defeated fighters into the countryside. To secure eastern Syria from any resurgence of

BELOW: Gunship crews had longer time at home in Florida or New Mexico between rotations to the Middle East after the end of the Afghan campaign in August 2021, as only one AC-130 detachment had to be sustained in theatre. (USAF)

RIGHT: Gunship crews got plenty of 'business' during the first three years of Operation Inherent Resolve but as so-called Islamic State (ISIS) fighters were driven from their strongholds there were fewer targets to be attacked. (USAF)

RIGHT: Targets for AC-130s included oil pumps used by so-called Islamic State (ISIS) to extract oil to fund their military campaign across Iraq and Syria. (US DOD)

BELOW: AC-130s attacks on so-called Islamic State (ISIS) oil production sites were credited with severely damaging its ability to extract oil to sell to fund their military campaign across Iraq and Syria. (US DOD)

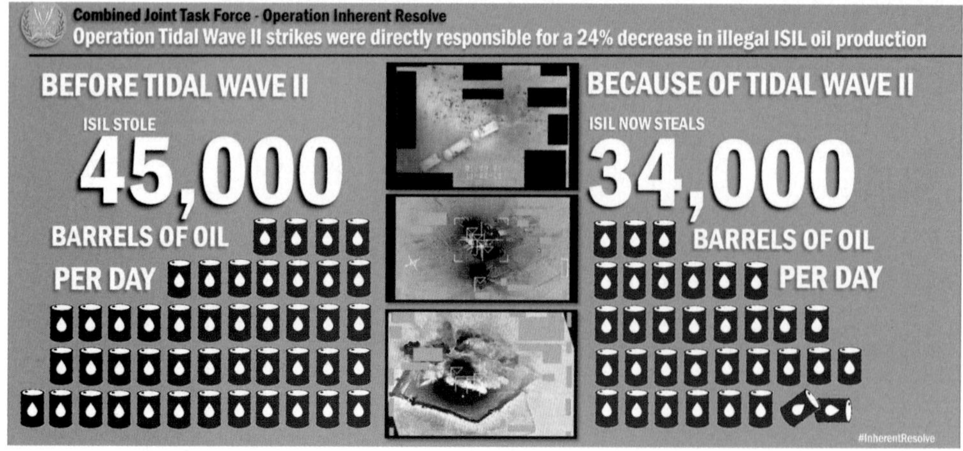

the organisation, the US military established a series of outposts in the country where US and allied special forces teams were based.

Combined Joint Task Force - Operation Inherent Resolve
Operation Tidal Wave II strikes were directly responsible for a 24% decrease in illegal ISIL oil production
BEFORE TIDAL WAVE II
ISIL STOLE
45,000
BARRELS OF OIL
PER DAY
BECAUSE OF TIDAL WAVE II
ISIL NOW STEALS
34,000
BARRELS OF OIL
PER DAY
#InherentResolve

US airpower was deployed to secure these bases from attack by ISIS fighters, pro-Iranian militias, Syrian government troops, and their Russian allies. Nighttime security patrols were flown over these bases by AC-130s and armed drones.

During the evening of February 7, 2018, a force of 500 pro-Syrian government fighters consisting of local militiamen, Syrian Army regulars, Shia militants from Liwa

Fatemiyoun and Liwa Zainebiyoun, and Russian mercenaries from the infamous Wagner Group, launched an assault on a joint US-Kurdish base near Khasham in eastern Syria. According to a Pentagon statement, the pro-government troops, supported by T-72 and T-55 tanks, first shelled the base with artillery, mortars, and rockets in a 'coordinated attack'. Around 20–30 shells landed within 500m of the base.

US special forces commanders called up airpower to respond, including AC-130 gunships, F-22 Raptor, and F-15E Strike Eagle fighter jets, MQ-9 Reaper unmanned combat aerial vehicles, AH-64 Apache attack helicopters, and B-52 bombers. Nearby American artillery batteries, including M142 HIMARS rocket launchers, shelled Syrian forces as well. The clashes lasted four hours and saw more than 100 Syrian pro-government fighters killed, with one SDF fighter injured, according to the coalition. No US troops were reported killed or wounded.

The rapid deployment of overwhelming US aerial firepower had the desired effect and there were no more attempts by Syrian government forces and their Russian allies to threaten the US presence.

Regular exercises and demonstrations of force were

ABOVE: Ali Al Salem Airbase in Kuwait was the home to the task force of US Air Force Special Operation Command aircraft supporting Operation Inherent Resolve. (USAF)

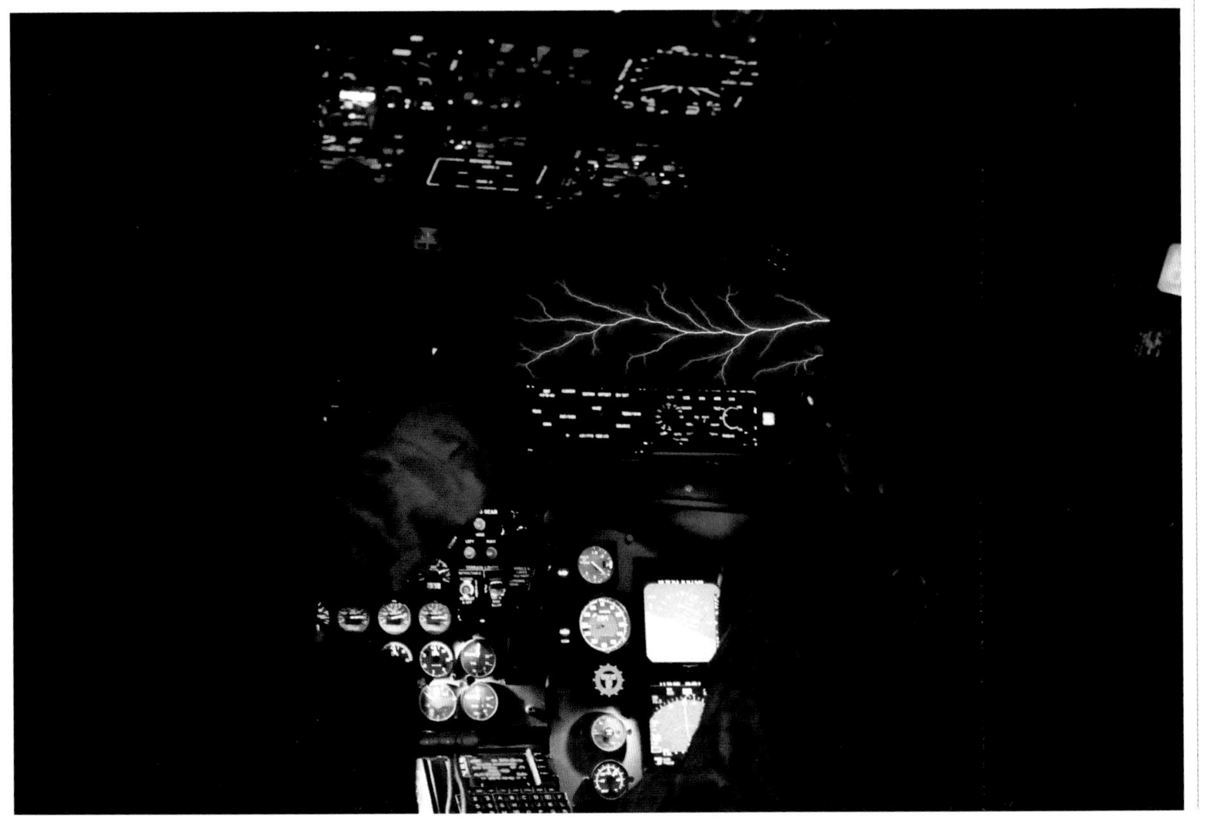

LEFT: Lightning illuminates the sky as an AC-130 heads into Iraq for an Operation Inherent Resolve mission in 2023. (USAF)

ABOVE: AC-130 and MC-130 Special Operations aircraft were based at Ali Al Salem Airbase in Kuwait throughout Operation Inherent Resolve. (USAF)

RIGHT: US special operations force teams on the ground in eastern Syria worked with pro-US Kurdish militia forces to prevent a resurgence of so-called Islamic State (ISIS) in the region, including calling down AC-130 fire on suspected Jihadi hideouts. (US DOD)

ABOVE: The AC-130U bore much of the brunt of Operation Inherent Resolve missions until the aircraft was retired in 2019. (USAF)

conducted by US troops in Syria to reinforce the deterrence aspect of their airpower. In March 2022, the US-led Special Operations Joint Task Force-Levant (SOJTF LEVANT) conducted a live-fire exercise with an AC-130J gunship in eastern Syria.

"Exercises like these establish aerial dominance and enhance readiness that enables our SDF partners to ensure the enduring defeat of Daesh (Islamic State)," SOJTF LEVANT said in a social media post, accompanied by a video clip of the gunship raking targets with its cannons. It concluded by saying, "we are determined to continue working together to build a secure, peaceful and prosperous northeast Syria."

Hamas 2023

In the aftermath of the Hamas attack on Israel on October 7, 2023, pro-Iranian militia groups staged a series of rocket and drone attacks on US bases across Iraq and Syria. This prompted the US military to step up its AC-130J self-defence patrols across the region. Each night, gunships of the 73rd SOS flying over US bases under threat.

On November 21, 2023, the major US outpost at Al Assad airbase in western Iraq came under attack with a ballistic missile. "Immediately following the attack, a US AC-130 aircraft in the area conducted a self-defence strike against an Iranian-backed militia vehicle and a number of Iranian-backed militia personnel involved in this attack," a Pentagon spokesperson announced. "This self-defence strike resulted in some hostile fatalities."

"We were able to identify the point of origin of these attacks because an AC-130 was up already in the area and therefore was able to respond," said the spokesperson. "They were able to take action because they saw the militants. They were able to keep an eye on the movement of these militants as they moved into their vehicles and that's why they were able to respond."

The AC-130 patrols over US bases in Iraq and Syria seemed to hark back to the early days of the Vietnam conflict in the mid-1960s, when AC-47s protected US Green Berets in jungle bases from Vietcong attack. The technology available on a 2024 era AC-130J is way in advance of that installed on the original Spooky gunship, but impact on enemy forces of gunship delivered firepower is just as devastating.

BELOW: AC-130s flew 'top cover' for US and coalition raids on hideouts of ISIS insurgents during Operation Inherent Resolve. In this image, the US special forces assault force can be seen approaching the target on the bottom right. (US DOD)

USAF Fixed Wing Gunships

Past, present and future

RIGHT: Old and the New. An AC-47D owned by the American Flight Museum in Topeka, Kansas, and USAF AC-130J Ghostrider conduct a gunship legacy flight during the Air Venture Oshkosh 2021 event at Wittman Regional Airport in Wisconsin. (USAF)

Sixty years ago in December 1964, the first ever operational US Air Force gunship mission was flown over South Vietnam. Within weeks, the first Douglas AC-47D Spooky gunship squadron was carving a place in history.

Less than three years later the first Hercules was being modified into a gunship and it was soon in action over Southeast Asia. The rest, as they say, is history.

Later derivatives of the AC-130 gunships have seen action in almost every one of America's wars through to the current day. Grenada, Panama, Iraq, Bosnia, Somalia, Kosovo, Afghanistan, Iraq, and Libya are all battle honours of the USAF's gunship squadrons.

The gunship is a quintessential American weapon system. The USAF pioneered the development of the gunship, and it has continued to invest in sustaining its unique capabilities. Few nations have the same ambitions for their armed forces and the gunship is a good fit for the Pentagon and White House.

In Vietnam, the gunship was an essential weapon to defend isolated jungle camps against Vietcong attacks and then take the fight to communist supply columns flowing south down the Ho Chi Minh Trail.

BELOW: Hurlburt Field Memorial Air Park contains more than 20 classic Air Commando aircraft, including three gunships, to preserve the history of America's unconventional warfare aviators. (USAF)

Soon after the fall of Saigon in 1975, the USAF had fitted its gunships with air-to-air refuelling to allow the AC-130 to become a key power projection tool. Whenever the US injects its armed forces into a new combat zone, far from home, the AC-130 is often the first aircraft to arrive in the scene.

The ability of the AC-130 to loiter for extended periods over combat zones to protect lightly armed contingents of paratroopers or special forces is highly prized. Once US forces became bogged down in long conflicts in Iraq and Afghanistan, the gunship proved to be the essential aircraft that was called on to protect isolated outposts. This was returning full circle back to the Vietnam era AC-47.

LEFT: Major General Mark Hicks, Air Force Special Operations Command director of operations, speaks during the AC-130H Spectre gunship retirement ceremony, May 26, 2015, at Cannon Air Force Base in New Mexico. Hicks then piloted the gunship to its final destination at the Davis-Monthan Air Force Base 'boneyard' in Arizona. (USAF)

In the intervening 60 years, the technology employed in USAF gunships has been at the forefront of military hardware. The science of gunships is remarkably simple and has not really changed over the past six decades. The pylon-turn around a target is an amazingly simple concept that is still used to this day to devastating effect.

However, the sensors, communications, defensive and aiming systems employed in 21st century gunships has been transformational. The sensor technology employed on Vietnam era gunships was innovative. First generation AC-130s and AC-119s employed new thermal imaging and image intensifying sensors that were soon in widespread use on other aircraft.

Gunships had the space to take large and heavy first versions of

BELOW: US Air Force special operations aircraft landed on Highway 63 during Exercise Emerald Warrior 24 FTX II in Bono, Arkansas, August 4, 2024. The objective of the exercise was to train aircrews to operate from improvised air strips when traditional airfields may be unavailable or under threat. (USAF)

ABOVE: Spectators watch as AC-130H Spectre gunship, nicknamed *Excalibur*, taxis down the flightline for its final time, May 27, 2015, at Cannon Air Force Base in New Mexico. (USAF)

these sensors and soon proved the concepts that in subsequent iterations were miniaturised to allow them to be installed on modern attack helicopters and fast jets.

In the 21st century, more revolutionary technology was installed on the AC-130W and AC-130J gunships to turn them into precision strike platforms. These new generation gunships fielded guided missiles to allow them to strike at targets from stand-off ranges. Just as importantly, the new generation of sensors and weapons could be installed on roll-on-roll-off pallets, without requiring complicated and expensive structural engineering changes to airframes.

This fundamentally changed the economics of designing and building gunships. So, when the USAF refreshed its gunship force with the AC-130J a decade ago, it could afford to buy more than 30 of the aircraft.

The future place of the gunship in the USAF looks secure. However, the ending of the US presence in Afghanistan in 2021 and the emergence of great power competition with Russia and China is forcing the USAF to re-imagine how it will use gunships.

No End For Howitzer

In 2023, suggestions emerged that the 105mm cannon would be stripped out of the AC-130J and more stand-off missiles would be installed. Other improvements being eyed included advanced active electronically scanned array radar for improved tracking of ground targets and a series of communications and

networking upgrades to better tie into command-and-control networks.

The idea to lose the 105mm cannon was quickly dropped because in the end the essential element of an effective gunship is the ability to put down massive amounts of firepower against targets with pin-point accuracy.

Despite trends to more precision weapons, the formidable firepower of the AC-130 cannot be equalled. There is just nothing like it. Those on the receiving end of gunship firepower from Vietnam to Afghanistan have come to fear the arrival overhead of a gunship. The sound of an AC-130 is distinctive and when tracer fire starts to arc to earth in its distinctive 'cone' those on the ground realise it is time be somewhere else.

The USAF has to date been the most committed user of the gunship. After the end of the Southeast Asia conflict, surplus AC-47s and AC-119s were transferred to the South Vietnamese, Laotian and Khmer air forces. Some of the AC-47s that escaped from the fall of America's allies to the communists in 1975 ended up in Thai, Philippine, and El Salvadorian service. Columbia, Indonesia, South Africa, and Uruguay all converted their own C-47s into gunships. These were simple conversions and could easily be conducted by these countries.

No other air force has been able to afford to follow the USAF to adopt gunships based in the C-130 Hercules. Britain's Royal Air Force briefly investigated acquiring AC-130s in the 1990s but the costs were considered unaffordable. The new generation of gunships with palletised sensors and weapons might tempt other air forces to field AC-130 gunships. Lockheed Martin is already marketing the idea around the world so new gunship operators might soon step forward.

There is an obvious tendency to focus on the impressive technology incorporated in the USAF gunships, but their commanders repeatedly say that the key component are the crews who fly them.

Crews Are The Key

Accounts of gunship operations repeatedly indicate that the aircraft's crews are instrumental in overcoming technical or tactical problems to get the mission done. The USAF call this the 'Air Commando spirit'. Adapt, improvise, and overcome, has been the ethos of the Air Commandos who crew gunships since the 1960s. This esprit de corps is hard to foster and easy to lose.

The modern USAF special operations community values its veterans and makes great efforts to preserve its heritage. Gunship heroes are honoured. Medal of Honor winner, John Levitow, has a special place in the Air Commando 'hall of fame', as the first enlisted airman to win America's highest award for gallantry and the only gunship crewman to be so honoured to date. Ron Terry was one of the key experts who brought the first gunships into service and then was instrumental in turning the AC-130 concept into reality. Known as the 'Father of the Gunship', he was lauded both for his skill at fighting Pentagon bureaucracy and taking

ABOVE: US Airmen render a salute for the posting of the colours during the 27th Special Operations Wing's change of command ceremony at Cannon Air Force Base in June 2017. The New Mexico airbase is one of two that currently hosts gunships. (USAF)

BELOW: In future conflicts, USAF gunships will have to operate in new and innovative ways, such as operating from road strips, to avoid enemy attacks on air bases. (USAF)

ABOVE: Hundreds of spectators lined the flightline to witness the final take-off of the AC-130H Spectre gunship, nicknamed *Excalibur* on May 27, 2015, at Cannon Air Force Base in New Mexico. (USAF)

RIGHT: Many former members that flew or maintained AC-130H Spectre gunships gather at the aircraft's retirement ceremony, May 26, 2015, at Cannon Air Force Base in New Mexico. As each campaign involving the aircraft was acknowledged, the veterans were prompted to stand to be properly recognised for their efforts. (USAF)

the controls of experimental gunships over Vietnam. He is described in USAF archives as a "subtle blending of tact and tenacity, self-confidence and openness, intelligence and common sense, and most significantly... uncommonly convincing..."

The USAF gunship community of serving personnel and veterans is tightknit. They are keen to tell the story of their unique weapon system and pass on the flame to future generations of Air Commandos.

At Hurlburt Field in Florida – the home of the gunship for more than 50 years – is a unique museum to honour previous generations of Air Commandos. The Hurlburt Field Memorial Air Park houses a collection of more than 20 classic Air Commando aircraft and helicopters, including an AC-47D, AC-130A, and AC-130H. In April 2024, the park re-opened to the public after being closed for 20 years.

"Today's grand opening is really a celebration of what Air Commandos are all about, this park and the people who flew these aircraft ... they have a story to tell," Colonel Patrick Dierig, 1st Special Operations Wing commander said during the re-opening ceremony. "We want to take the opportunity to open the gates and open that history up to the public, so that we can plant the seeds for future Air Commandos."

"As we view this crown jewel of our history, we see our heritage from two perspectives, our Air Commandos and our iron," said Lieutenant General Tony Bauernfeind, Air Force Special Operations Command Commander, during the ceremony. "While the [aircraft] physically looms largest in the air park, the stories of our men and women on the bronze placards speak volumes of the true inspiration and carry the heaviest weight."

This commitment to preserving the history of the gunship community has not always been so strong. In a sign of how rapidly gunships were brought into service at the height of the Vietnam War, little time or effort could be spared to preserve the history of the first generation of gunships. There was a war to be fought. For many years none of the original AC-47s or AC-119s were thought to have survived the defeat of America's allies or neglect after being returned to an air base in the Philippines. The AC-47s and AC-119s on display today in museums around the US or restored to flight are all conversions of non-gunship airframes.

In a sign of the tenacity of Air Commando veterans, several hunted for years to track down the fate of those original gunships. Earlier this century when Tan Son Nhut airport outside Ho Chi Minh City, former Saigon, was being re-developed. Eagle eyed AC-119 veterans spotted the distinguished shape of one of their old aircraft on the airfield ramp in Google Earth satellite images. An expedition was mounted to Vietnam to investigate and possibly return the last surviving original AC-119 for display in the United States. The Vietnam People's Air Force had used aircraft for several years after 1975 and then stored in a hanger. The authorities in Vietnam, unfortunately did not grant approval for the return of the aircraft. They said wanted to keep it, as it was the only gunship they held among their collection of abandoned US aircraft. The lure of the gunship history is strong – even among its former enemies.

ABOVE: The AC-47D Spooky of the American Flight Museum in Topeka has been restored in the markings of John Levitow's aircraft from the Vietnam War, in tribute to the Medal of Honor winner. (USAF)

LEFT: The only surviving AC-119K *Stinger* was discovered at a Vietnamese People's Air Force base in Ho Chin Minh City, formerly Saigon, in 2006 by a group of gunships veterans using satellite imagery. A request to return it to the US was denied by the local authorities who wanted to keep the aircraft in Vietnam. The aircraft can be seen on the bottom right. (GOOGLE EARTH)

Tracing Gunship History

Finding Documents and Imagery

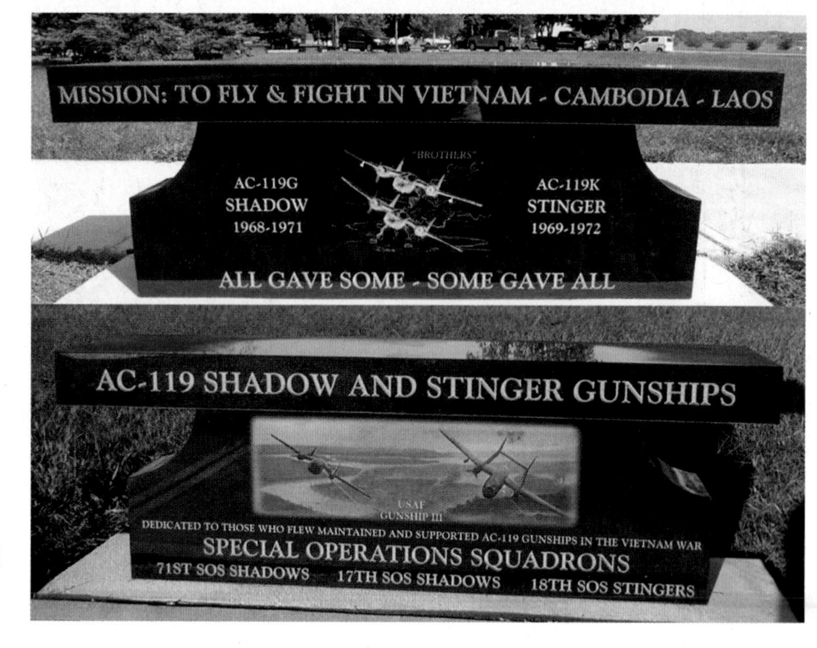

RIGHT: The AC-119 Shadow and Stinger Gunship Memorial at the National Museum of the USAF. (USAF)

In the sixty years since the USAF started using fixed wing gunships in Southeast Asia it has amassed an impressive record.

To compile this publication, we have tapped into official US military records and imagery archives, as well as accessing the resources of gunship veteran communities.

Gunship veterans have created several important resources for those looking back at their history dating back to the Vietnam conflict. These include the associations of AC-130 Spectre veterans and AC-119 veterans, who have created websites full of impressive documents and records, at www.spectre-association.org and www.ac119gunships.com

The Air Command Association has also put its impressive journal online, at www.aircommando.org, which contains accounts from Air Commando veterans going back to World War Two.

The impressive photography used in this publication is mostly provided by the photographers of the USAF Public Affairs and US Joint Combat Camera organisations. Over the decades, they have been on the frontline recording gunship operations in the combat zones. Their outstanding work can be seen at the Defense Visual Information Distribution Service website www.dvidshub.net and the USAF website, www.af.mil/News/Photos

Many of the Vietnam-era images are held in the US National Archives and can be accessed via www.archives.gov

There are also several highly informative books and articles about the history of gunships, many of which were vital in the research for this volume, including:

Development and Employment of Fixed-Wing Gunships 1962-1972, by Jack S. Ballard, Office of US Air Force History, Washington DC, 1982

C-130 Hercules Variant Briefing Part 1 & 2, World Air Power Journal, Vol 6 & 7, Editors: David Donald and Jon Lake, Aerospace Publishing London / Airtime Publishing, 1991

Eagle Down: The Last Special Forces Fighting the Forever War, Jessica Donati, Public Affairs, 2021

Air War over Southeast Asia - A Pictorial Record, Vol.1, 1962-1966 by Lou Drendel, Squadron Signals Publication, 1982

Shadow and Stinger: Developing the AC-119G/K Gunships in the Vietnam War, William Pace Head, Texas A&M University Press, 26 Feb 2007

Vietnam Air Losses, USAF/USN/USMC, Fixed-Wing Aircraft Losses in Southeast Asia, 1961–1973, Hobson, Chris, North Branch, Minnesota, Specialty Press, 2001

Air Power in Three Wars, General William Momyer, (US Air Force, retired), US Government Printing Office, 1983

Not a Good Day to Die: Untold Story of Operation Anaconda, Sean Naylor, Penguin, 2006

Spectre Stalks the Night, Tim Ripley, United States Air Force Yearbook, RAFBFE Publishing, 1994

Project CHECO. Contemporary Historical Evaluation of Combat Operations: Fixed Wing Gunships in Southeast Asia, HQ Pacific Air Force, 30 November 1971

Gunships, A Pictorial History of Spooky, Larry Davis and Don Greer, Squadron/Signal Publications, 1982

BELOW: AC-130A, 54-1623 'Ghost Rider', is preserved at the Aviation History and Technology Center at Marietta in Georgia. (THOMSON200)

CONTENT

AEROPLANE YEARBOOK 2024-25

22

6 **Welcome**

8 **Preservation Review of 2024**
It's been a busy year on the aviation heritage scene — we look back on the big events

14 **Vulcan XL426**
The RAF's Vulcan Display Flight kept XL426 flying despite reservations among some of the top brass. But how, exactly, did it happen?

22 **Geoffrey Stephenson**
Shot down over the Dunkirk beaches, No 19 Squadron's CO was a greatly respected aviator among his peers — Douglas Bader included

32 **Avro Transport Co**
The pioneering purveyor of Britain's first regular domestic passenger air service

40 **Typhoon restoration**
The autumn of 2024 saw one of the most significant milestones yet in the return to flight of Hawker Typhoon RB396. What better opportunity to find out how the project's going?

46 **Elba Comet disaster**
Documents from the de Havilland archive detail the immediate aftermath of a terrible tragedy

54

62

AEROPLANE YEARBOOK 2024-25

ISBN: 978 1 83632 022 7
Editor: Ben Dunnell
Senior editor, specials: Roger Mortimer
Email: roger.mortimer@keypublishing.com
Cover Design: Paul Sander
Design: Panda Media
Advertising Sales Manager: Sam Clark
E-mail: sam.clark@keypublishing.com
Tel: 01780 755131
Advertising Production:
Becky Antoniades
E-mail: rebecca.antoniades@keypublishing.com

SUBSCRIPTION/MAIL ORDER
Key Publishing Ltd, PO Box 300, Stamford, Lincs, PE9 1NA
Tel: 01780 480404
Subscriptions e-mail: subs@keypublishing.com
Mail Order e-mail: orders@keypublishing.com
Website: www.keypublishing.com/shop

PUBLISHING
Group CEO and Publisher: Adrian Cox

Published by
Key Publishing Ltd, PO Box 100, Stamford, Lincs, PE9 1XQ
Tel: 01780 755131 **Website:** www.keypublishing.com

PRINTING
Precision Colour Printing Ltd, Haldane, Halesfield 1, Telford, Shropshire. TF7 4QQ

DISTRIBUTION
Seymour Distribution Ltd, 2 Poultry Avenue, London, EC1A 9PU
Enquiries Line: 020 7429 4000

KEY Publishing

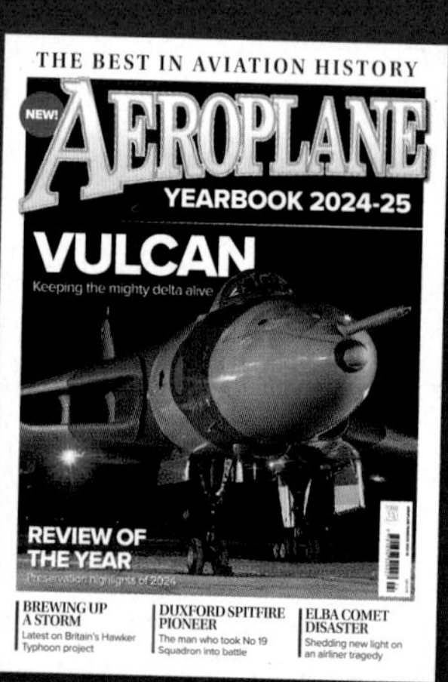

Cover image by Simon Jenkins/AirTeamImages.com

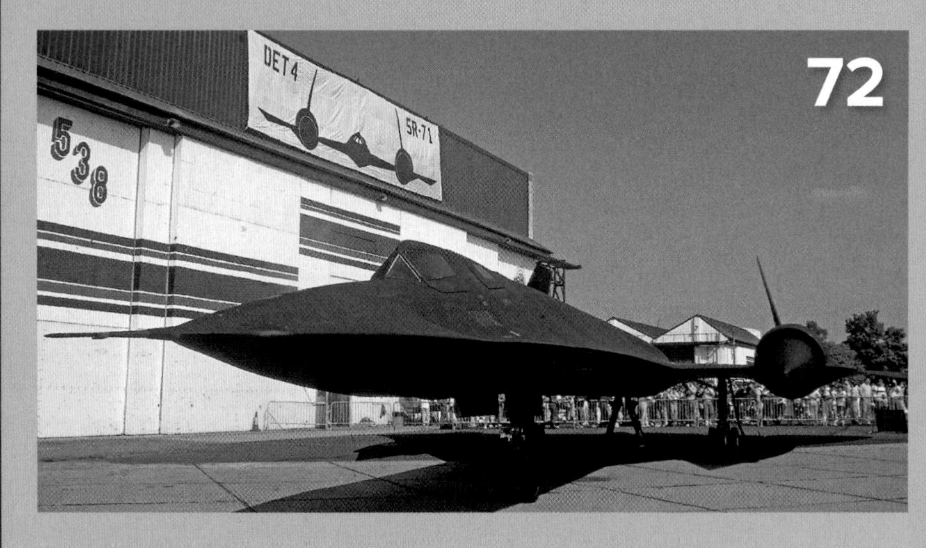

54 Lightnings in Singapore
The Far East years of No 74 Squadron, and a theatre of operations for English Electric's jet like no other it served in

62 IGN B-17s
The French geographical organisation which kept a fleet of veteran Fortresses operational decades longer than most

72 SR-71 in the UK
Fifty years on from the first SR-71 visit to these shores, how did the 'Habu's' association with the UK begin?

80 Fundacja Eskadra
We visit Warsaw to look at a new classic jet operator that's already making waves

88 Concorde 'Delta Golf'
Test-flying the first British production-standard example of the supersonic airliner

94 Last RAF Buccaneers
Memories of the mighty strike jet's final RAF service days from those who flew it

104 *Aeroplane* meets... Dave Mackay
The first Scottish astronaut recalls flying everything from Shuttleworth's Blériot XI to Virgin Galactic's SpaceShipTwo

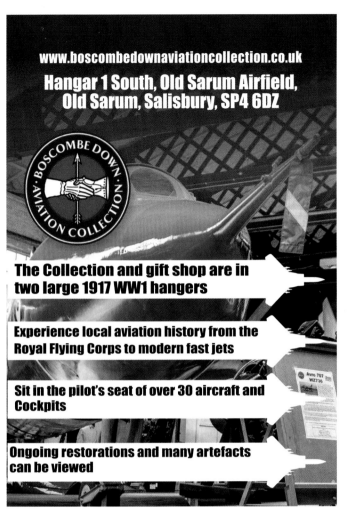

WELCOME

AEROPLANE YEARBOOK 2024-25

CONNECT WITH US!

AEROPLANE

www.facebook.com/AeroplaneMonthly

@HistoryInTheAir

KEY.AERO

It's a pleasure for the *Aeroplane* team to bring you our Yearbook 2024-2025, featuring brand-new articles and the best of our historic magazine from the year gone by. Find out more about some of the most famous aircraft of all time — Concorde, thanks to one of its last surviving test pilots, the Vulcan, in the form of the RAF's initial preserved flying example, the SR-71 'Blackbird', as we marked the 50th anniversary of its debut British visit, and many more. Take a behind-the-scenes look at how de Havilland responded to the Comet disaster off Elba, discover the UK's first domestic passenger airline, and head into space with Scotland's first astronaut. And, on the preservation front, learn what's new with the restoration to airworthiness of Hawker Typhoon RB396.

This is just a taste of what's inside — and what you can find in *Aeroplane* every month. It's always a great read. Go to pages 12-13 and subscribe now!

Ben Dunnell, editor

The D-Day 80th anniversary commemorations on both sides of the Channel provided some of 2024's aviation heritage highlights. Over the Normandy coast, Tim Savage's Western Air Lines DC-3, NC33644 — one of the D-Day Squadron aircraft visiting from across the Atlantic — leads the Chalair C-47B F-AZOX, with a gaggle of warbird fighters joining behind: two P-51D Mustangs, two Spitfires and a Hurricane. USAF

AEROPLANE
ESTABLISHED 1911

Aeroplane traces its lineage back to the weekly *The Aeroplane*, founded by C. G. Grey in 1911 and published until 1968. It was re-launched as a monthly in 1973 by Richard T. Riding, editor for 25 years until 1998.

PRESERVATION REVIEW OF 2024

Chronicling an extremely busy year in the aviation heritage world, with first flights and notable projects galore

WORDS: BEN DUNNELL

The deaths of Battle of Britain Memorial Flight pilot Sqn Ldr Mark Long, killed in the crash of Spitfire IX MK356, and Air Leasing/Ultimate Warbird Flights boss Richard Grace, following a lengthy illness, cast a pall over 2024 on the historic aircraft scene. Both will, it goes without saying, be deeply missed. But we should also recall some very welcome developments, of which the saving of the last Blackburn Beverley by the Solway Aviation Museum at Carlisle ranks as the most heartwarming. Some understandably doubted whether crowd-funding could come to the rescue of what is, after all, not the best-known type out there, but an extremely well-run campaign drummed up the necessary support, and secured the future of an aeroplane too often forgotten and ignored.

In fact, there was a lot of positive activity among the UK's independent museums in 2024, with new exhibits aplenty and all the added public interest that accompanies them. In a similar way, the D-Day 80th anniversary brought aviation heritage into the wider headlines in a positive fashion. If many years end up being dominated story-wise by newly rebuilt Spitfires — not that there weren't a few of those in the past 12 months — the fact that such as the 'Bev', multiple C-47s/DC-3s, the Martin Mars and numerous Mosquitos, static and flying, occupied 2024's limelight came as a refreshing change.

BELOW: Beverley C1 XB259 partially dismantled at Fort Paull before its gradual move to Carlisle. KIERON PILBEAM

JANUARY

8 Vampire T11 XE920/N920DH made its first flight for nearly 20 years at Ogden, Utah. The ex-RAF trainer is owned by the Flying History Foundation of Preston, Idaho.

16 The RAF Battle of Britain's Memorial Flight received Spitfire XVI TE311 back from a two-year major service with The Spitfire Company at Biggin Hill.

30 At Ardmore, New Zealand, Rob Mackley's 83-year-old Lockheed 10 Electra ZK-AFD completed its maiden post-restoration flight.

FEBRUARY

1 A crowd-funding campaign is launched by the Solway Aviation Museum to save the sole surviving Beverley C1, XB259, a previous purchase and move of which from its home at Fort Paull had fallen through.

8 The world's sole airworthy Hawker Demon, K8203/G-BTVE, is cancelled from the UK register on its sale to Kermit Weeks.

27 VH-3D BuNo 159358 goes on show at the George H. W. Bush Presidential Library and Museum in College Station, Texas. The helicopter had been used as 'Marine One' by both President Bushes.

INTREPID MUSEUM

MARCH

14 **Ex-British Airways Concorde G-BOAD arrives back at the Intrepid Museum in New York by barge, after 14 months of conservation work at the Brooklyn Navy Yard.**

18 **The fourth airworthy Mosquito to emerge from the Avspecs workshops at Ardmore, New Zealand, T43 NZ2308 for Lewis Air Legends of San Antonio, Texas, takes to the air. Steve Hinton is at the controls of the former Royal New Zealand Air Force machine.**

APRIL

3 The Solway Aviation Museum announces it has passed its £60,000 fundraising target for the acquisition and move of Beverley XB259.

15 KC-10A Extender 84-0191, a veteran of the 1986 Operation 'El Dorado Canyon' raid on Libya, arrives at Wright-Patterson AFB, Ohio for the National Museum of the US Air Force.

17 Ownership of Miles Messenger G-AKIN transfers to Alan and Phil Hardwick, who will keep up its unbroken 72-year run of residence at the Northamptonshire airfield.

18 Roll-out at the Bentwaters Cold War Museum of T-33A 51-9252, freshly restored as an 81st Tactical Fighter Wing aircraft based at the Suffolk airfield.

18 The Gatwick Aviation Museum at Charlwood receives its first new aircraft exhibit for 16 years, in the shape of Jaguar GR1 XX967, formerly an instructional airframe at Cosford.

22 The latest Spitfire to fly is two-seat IXT EN570/LN-AOA, rebuilt by The Spitfire Company at Biggin Hill for Norwegian Flying Aces. A fortnight later it's delivered to its base at Notodden.

MAY

5 **At Sywell, CA-18 Mustang Mk21 G-JERK — painted as 361st Fighter Squadron CO Donald Strait's wartime P-51D *Jersey Jerk* — makes its first flight in Britain following importation from Australia for Fighter Aviation Engineering.**

NIGEL HARRISON

10 What had been the last Hunter operating in Switzerland, the Hunterverein Obersimmental's F58 J-4040/HB-RVS — painted as the famed J-4015 'Papyrus' — returns by road from Altenrhein to its base at St Stephan, where it has become a static exhibit.

13 Newly acquired Hawk T1 XX265 is unveiled by the North East Land, Sea and Air Museums in Sunderland.

14 King Charles III unveils Apache AH1 ZJ224 at Middle Wallop's Army Flying Museum. It is the sole ex-Army Air Corps Apache preserved in the UK.

25 Spitfire IX MK356 of the Battle of Britain Memorial Flight crashes near RAF Coningsby, with the loss of pilot Sqn Ldr Mark Long. The BBMF's fighters end up remaining on a 'flying pause' for the rest of the display season.

25 The Dutch Hawker Hunter Foundation announces it is ceasing operations and selling Hunter T68 G-EHLW — another nail in the coffin of preserved Hunter activity in Europe.

27 Spitfire IX TE517 arrives with its new owner, Ali İsmet Öztürk's MSÖ Air and Space Museum at Sivrihisar, Turkey, following a ferry flight from Sywell. It goes on to be repainted in Turkish Air Force colours.

JUNE

5 The Michigan Flight Museum — formerly the Yankee Air Museum — at Ypsilanti confirms the sale of its B-17G Flying Fortress 44-85829/N3193G *Yankee Lady*. Later in the year the bomber is shipped to Avspecs in New Zealand for restoration.

6 The 80th anniversary of D-Day, and participation in a 56-aircraft flypast along Normandy's Omaha Beach marks a high point of the D-Day Squadron's trans-Atlantic tour by four DC-3s/C-47s, which also undertook numerous commemorative parachute drops and event appearances.

6 Aero Legends' second two-seat Spitfire IXT, MJ444, completes its maiden flight after rebuild by the Duxford-based Aircraft Restoration Company.

16 The crash at Chino, California, of the Yanks Air Museum's Lockheed 12A Electra Junior N93R claims the lives of crew members Frank Wright and Michael Gilles.

DAVE BROCKLEHURST

24 Prone-pilot Meteor F8 testbed WK935 is moved from storage at the RAF Museum Midlands at Cosford to the Newark Air Museum in Nottinghamshire. There it goes on show alongside Reid & Sigrist Desford VZ728/G-AGOS, also used for prone-pilot experimental work.

27 Lancaster 10P (AR) KB882, a wartime combat veteran owned by the National Air Force Museum of Canada, is unveiled at the Base 31 facility at Picton Airport, Ontario.

28 Built up by Peter Smith in Lancashire, the fuselage of the Whirlwind Fighter project's replica Whirlwind I arrives at the Kent Battle of Britain Museum at Hawkinge, and goes on to be mated with the nose and cockpit section.

DAVID WHITWORTH

31 Almost exactly nine years after being damaged in an emergency landing at Biggin Hill, Spitfire IX MK912 — now owned by Matthew de Morgans — flies again from the Kent airport.

JULY

8 Another new historic transport for Australia's Historic Aircraft Restoration Society — a Douglas DC-2, VH-CDZ — arrives at HARS' Shellharbour Airport museum facility.

15 Major components of Beverley XB259 begin being road-transported to Carlisle Airport from Fort Paull.

19 A Jaguar arrives back at the former RAF Coltishall — GR1 XZ384, which never actually served at the Norfolk station. It becomes part of the Coltishall Heritage Centre.

22 The world population of airworthy Helldivers is doubled when SB2C-5 BuNo 83393 of the Fagen Fighters WWII Museum takes to the air at Granite Falls, Michigan.

AUGUST

8 Another flying Helldiver joins the scene: Jim Slattery's SB2C-1A, BuNo 75552, with a maiden flight at Colorado Springs where its restoration was completed by West Pac.

21 Martin JRM-3 Mars C-FLYL *Hawaii Mars* undertakes a much-publicised final flight from its long-time base at Sproat Lake, British Columbia to Patricia Bay adjacent to Victoria International Airport, where the immense flying boat will be preserved by the British Columbia Air Museum.

24 A huge boost for the Cambridgeshire-based Stirling Aircraft Project, with the delivery of a large fuselage section from Stirling IV LK142, previously exhibited at Condé-Vraux in France.

DEREK HEYES

SEPTEMBER

9 Ex-Securité Civile Conair Turbo Firecat F-AYKM flies for the first time in the ownership of the Montélimar-based Musée Européen de l'Aviation de Chasse.

13 Thom Richard announces the sale of his TP-40N Warhawk *American Dream* to the Mid-America Flight Museum in Mount Pleasant, Texas.

16 On loan from the RAF Museum, Comper Swift G-ACGL joins the Hooton Park Trust's displays at the historic site near Ellesmere Port — the location where Nicholas Comper set up his eponymous aircraft company.

21 At the Planes of Fame Central Coast AirFest at Santa Maria, California, two Mosquitos fly together or the first time in more than 37 years: the Somers Warbird Collection's FBVI PZ474 and Lewis Air Legends' T43 NZ2308.

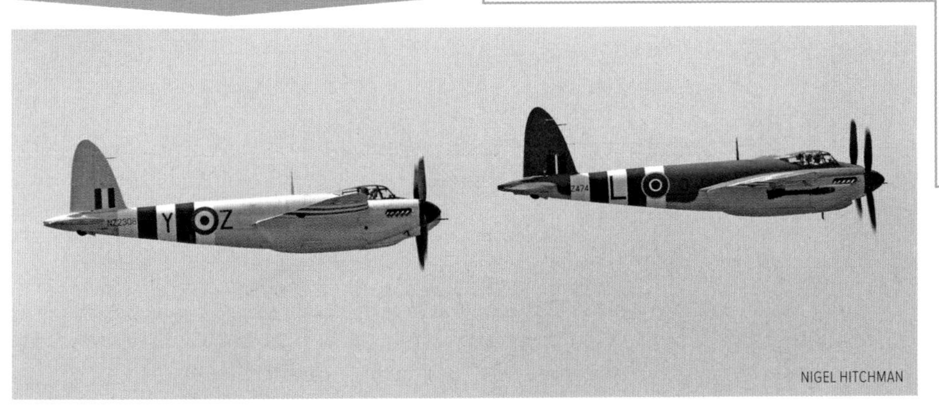
NIGEL HITCHMAN

OCTOBER

1 FG-1D Corsair BuNo 92013 joins the Intrepid Museum in New York on loan from the National Naval Aviation Museum.

3 The RAF Station Czechoslovakia organisation at Podhorany in the Czech Republic reveals that it has bought Anson I MH120/ZK-RRA — the sole airworthy specimen of the mark — from Bill Reid in Omaka, New Zealand. It should arrive in the new year.

5 Military Aviation Museum founders Gerald and Elaine Yagen announce a gift to the Virginia Beach-based museum of more than $100 million, including its buildings, the aircraft collection and an endowment for future maintenance.

9 Another Mustang for the UK: 517 Ltd's P-51D 45-11553/G-FSID *Shangri-La* arrives at Sywell from the USA.

13 A big day for the de Havilland Aircraft Museum at Salisbury Hall, with the formal roll-out of Mosquito FBVI TA122 on completion of a restoration project that lasted more than 40 years.

15 Richard Grace, display pilot, engineer and director of Sywell-based Air Leasing and Ultimate Warbird Flights dies aged 40 after illness.

18 Spitfire VIII MV154/VH-A58 makes its initial flight since being exported from the UK to Australia — and repainted as RAAF ace Clive Caldwell's mount — at Archerfield Airport near Brisbane.

21 The Avro Heritage Museum at Woodford announces plans for a new building, able to house exhibits such as Shackleton AEW2 WR960 under cover.

22 Javelin FAW9 XH767 leaves Elvington's Yorkshire Air Museum for the East Midlands Aeropark, in a journey that saw parts of Shackleton MR2 WR963 starting to move from Coventry to Elvington.

22 A fascinating new exhibit for the ever-expanding Pima Air and Space Museum in Arizona: EP-3E Aries II BuNo 156511, the aircraft involved in 2001's 'Hainan Island incident' in which it collided with a Chinese J-8 II fighter.

23 Tucano T1 ZF372 becomes the latest ex-RAF training type to augment the Newark Air Museum's inventory.

NOVEMBER

1 The Newark Air Museum announces that Swift FR5 WK277, which had been on long-term loan from its private owner, will be moving to the South Wales Aviation Museum at St Athan.

SUBSCRIBE TODAY!

Aeroplane is still providing the best aviation coverage around, with focus on iconic military aircraft from the 1930s to the 1960s.

/collections/subscriptions

**Free 2nd class P&P on BFPO orders. Overseas charges apply.*

THE LONG GOODBYE

It's now 40 years since the RAF's Vulcan Display Flight embarked on its debut airshow season, keeping Vulcan XL426 flying despite reservations among some of the top brass. But how, exactly, did it happen? **WORDS:** BEN DUNNELL

"I thought the Royal Air Force had said 'goodbye' to the Vulcan…" AVM John Price wasn't wrong. The Assistant Chief of the Air Staff for operations was responding to the proposal that one example of the Avro bomber be kept flying for the 1984 airshow season, when all its brethren had finally been phased out. Yet despite his nagging doubts, it happened. What's more, it carried on.

Those behind the establishment 40 years ago of the Vulcan Display Flight had strictly limited ambitions — officially, at least. Behind the scenes there were, as Price put it, "ideas in the air for further displays in 1985", not that anyone was admitting it in public. Getting the enterprise going required a degree of sensitivity, playing down the costs and burdens involved, lest those on high consider it too great a drain on restricted resources. But operating Vulcan XL426 as a piece of flying heritage would have a lasting effect, even if its own period in the limelight was brief.

None of this, surely, would have happened had it not been for the Falklands War. Without it, the final 36 Vulcan B2s would have been retired at Waddington on 30 June 1982, and that would have been that. Instead, as is well-known, 24 were given a reprieve until the end of Operation 'Corporate', among them six converted into K2 tankers to provide extra air-to-air refuelling capacity. The force's exploits in the South Atlantic, especially the 'Black Buck' bombing raids, need not be recounted here. But as 'Corporate'

> ***"Operating XL426 as a piece of flying heritage had a lasting effect"***

came to a successful end in June 1982, consideration was being given to running on a single Vulcan tanker squadron — with a secondary maritime radar reconnaissance capability — until late 1983 or early 1984, easing the burden on the Victor K2 fleet and filling the gap until arrival of the VC10 tanker.

The last two Vulcan bomber units carried on a little longer than planned, too, No 101 Squadron disbanding in August 1982 and No 44 Squadron at the year's end. But approval was given for No 50 Squadron, still Waddington-based, to hang on until 31 March 1984. At its disposal were the six tankers, one of which now lacked a Mk17 hose-drum unit but could still be used for continuation training, and could theoretically have been fitted with the HDU from one of the other K2s if they were in extended servicing. It also had two B2s for training purposes and, in an emergency, the MRR function. While these aircraft were still going about their active business, in the summer of 1983 initial discussions took place about keeping a Vulcan for the airshow circuit, and what it might entail.

At Strike Command HQ, Wg Cdr R. K. Grinter put together a paper detailing the options. Having examined the fatigue index (FI) figures for each airframe in the fleet, he saw K2 XH560 as "the most suitable aircraft for the display role", since it was projected to have 64 FI remaining as of 1984. Using information gathered from 1982's Vulcan displays, XH560 would reach the limit of its fatigue

OPPOSITE PAGE: One of the earliest show appearances for Vulcan XL426 in 1984 was at RAF Mildenhall's Air Fete, held that year on the second weekend in June to accommodate a visit by the USAF Thunderbirds. KEY/DUNCAN CUBITT

BELOW: On the ramp at Mildenhall, awaiting its afternoon slot. Performances at USAF shows in 1984 — this one aside, XL426 flew at Alconbury, Lakenheath and Wethersfield that year — as well as those staged by the other UK services and civilians came out of the allocation of 10 displays to the RAF Participation Committee. Those at the RAF's own events did not. USAF

ABOVE: XL426 in service with No 50 Squadron, being refuelled by the aircraft that was intended until late in 1984 to replace it as the display Vulcan, XH560. Ultimately, a lack of hours remaining on '560 saw it being consigned to the Marham dump. GLENN SANDS COLLECTION

life in 1993, or even 2000 if fewer performances were flown and additional limitations placed on the aircraft. Another tanker, XH558, was proposed as a reserve, with 46 FI left. Either would need reconversion back to B2 standard.

High-level support came from ACM Sir David Craig, Strike Command's Air Officer Commanding-in-Chief. A former Vulcan pilot and squadron CO, without Craig the proposal might never have come to anything. "I know we share the view that there would be merit in running-on a Vulcan for display purposes", he wrote to the Air Member for Supply and Organisation, Air Marshal Sir Michael Knight. "Two of the principal reasons for retaining a Vulcan are the aircraft's historical importance and its PR value. On the historical side, the Vulcan symbolises the V Force and the era of airborne nuclear deterrence which was the cornerstone of our defence policy for many years... The aircraft has obvious historical interest, but perhaps the overriding argument for retaining one in flying condition is the grip it has on the imagination of the general public and therefore its value in promoting public interest in the Royal Air Force."

In Knight, who had been AOC No 1 Group at the time of Operation 'Corporate', and thus responsible for the Vulcan and Victor forces, he found another supporter. Craig estimated the annual cost for 120 hours' flying a year as around £340,000, of which some £260,000 would go towards fuel. He mused, "Perhaps there could be some mileage in looking for sponsorship for the Vulcan from one of the aviation fuel companies; Shell or BP for example!"

He had other ideas about how to make the outlay more palatable. In an earlier draft, Craig suggested it might be possible to offer the display Vulcan to the Ministry of Defence (Procurement Executive) "for limited trials use in the winter months as a way of offsetting some of the cost". Given the limited annual hours and fatigue life, and the need to retain crew currency, this was a non-starter. But now he opined that while it would be best to configure the aircraft externally as a B2 by removing the HDU, "the bomb bay tanks and other AAR modification could be retained so that the aircraft could be recovered in the tanker role in an extreme emergency. A potential for AAR use in war could help a little presentationally". That thought, too, was put to one side. But the general idea was gaining momentum.

This is not to say it met with universal approval. Air Cdre Michael Stear, in charge of plans at Strike Command, said it "would be an admirable project", but was anxious that "we might thereby set a precedent for perhaps equally deserving cases, such as the Hunter and later the Lightning". He worried about the plan to use Victor crews with prior Vulcan experience, saying their availability would be insufficient, and that the "totally different flying characteristics of the aircraft [...] do not lead to a direct read across of flying skills and hence continuity", with a resulting safety concern. "In practical terms", Stear wrote, "I believe that it would be very difficult to retain Vulcan experience in the Victor force for the necessary length of time", especially if a Vulcan were to be kept flying into the early 21st century, which he doubted was practical anyway. And he felt it would be too great a drain on personnel and finances. "I suggest", he concluded, "that it would be unwise to pursue the project further."

But what Craig called "prudent provisional planning" for both 1984 and beyond had been going on "in the expectation of a green light", and by the end of 1983 things were beginning to firm up. It had been suggested that the aircraft should be based at Marham, co-located with the Victor force. However, with a view solely to 1984, it was felt better to keep the aeroplane at Waddington. In a similar vein, B2 XL426 was earmarked as the display machine, for XH560 would still be in use with No 50 Squadron until the end of March, and then needed conversion back into a B2. British Aerospace was asked what work would be required.

A final decision had to be reached without too much delay, for the last batch of Vulcan disposals needed arranging, and all the manning and engineering implications working through. By 12 March 1984, when No 50 Squadron had less than three weeks to run, the AOC-in-C had agreed to the retention of three airframes for that season. B2 XL426 would be the display aircraft, with 160 flying hours or 15 FI remaining — "the display consumption rate", it was noted, "is 7.75 FI per annum". Once returned to B2 configuration, K2 XH560 was its proposed long-term replacement, with eight years' fatigue life left, while K2 XH558 would act as its 'Christmas tree' spares source. In addition, K2 XJ825, which became a battle damage repair training aid at Waddington, was able to donate parts.

“ David Craig said, 'A potential for AAR use in war could help...' ”

A need was identified for a minimum of two display pilots, and three pilots overall. Coming straight from No 50 Squadron, Sqn Ldr Bill Burnett was earmarked as flight commander and lead display pilot. Soon to join him as second pilot was Flt Lt Paul Millikin, then a qualified flying instructor on the Victor, who had displayed the Vulcan in 1979-80. The co-pilot, navigator and air electronics operator were to be ex-No 50 Squadron personnel staying at Waddington in the short term as members of the 'rear-guard party' for Vulcan deliveries on disposal. Aiding the wider manning situation, groundcrew posted to Waddington for the benighted Nimrod AEW3 programme could be made available while it continued to be delayed.

Ten Vulcan displays were allocated to the RAF Participation Committee for 1984, but others were to be authorised in support of Strike Command taskings, including the RAF's own shows. This, said the Air Member for Personnel, Air Marshal Sir Thomas Kennedy, was "especially welcome because following an accident to a Red Arrows aircraft in Cyprus on 21 March, and the decision to recruit a new team member and restart training, there will be a delay in the start of the Red Arrows display season". He noted that about 10 shows would be lost, so the proposed Vulcan appearances would compensate almost exactly. But it was now mid-April, with just weeks to go before the season.

What's more, there were still doubters — notably AVM John Price, as quoted at the start. In his role as ACAS (Ops), he wrote on 25 April, "I have mixed feelings. On the one hand I welcome the attention to the Royal Air Force which will be engendered through Vulcan displays. On the other hand [...] the public may find it odd that we are

BELOW: On display at St Athan's Battle of Britain 'At Home' Day in September 1984, one of the last shows of the season. ADRIAN M. BALCH

Applied just behind the RAF roundels on XL426's nose — as here at Alconbury in August 1984 — was the black panther's head emblem of No 1 Group, under whose 'umbrella' the aircraft was placed. This served to represent all Vulcan squadrons. KEY/DUNCAN CUBITT

With hindsight, XL426 was an obvious choice as a short-notice option for the VDF's inaugural 1984 season since it had never been converted into a tanker. As a standard B2, it was used by No 50 Squadron for training purposes. GLENN SANDS COLLECTION

still flying one ... At a time of great manpower and financial difficulty, the proposal comes rather oddly. All that said, at the end of the day I would go along with the AOC-in-C — but I would somehow try to let him know that the idea caused the raising of a quizzical eyebrow". Price added that the Chief of the Air Staff, ACM Sir Keith Williamson, had "strong views" on the matter.

But it was already too late, and there was no eleventh-hour show-stopper. So it was that the Vulcan Display Flight came into being. "We were initially the Vulcan Historical Flight, or VHF", recalls Bill Burnett today, "but it became the VDF". He was simultaneously engaged with getting the flight going and heading up the disposal effort, which included ferrying XM571 to Gibraltar that May. "The AOC's approval display was also done in May. It was all controlled through No 1 Group HQ at Bawtry — they were in charge of us. But we would think of places to go and

XL426 ALIVE IN '25

The Vulcan Restoration Trust will be hosting several events involving XL426 at its London Southend Airport base during 2025, all allowing close-up access to the aircraft. For more details, visit www.avrovulcan.com

do. The first public display was at Honington, a No 9 Squadron standard parade, on 23 May."

XL426 ended up giving far more than 10 displays in 1984. It performed at major events such as RAF Mildenhall's Air Fete '84, the RNAS Yeovilton Air Day and the International Air Tattoo-organised TVS Air Show South at Bournemouth, which took up the Participation Committee's allocation, but on top of that were RAF open days and Battle of Britain 'At Home' Days. Serviceability, says Bill Burnett, was "excellent... We had a dedicated team, and if we had a problem we'd talk it through and sort it. We knew what was wrong, what was right and what to do."

As the year's commitments came to an end, on 17 September Bill flew XH558 to Marham, marking it in his logbook as the aircraft's final flight. The intention was still for the VDF to eventually take up residence at the Norfolk base, alongside the Victors, from which crew members would be drawn. There, '558 was to be plundered for spares and end up on the dump. The very next day, Wg Cdr M. R. Smith at Strike Command wrote to colleagues, describing the "conspicuous success" of the 1984 season and how the AOC-in-C had decided to continue operating XL426 for 1985, still based at Waddington in the immediate term. He sought comment on the plan. The notion put forward in one earlier proposal that the servicing cadre "could be [...] absorbed into the Battle of Britain Memorial Flight" had long been forgotten.

> ***"If we had a technical problem we'd talk it through and sort it"***

But there was soon some doubt over which airframe would act as the future follow-on. Looking into XH560's records, it was discovered that just 160 flying hours remained before the need for a major service. The equivalent figure for XH558, by contrast, was 600 hours. A signal from Waddington's station commander on 14 October pointed out that delays to the arrival of the Nimrod AEW3 meant the "present experienced team" which serviced XL426 "could be made available" to convert a K2 into a B2 between 5 November and 20 December. Thereafter, they were "likely to be dispersed to other duties". Advice was requested as to which aircraft, XII558 or XH560, would be involved.

Given the available hours, the choice was clear. Bill Burnett recounts, "On 14 November with Paul Millikin, I flew '558 back from Marham to Waddington so it could be converted back to a B2. On 29 November I delivered '560 to

ABOVE: Opportunities to view XL426 at its Southend home are numerous.
KEY/JAMIE EWAN

Marham". There it finished up on the dump, though the cockpit was preserved. XH558, meanwhile, entered conversion. The HDU and most other refuelling apparatus was taken out, though one of the tanks which had been added in the bomb bay as part of the K2 fit-out had to be retained for weight and balance reasons, since it was not possible to reinstate the electronic countermeasures equipment which had been deemed surplus for the tanker role.

Held in reserve for 1985, XH558 was repainted at Kinloss that autumn, prior to returning to Waddington. Somehow, despite an acute lack of personnel, the VDF stayed active to allow a smooth aircraft change-over. Bournemouth, again for TVS Air Show South, saw the maiden VDF outing of '558 over the weekend of 31 May-1 June 1986. A fortnight later, nearly out of hours, XL426 gave its final display at RAF Coningsby's open day on 14 June. It had only a couple of flights still to make. Since Waddington's runway needed resurfacing, the VDF transferred temporarily to Scampton, '426 being ferried there on 27 July. Then, a deal with a French consortium having collapsed, the aeroplane was purchased by Roy Jacobsen, who already owned XM655 at Wellesbourne Mountford. Despite the plans he had for airworthy operation in civilian hands, the delivery flight to Southend on 19 December 1986 was '426's last. But at least it has been preserved there, and in taxiing order, thanks to the splendid efforts of the Vulcan Restoration Trust.

> ***"It's remarkable the VDF carried on beyond a single display season"***

Given all the pressures on the defence budget, even while the Cold War was still 'on', it is remarkable that the single Vulcan display season in 1984 carried on into a second year, and then a third, and way beyond. In this, again, Sir David Craig was instrumental. He became Chief of the Air Staff in October 1985, which was good news for the VDF. Having an ex-Vulcan man in the top job headed off a lot of the objections from other quarters, especially among those senior officers whose background had solely been in fast jets. It was no coincidence that when he moved upwards to become Chief of the Defence Staff in 1988, the pressure to stop flying XH558 mounted, never really to decrease until eventually it was sold off.

But what those early display outings with XL426 had proved was the Vulcan's special — almost unmatched — place in the British public's affections. David Craig recognised that earlier than most. "In the same way that the Battle of Britain Memorial Flight so successfully recalls the RAF's years of wartime effort", he wrote, "a Vulcan would dramatically symbolise the era of the V-Force". That it did, and even without a flying example, the aircraft still does today. A

Thanks to Richard Clarkson and Jen Paszkowski of the Vulcan Restoration Trust.

BELOW: Some felt the Vulcan display shouldn't have been continued beyond 1984, but come the 1985 season — this is Air Fete '85 at Mildenhall — XL426 was back again. The Vulcan Display Flight badge was applied to the nose undercarriage door. USAF

'FULL OUT' AT EVERYTHING

That description of Geoffrey Stephenson, whose time as CO of the RAF Duxford-based No 19 Squadron came to a premature end in 1940, sums up one of the qualities that made him such an outstanding fighter pilot. Seventy years on from Stephenson's death, testing a new F-100 Super Sabre in the USA, his biographer casts fresh light on a career that spanned several combat aircraft generations **WORDS:** JOHN SHIELDS

It was a bright, cool, November 2019 afternoon in downtown Montgomery, Alabama — the Saturday of the Veterans' Day weekend — and I found myself at the Oakwood Cemetery Annex preparing for the following day's Anglo-French Remembrance Sunday parade. As the senior RAF officer at the nearby Maxwell Air Force Base, I would be leading the event, and I thought a quick recce of the site before the big occasion would be prudent. My recent arrival from Blighty and my studies at Air War College had kept me busy to date, so, as a result, this was my first visit to the largest Commonwealth War Graves Commission cemetery in the US. What I found that afternoon would have a profound and lasting effect on me.

As I took in the peaceful vista, I walked among the well-kept graves and read the names of the 78 young airmen who were killed during their flying training at Maxwell and Gunter Fields between 1941 and 1943. However, I stumbled across one with a subtly different design. It was not from the Second World War but the 1950s, and marked the resting place of a 44-year-old air commodore rather than a trainee. Who was G. D. Stephenson CBE, and why was he buried in Alabama in 1954? I vowed to find out as much as I could and tell the story to the Remembrance Sunday audience the following day.

My internet research that evening revealed the remarkable life of Geoffrey Stephenson. The following day, I talked about Stephenson's early days at Cranwell, his friendship with Douglas Bader, commanding No 19 Squadron and flying Spitfires, Dunkirk, and his time as a prisoner of war. I ended with Stephenson's post-war career and his steady rise to the rank of air commodore before his fatal Super Sabre crash. It was clear that the attendees, some of whom had been coming to the Remembrance Sunday event for over 20 years, were unaware of Stephenson or his extraordinary journey. I vowed to keep his memory alive on this side of 'the Pond,' but I also wanted Stephenson's family to know he was not forgotten. The project ballooned beyond my expectations and would lead me to write his biography.

Geoffrey Stephenson was the eldest of four children born in 1910 to a wealthy north Lincolnshire farming family. However, their comfortable life would soon be shattered with the arrival of the First World War. Stephenson's father, already a decorated Boer War veteran, and most of his uncles were called up. Not all would return. His father was wounded during the German spring offensive of 1918. He was lucky; he survived, but three of his uncles paid the ultimate price.

As part of his recovery, Stephenson's father became the army's chief instructor at the Agricultural Training Farm at Ballyfair, Ireland. The family headed to Ireland, where Geoffrey continued his private education at Castle Park School in Dublin. Stephenson spent the next six years in Ireland, much of it on his own following the Irish War of Independence and the subsequent civil war, which forced his family's return to England. At the age of 14, Geoffrey came back to complete his studies at Shrewsbury School. Stephenson was bright, sporty and of the right pedigree — just the type of chap the RAF needed for its officer cadre. However, there was a problem.

Back in 1928, there were only two intakes of two dozen students each year to the RAF College at Cranwell. It was a highly competitive process, and attendance at the college was not gratis — the officer cadets had to pay fees to attend the two-year course. Ordinarily this would not have been an issue for an affluent farming family, but Stephenson's father had mismanaged their finances through several poor investments. Thankfully, the RAF catered for this situation and scholarships were available for the correct type of candidate. Due to his father's decorated military service, Stephenson was eligible and was duly awarded one of the scholarships. Another, for that same Cranwell intake, went to a certain Douglas Bader. Through their common bonds, Stephenson and Bader became life-long friends.

> ***"He won the prize for best pilot at Cranwell, well ahead of Bader"***

During the two years at the RAF College, Stephenson performed well academically, sitting comfortably in the middle of the pack. However, in the air he excelled. He was a gifted aviator and won the R. M. Groves Memorial Prize for best pilot, comfortably ahead of his nearest rival, Bader. In Stephenson's end-of-course report from Cranwell, the RAF College commandant AVM Arthur Longmore wrote, "smart efficient Cadet Sergeant who set a fine example to others by his energy and enterprise in work and sports. Will make a valuable officer and good mess mate."

Upon graduation from Cranwell in July 1930, Stephenson and Bader both headed to No 23 Squadron based at RAF Kenley, which flew the single-seat Gloster Gamecock biplane fighter. In addition to affiliation sorties with bomber squadrons, co-operation exercises with the army and air-to-air gunnery, the squadron performed formation aerobatics. Despite being junior pilots, Stephenson and Bader were both involved in this, supervised by one of the flight commanders, Flt Lt Harry Day.

In June 1931, the No 23 Squadron trio headed to the highest-profile display of the year, the Hendon Pageant. Day and Bader flew

ABOVE: Gp Capt Geoffrey Stephenson CBE ADC circa 1949 as the 23rd commandant of the Central Flying School.
CFS ASSOCIATION ARCHIVES

OPPOSITE PAGE: Stephenson's rebuilt former mount, Spitfire Ia N3200, now owned by the Imperial War Museums.
GEORGE ROMAIN/ARC

CLOCKWISE FROM RIGHT: A cheery Flight Cadet Stephenson looking resplendent in his RAF mess dress at Cranwell. STEPHENSON FAMILY ARCHIVE

Cranwell flight cadets learning about aero engines, with the ever-attentive SNCO supervising in the background. Douglas Bader is on the left leaning forward with Stephenson second from right. STEPHENSON FAMILY ARCHIVE

From left to right, Plt Off Bader, Flt Lt Harry Day and Plt Off Stephenson stand in front of a No 23 Squadron Gloster Gamecock during the 1931 Hendon display.

in the formation routine, with Stephenson relegated to the reserve pilot role. Although Geoffrey may have been disappointed, his time would soon come. "Two months later", said the squadron record, "on 22 August [...] at Cramlington in Northumberland, Bader and Stephenson, flying the pair together for the first time in public, fashioned a sequence over the top of the airfield which set the great northern crowd alight."

Moreover, Stephenson's tactical flying skills were recognised too. After the successful squadron air firing camp earlier in the year, Stephenson was selected to compete in the Brooke-Popham Cup and "proceeded to Sutton Bridge for best firer's competition". He impressed his seniors. In his 1931 confidential report, his squadron commander assessed Stephenson as an "exceptional" flyer. He highlighted,

> ***"Stephenson's luck had held despite a few close calls"***

"his energy and enterprise are a fine example, smart and efficient and a great asset. 'Full Out' at everything". The Kenley station commander, Wg Cdr Robinson, suggested Stephenson was "a keen and energetic officer of the right type."

Despite the accolades and their natural ability, Stephenson and Bader were still inexperienced, with relatively few flying hours — less than 500 hours' total. To be a truly experienced pilot, you need maturity, ability and luck. So far, Stephenson's luck had held despite a few close calls. During an aerobatic practice, he "fell out of a slow roll but luckily was just beyond the end of the Kenley escarpment and had enough space to recover". On another occasion, his engine failed, resulting in a "forced landing in the grounds of a country estate". Stephenson had been fortunate. Others would be less so. A change in aircraft type and an impetuous

approach to flying would prove to be the undoing of his best friend. In mid-1931, the squadron retired its Gamecocks and replaced them with the larger, heavier, but faster Bristol Bulldog. The bulkier Bulldog was more of a handful than the Gamecock, and Bader's near-fatal crash in December 1931 put paid to the Stephenson and Bader flying duo for now.

While they barely survived their first tour, many of their Cranwell cohort would not be so lucky. By the end of 1931, less than 18 months after their Cranwell graduation, five — nearly a quarter — of Stephenson's graduating class would be dead, four due to flying accidents. A month after Bader's crash, Stephenson headed to Iraq, a career-enhancing opportunity to broaden the young officer's perspective.

There Stephenson initially worked as the adjutant in an RAF armoured car company, a forerunner to today's RAF Regiment, based out of Basrah (now spelled Basra) in the south of the country. The turmoil had, by this stage, died down. Nevertheless, the unit still regularly sent Rolls-Royce armoured cars for extended policing patrols into the desert.

At RAF Hinaidi, outside Baghdad, he took a more refined appointment as the staff officer to AVM Charles Burnett, Air Officer Commanding Iraq Command. There would be some flying, but it was of a sedate nature in older, more docile aircraft on simple transits with senior officers as his passenger. He emerged a more mature, experienced and wiser officer and pilot. There was always an inherent risk in flying military aeroplanes in an unforgiving environment, but less so than in a testosterone-laden front-line fighter squadron. It would be another eight years before Stephenson piloted another fighter, a decision that may have prolonged his life.

After nearly three years away from home, in late 1934 Stephenson attended the Central Flying School at Wittering to become a flying instructor. Despite an extended period without a regular flying appointment, he had lost none of his innate skills. Of a course of 29, he was the top student and the only pilot to graduate with an A2 qualification, signifying above-average performance in the air and on the ground. Stephenson plied his trade at Cranwell for the next 18 months.

Given his natural talent, he soon rejoined the CFS, now at Upavon, to train would-be flying instructors. The CFS tour allowed Stephenson to be upgraded to the coveted A1 exceptional instructor categorisation, as well as familiarising himself once again with formation aerobatic displays. Flying Avro Tutors, the 1937 CFS three-ship aerobatic team was led by Flt Lt 'Tubby' Mermagen with Stephenson and Sgt Colin Scragg on his wings. They performed at Hendon's last RAF Display.

Stephenson was promoted to squadron leader in October 1938 and headed off to another career-enhancing outer office appointment in the Inspectorate of the RAF, working directly for the now ACM Burnett, his former boss in Iraq. A few months after the outbreak of the Second World War, Stephenson finally headed back to a fighter cockpit and command. Arguably, it was the station, squadron and aircraft that would define him — Duxford, No 19 Squadron and Supermarine's Spitfire.

Allocated to Fighter Command's No 12 Group, No 19 Squadron had converted to the Spitfire in August 1938. Stephenson took command in January 1940, during the 'Phoney War.' That initial respite in early 1940 over southern England, where the operational tempo was low and the enemy rarely present, would be short-lived but essential in

LEFT: In July 1930, Stephenson, Bader and 19 other flight cadets graduated from Cranwell. By the end of 1932, five of the graduates would be killed. RAF COLLEGE CRANWELL ARCHIVES

BELOW LEFT: In the cockpit of his Cranwell-based Armstrong Whitworth Siskin trainer. STEPHENSON FAMILY ARCHIVE

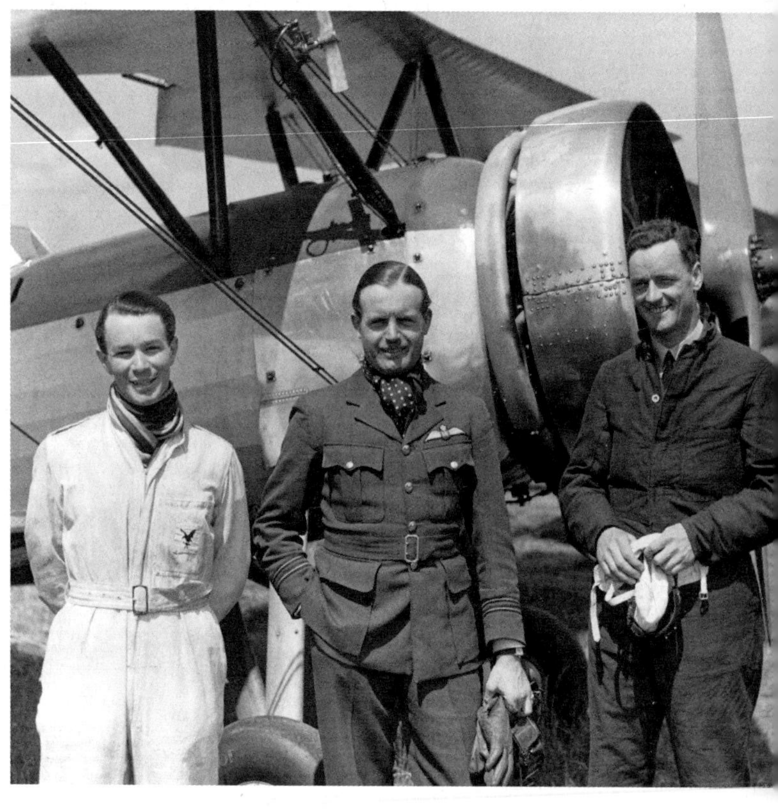

ABOVE: Iraq in the early 1930s, and Geoffrey cleans his shotgun. As expected from a fighter pilot, he was a naturally competitive individual and a keen shot, as ably demonstrated by his participation in the Iraq Rifle and Pistol Association's competitions. STEPHENSON FAMILY ARCHIVE

ABOVE RIGHT: The 1937 CFS display team. Standing in front of one of its Avro Tutors are, left to right, Flt Lts Geoffrey Stephenson and 'Tubby' Mermagen as well as Sgt Colin Scragg. STEPHENSON FAMILY ARCHIVE

preparing himself and his squadron for what was to follow. Moreover, it was also an opportunity to bring an old friend back onto front-line duties. Stephenson was instrumental in getting his old Cranwellian pal, Bader, back into a fighter cockpit. It was, therefore, no surprise that Fg Off Bader arrived on No 19 Squadron a mere month after Stephenson had taken over.

Bader had a difficult transition to the contemporary fighter world. Nevertheless, Stephenson still rated him as an exceptional pilot despite a few careless mishaps. His aggression and drive were evident, as was his relative inexperience in modern fighters and his frustration about being treated below his peer group. Thankfully, for Stephenson's sake, 19's sister squadron at Duxford needed a new flight commander. 'Tubby' Mermagen, the former CFS aerobatic team leader, was now commanding No 222 Squadron and only too happy to take the forthright Bader.

On 19 April 1940, just a few days after Bader's departure, three further Spitfire Is arrived at No 19 Squadron from No 8 Maintenance Unit at Little Rissington in the Cotswolds. One of the aircraft was N3200, which came off the Supermarine production line at Woolston in Southampton on 25 November 1939 and flew for the first time four days later. With its acceptance checks completed, the aircraft was ferried north on 2 December 1939 to Little Rissington, where it stayed for more than four months before heading east towards its new home at Duxford with 19. It would not be long before it was in action on its only operational mission.

May 1940 saw the end of the 'Phoney War' as Germany pushed relentlessly west through Belgium, the Netherlands and France,

> ***"The belly-landing caused little damage to the Spitfire"***

leading to the British Expeditionary Force's chaotic withdrawal towards Dunkirk. Fighter Command elected to preserve its Spitfires in the UK, relying on Hurricanes to operate on the continent. No 11 Group Spitfires worked initially in small formations that ranged over northern France, but they were outnumbered by their Luftwaffe counterparts and losses soon mounted. As a result, No 12 Group units were ordered forward and to operate in squadron-strength patrols. Stephenson's No 19 Squadron was first up and deployed to Hornchurch on the evening of 25 May 1940.

Sunday 26 May 1940 saw an early start for No 19 Squadron. At 07.40hrs, 12 Spitfires — led by Stephenson in N3200 — launched from Hornchurch and headed south-east towards Dunkirk. The weather was fine, but navigation was made all the easier by the black plumes of smoke rising from Dunkirk. The initial patrol was conducted at medium altitude, but the cloud structure at height made manoeuvring the formation problematic. Stephenson, leading the three aircraft of Red section, brought the remaining sections — Blue, Yellow and Green — down to 6,000ft to operate in clearer weather and in sight of the carnage below. It was not long before they spotted the enemy.

At the easterly point of their patrol, they turned west to track back down towards Dunkirk. In the distance, they spotted a group of aircraft coasting out into the English Channel: a formation of 21 Junkers Ju 87 Stuka dive-bombers from Sturzkampfgeschwader 76 setting up to attack the beach-head from the English Channel. Stephenson elected to attack from astern, in compliance with the standing Fighter Command tactics. However, he had not factored in the slow speed of the Stuka. The No 19 Squadron formation barrelled into the Ju 87s with significant overtake, compressing the available time to track and engage their opponents. As the leader, Stephenson had more time than his squadron-mates and managed to fell one Stuka. He had opened the account, but the ensuing dogfight was a chaotic affair.

The combat reports from those who made it home are, at times, contradictory as individuals tell their own personal brutal and fleeting fights for survival and glory. The 12 Spitfires and 21 Stukas were quickly joined by 30 Messerschmitt Bf 109s, which swooped into the melee. The German fighters included the 2. Staffel of Jagdgeschwader 2, the famed 'Richthofen' fighter wing, and among their number was Erich Rudorffer, a 22-year-old Oberfeldwebel with four kills already to his name. By the end of the dogfight, Rudorffer would be an ace, with Stephenson added to his tally. Although heavily outnumbered, No 19 Squadron more than held its own. It achieved six kills — two Bf 109s and four Ju 87s — but lost two Spitfires. One of Stephenson's wingmen, Plt Off Peter Watson, was shot down; wearing a black flying coverall, he was seen parachuting from his stricken aircraft. Sadly, he did not survive. Another wounded Spitfire exited the fight, descending towards the French coastline streaming glycol. By subsequent deduction, this was confirmed to be Stephenson in N3200 heading towards the beach at Sangatte.

The post-dogfight photographs of a forlorn N3200 sat on the French beach testify to Stephenson's innate flying skills. The belly-landing was well-executed with little damage to the aeroplane. As a result, Stephenson stepped out unhurt. Now standing in his rather obvious white flying coverall, Stephenson had to change clothes and move quickly away from the stricken Spitfire. Before heading south into the French countryside, he exchanged a few personal items for civilian attire with French onlookers and some retreating British engineers. His memoir, *I Walk Alone*, details his journey across terrain and places his father would have been familiar with from the First World War.

On 2 June, after eight days on the run, a beleaguered Stephenson entered Brussels to seek assistance from the US embassy. However, to maintain neutrality, the American diplomats had limited options to support British forces in this predicament. Stephenson was turned away hungry, tired and haggard. He stood out and had little means to buy food or communicate — he was out of options. He took the difficult decision to hand himself in and made his way to a Luftwaffe base on the outskirts of the Belgian capital. He was treated well and was soon on his way to captivity. Little did he know it would be another five years before he tasted freedom.

❖

His first PoW camp was Dulag Luft at Oberursel, just outside Frankfurt. It was a transit camp for all captured airmen, where they were interviewed to understand their intelligence value. Those of limited utility were processed quickly and sent to one of the larger, more permanent facilities. After processing, Stephenson was reunited with one of his old No 23 Squadron flight commanders. Harry Day, now a wing commander, was the camp's senior British officer and responsible for easing the new inmates into the routine.

Stephenson spent a few months at Dulag Luft. This extended period is perhaps unsurprising as a senior RAF officer and a Spitfire squadron commander would have interested the German authorities, but there was also a more practical reason for holding onto Stephenson. The surge in PoWs following Dunkirk had put pressure on the German system. Consequently, individuals were held at Dulag Luft until new facilities were available elsewhere. In September 1940, Stephenson was eventually transferred to Stalag Luft I at Barth on the Baltic coast.

Stalag Luft I was significantly larger and more chaotic than the simple, relaxed life at Dulag Luft. The relationship between the guards and PoWs was more adversarial and not helped by the antagonistic approach of Sqn Ldr Brian Padden, the senior British officer at Barth. After a failed escape attempt in February 1941, Padden was transferred to an

BELOW: German soldiers were initially able to inspect the force-landed Spitfire Ia N3200 on the Sangatte sands — but soon the No 19 Squadron fighter was increasingly submerged.

TOP: The RAF cohort at Colditz during the winter of 1942-43. Bader, as the senior airman, is in the centre of the front row while Stephenson is second from left in the front row. The designers of the 'Colditz Cock' glider are on the flanks of the rear row — Flt Lts Jack Best (right) and Bill Goldfinch (left). STEPHENSON FAMILY ARCHIVE

ABOVE: The early F-100As, as flown by Stephenson on his last flight in November 1954, had a small tail fin — such as 52-5773 at right. As a result, they were difficult to handle and had a notorious reputation among pilots. Following Stephenson's fatal crash, the USAF grounded the Super Sabre fleet. The aircraft were subsequently modified with a larger fin and longer wingspan, as on 52-5778 on the left, to improve stability. NASA

apparently more secure camp, thus promoting Stephenson to the senior British officer position. Stephenson had inherited a challenging environment, but his peers believed he was "doing a reasonable job under difficult circumstances."

During a search a couple of months later, Stephenson was caught in possession of a poem decrying Hitler, one he had confiscated from another prisoner. Since he was unwilling to tell the incensed German authorities who had actually written the poem, the Germans decided to make an example of Stephenson. He was initially sent to the 'cooler' for three weeks before going to another PoW camp, one specifically created to hold troublemakers.

In August 1941, Stephenson arrived at the camp that would be his home for the rest of the war: Oflag IVC, better-known as Colditz. Unlike the earlier camps, which predominantly housed British airmen, Colditz had a more multi-service, coalition feel to it, with members from all three armed forces plus Poles, Dutch and French. A year into his stay at Colditz, his old friend Douglas Bader joined him. Bader was a notorious 'goon-baiter' and Stephenson followed suit, often ending up in solitary confinement for his endeavours.

Colditz is renowned for being the home to the persistent escaper, but Stephenson, contrary to popular belief, was not one of them. He tended to operate in the supporting role rather than as the main act. However, as confirmed in his post-war MI9 debrief, he "made several abortive [escape] attempts from Oflag IVC". Although he does not add detail in the report, his diaries reveal clues to his escape activities. Not only did he act as a 'stooge' to

> ***"He went to a PoW camp created to hold troublemakers"***

maintain a look-out against prying Germans intercepting any nefarious escape activities, but he was active in tunnelling, carpentry and the 'Colditz Cock' glider project.

Colditz and its inmates were relieved by the US Army in April 1945. Stephenson's war was finally over. After a quick flying refresher, the now Wg Cdr Stephenson was gently reintroduced into the RAF. His initial post-war appointments were a couple of short command tours overseeing the draw-down and closure of the wartime bases at Bradwell Bay in Essex and Spilsby in Lincolnshire.

While there was order in his military life, his domestic situation was more turbulent. His engagement to his fiancée ended soon after his return from captivity. However, at Bradwell Bay, Stephenson met Maureen Menzies. Maureen was a 25-year-old single mother who had recently been informed that her husband, a Special Operations Executive agent, had been executed by the Nazis during the last weeks of the war. In among his academic studies as a student at the RAF Staff College, Stephenson and Maureen were married in June 1946 at Maureen's local parish church, St Mary the Virgin, a stone's throw from her parents' home in Burnham-on-Crouch, Essex. Bader was Stephenson's best man; daughters Victoria and Veryan followed soon afterwards.

Stephenson's career was back on track after his Second World War sabbatical. He was promoted to group captain a few days after his wedding and headed to a staff appointment at the headquarters of Flying Training Command. During the tour, he was appointed CBE and made an aide-de-camp to the monarch. His recent staff experience and previous instructional knowledge meant Stephenson was the obvious choice to return to CFS as the commandant.

Having spent two years in command at Little Rissington, Stephenson left the training world for another operational appointment overseas. In September 1950, the Stephenson family headed to Egypt, where Geoffrey led No 1 Sector from its headquarters at RAF Ismailia, on the western bank of the Suez Canal. Due to the increase in Egyptian nationalism and the associated rioting and disturbances, he spent the last year of his tour on his own while his family were evacuated to the safety of the UK. But there was good news as well.

Stephenson was promoted to air commodore in early 1953 and put in command of a key operationally focused unit: the Central Fighter Establishment, based at West Raynham in Norfolk. Before that, there were royal duties to attend to. Stephenson and Maureen attended the Queen's coronation in Westminster Abbey early that June,

LEFT: RAF Odiham in July 1953, and the newly coronated Queen Elizabeth II is escorted by Air Cdre Stephenson around the 300 aircraft comprising the static display of the RAF Coronation Review. STEPHENSON FAMILY ARCHIVE

and he was tasked with organising and executing the static display for the new monarch at the Coronation Review. Hosted at Odiham on 15 July, it consisted of a parade, a static display and a flypast, all of them on an unprecedented scale. Press footage shows Stephenson escorting the Queen around the static array of 321 aircraft. She returned to the royal dais to review the flypast, which lasted 27 minutes and contained 641 aircraft, comprising 47 formations of 26 different types from 43 bases. With his royal duties over, Stephenson headed off to Norfolk for what proved to be his last tour.

The CFE was created in the closing days of the Second World War and initially led by Richard Atcherley, one of Stephenson's flight commanders on No 23 Squadron in 1930. It was charged with increasing "the efficiency of the fighter aircraft and the man who flies it, in all roles in which day and night fighters can be used". This was a high-profile appointment that enhanced an individual's career, being "the place where every keen fighter pilot had dreams of being posted". Moreover, it allowed the commandant to fly in all the latest fighter aircraft. Stephenson undoubtedly relished command of CFE and the broad, varied and relevant tactical flying opportunities it presented.

Consequently, he was airborne most days. His subordinates regarded him as an active flyer, not a desk pilot.

While he had several thousand hours of flight time in his logbook dating back to the late 1920s, Stephenson's recent experience made him stand out from his peer group. He was generally considered to be one of the RAF's experts in jet fighters for exactly that reason as well as his longevity. He sampled the newest types of British jets, including the Hawker Hunter, Gloster Meteor and Javelin, de Havilland Venom and Supermarine Swift, as well as the US-designed North American F-86 Sabre. After an enforced hiatus during the Second World War, Stephenson was making up for lost time and led the RAF's fighter pilot cadre of the early 1950s by example.

As part of the CFE's remit, the unit conducted "liaison with Allied Air Forces to achieve maximum coordination of current thought and method". Consequently, it visited the US on an annual basis. The trip was not only about strategic leadership engagement, gaining insights into the latest developments in aviation research and visits to the aircraft manufacturers, but also a more practical element. The highlight was the time spent at the establishment's US Air Force equivalent, Air Proving Ground Command, at Eglin Air Force Base in the Florida panhandle. More importantly, it allowed Stephenson and his six-man team to fly in the USAF's most up-to-date jets. In 1954, the state of the art was the sleek, supersonic North American F-100A Super Sabre.

As their three-week US sojourn drew to a close, the CFE team found themselves at Eglin on the evening of 7 November 1954. The next day's plan was for two British pilots to fly the Super Sabre. Stephenson was to go first, chased by another F-100 in the hands of an experienced USAF pilot, Capt Lonnie Moore, a Second World War veteran who had recently returned from Korea as an F-86 ace. For the second sortie, Gp Capt Frederick Rosier would replace Stephenson and follow the same flight profile.

The schedule called for a 14.00 take-off for the first event. Consequently, the British pilots had much to cover ahead of their afternoon F-100 familiarisation sorties. The morning was spent with Lt Col Henry 'Baby' Brown, a World War Two P-51 Mustang ace and himself a former PoW, from the Super Sabre evaluation team. Brown's comprehensive briefing covered the F-100's background, handling characteristics and sortie details. There was much to take in as the Super Sabre's entry into service had been problematic, with the new fighter quickly gaining a reputation for its handling vices. These issues had recently claimed the life of North American Aviation's chief test pilot, Pearl Harbor veteran George Welch.

After the briefings, lunch and kitting-out, Stephenson and Brown walked out to their allocated aircraft — a silver-skinned F-100A, serial 53-1534. Brown assisted in firing

LEFT: Under ever blue skies, Stephenson's final resting place is at the Oakwood Cemetery Annex in Montgomery, Alabama — the largest Commonwealth War Graves Commission site in the United States. JOHN SHIELDS

ABOVE: The resurrection of N3200 to airworthiness by the Aircraft Restoration Company has ensured Stephenson's memory is perpetuated. Here, John Romain flies the fighter.
GEORGE ROMAIN/ARC

up the single-seat fighter. All went well until Stephenson took off. As soon as the Super Sabre rose off the Eglin runway, the aircraft began to 'porpoise', so much so that back on the runway's threshold Moore, sitting in the chase aircraft, thought it was about to crash. Fortunately, Stephenson eventually got the Super Sabre back under control.

The subsequent climb to altitude, supersonic run and descent passed without incident. The Super Sabres were now at 300kt, 15,000ft overhead Eglin and heading north back into the Florida countryside. The plan was for Stephenson to hand the lead over to Moore to allow the RAF pilot to practise close formation flying. As Stephenson was repositioning, Moore saw his aircraft start to porpoise once again. The American lost sight of the Briton's jet as it dropped back, still porpoising; this was the last time Moore saw Stephenson.

At Eglin Auxiliary Airfield number 2, members of a visiting F-86 squadron looked up to see a spinning F-100. The aircraft briefly recovered at about 5,000ft before re-entering a spin and crashing a mile or so north of the airfield. They had witnessed the final moments of Air Cdre Geoffrey Stephenson CBE.

> ***"Stephenson's death in the F-100 was tragic but it was not in vain"***

The Accident Investigation Board determined the primary cause was a loss of control, with two contributory factors: the "apparent instability of F-100 model aircraft", and the "pilot's inexperience with this type of control system". The early Super Sabres were challenging to fly, but an experienced pilot and instructor like Stephenson should have been able to deal with the marginal-stability flight characteristics. However, the situation was exacerbated by a technical problem. A faulty electrical connection between the trim button on the control column and the horizontal stabiliser materialised in flight. Although Brown checked the trim switch during start-up, it was discovered that due to improper assembly during manufacture, the electrical wire sheared from its plug, disconnecting the trim button from the horizontal stabiliser. The net result was that an aircraft already prone to stability issues needed even larger control inputs to control it. Therefore, it was inevitable it would be overcontrolled and induce the porpoising effect before losing control.

Following Stephenson's fatal crash, the Super Sabre fleet was grounded for several months, delaying the type being declared operational. The stability issues were mitigated by modifications, and the F-100 finally entered service. Stephenson's death was tragic but not in vain. The changes meant many future pilots survived their dalliance with the 'Hun'.

In keeping with British policy at the time, Stephenson was laid to rest at the nearest CWGC cemetery. On 10 November 1954, after a short service at Eglin's base church, his coffin was escorted by a party of RAF and USAF personnel and flown north to Maxwell Air Force Base before transferring the few miles to the Oakwood Cemetery Annex in Montgomery. Representing the RAF at the funeral was AVM Richard Atcherley, the senior RAF airman in the US, as well as Stephenson's former flight commander and CFE founder.

His enduring influence beyond his immediate family may have stopped at that point. However, a 1986 storm in the English Channel uncovered a secret it had been keeping for in excess of four decades, as Stephenson's Spitfire N3200 revealed itself from its sandy grave. Initially the wrecked fighter was displayed at a French museum, but was ultimately selected for rebuild. After a two-year restoration, N3200 returned to the air from its old Duxford base in 2014 with John Romain at the controls. The following year, N3200 was generously donated to the Imperial War Museums, where it continues to fly and is a popular attraction on the display circuit. The Aircraft Restoration Company's new hangar was named in Stephenson's honour.

Geoffrey Stephenson's life was short and eventful, but his enduring legacy lives on today over the skies of Duxford and at every Remembrance Sunday at his final resting place in Montgomery, Alabama. Lest we forget.

Spitfire Pilot — Air Commodore Geoffrey Stephenson is published by Pen & Sword.

BELOW: N3200 has now spent far longer at Duxford as a preserved warbird than ever it did in RAF service. GEORGE ROMAIN/ARC

AVRO'S AIRLINE

In the early, pioneering days of commercial travel following the Great War, it was the Avro Transport Company that stole a march on its competition and offered Britain's first regular domestic passenger air service **WORDS:** NEVILLE DOYLE

Aeronautics advanced so rapidly during the First World War that, when hostilities ended in November 1918, it took nearly six months of hard graft to frame the rules and regulations necessary for the resumption of civil aviation, although, as a special concession, flying was allowed over the Easter weekend of 1919 in 'service-type' aircraft only, and within a radius of three miles of the aerodrome. The Air Navigation Regulations were published on 30 April, after much effort by Gen Frederick Sykes, the controller general of civil aviation, and his tiny staff. Civil flying, internal to the UK only, was permitted from the following day. With considerable publicity, aircraft took off for a variety of destinations.

The first was scheduled to leave Hendon at midnight on the 30th to fly copies of the *Daily Mail* to Bournemouth along a route "marked out with searchlights", but mist delayed the start until 04.20hrs, and the flight by the Aircraft Transport & Travel Airco DH9 ended prematurely on Portsdown Hill near Portsmouth, leaving the pilot, Capt Howard Saint, with a fractured jaw and his passenger, Capt Donald Greig, severely shaken. At about 10.30 Lt Cyril Uwins left Bristol's Filton aerodrome in a fast Bristol 27 biplane — an F2B Fighter with an enclosed passenger cockpit — with his passenger, Herbert Thomas, "sitting in a warm closed-in coupe, in which a writing desk is installed". They reached Hounslow in 58 minutes to make "the first flight along one of the new national air routes."

The Air Ministry's "new national air routes" joined London to other parts of the country via existing RAF stations, but they were just lines on paper with no plans for regular services, although some dismay was felt by the more progressive elements in towns not connected to any of them. Blackpool was one such. After the enthusiasm of the opening days, interest turned to imminent attempts at the vastly more hazardous adventure of flying the Atlantic, but considerable space, especially in local papers, was still devoted to the mystique of flying as experienced by ordinary people "indulging in aerial locomotion" for the very first time, because the only outlet for commercial aviation, despite the great hopes, turned out to be joy-riding and the odd air taxi.

ABOVE: A variety of markings are displayed on these three 504s. In the foreground is E3292, later G-EADI, and behind it is D9340, fleet number 15, which became G-EAFS, with its serial writ large on its fuselage flanks.

One of the best machines for joy-riding was the Avro 504K, available in large numbers at low cost from war surplus stocks and its makers. A. V. Roe & Co bought some back from the government and formed the Avro Transport Company to operate them commercially. Its machines usually had the 110hp Le Rhône rotary engine, although others could be fitted such as the Clerget. For civilian flying the relatively high fuel consumption and an oil consumption of some three gallons per hour reduced the payload on a long trip. Nevertheless it was very suitable for joy-riding, which proved to be a popular entertainment, and there was keen competition for the sites with the best prospects, such as Blackpool's miles of golden sand, for which both Avro and Sopwith were negotiating.

> ***"For Mr Harbottle, the town clerk, 'It was like riding on velvet'"***

But the deputy town clerk told a reporter that Blackpool had a much better object in view than being first in the air with joy-rides: "Before that we place the safety of the public and a service that will be adequate... We are hoping, also, that if it results in a civil aerodrome here the Government will recognise it as one of the official stations. It would make an excellent station, say, for flights to and from Belfast..." In the end Avro won the day, but it is reasonable to suppose that the promise of a regular daily air service between Blackpool and the Manchester 'air station' at Didsbury, on one of the new routes, did much to tip the scales in its favour.

On Saturday 10 May 1919, members and officials of the Blackpool Corporation were taken by car to Manchester to return, later in the day, in four Avro 504Ks. A huge throng awaited them, making "a deep black line along the sands, on the Promenade and on the Victoria Pier". When the first three machines emerged from the thundery haze, "there was a yell from the crowd of 'here they are'". As soon as they landed, the crowd, "hitherto admirably controlled by the police and special police [...] at once flooded the sands and swarmed around the machines." For Mr Harbottle, the town clerk, "It was a pleasurable sensation like riding on velvet... a rather weird feeling when the machine banked, and a motion like a motor-car going over a hump when the aeroplane rose and fell..." "The towns looked like toy shops", added Mr Furness of the transport department. Councillor Bean, meanwhile, "saw something like a match-stick peeping up through the haze. It was the Tower..." When Chief Constable Pringle descended

OPPOSITE PAGE: Fleet number 6 in the Avro Transport Company's inventory of 504Ks flies past the 'booking office' on Birkdale Palace aerodrome, Southport, in mid-1919. The aircraft still carries its military serial number, E3292, on its rudder; a civil registration, G-EADI, has yet to be applied.

ALL VIA PHILIP JARRETT

ABOVE: Crowds surround three 504s on Blackpool's fairground pleasure beach in 1919, with Hiram Maxim's massive roundabout in the background on the right.

from the third Avro he was handed a telegram authorising the use of the sands at South Shore, opposite the Star Inn, for flying.

The fourth aeroplane was half-an-hour late due to a lack of revs from the engine of the original aircraft and the lack of a map on the part of its replacement's pilot, but eventually, in the delightful prose of the contemporary journalist, it "arrived over Blackpool at a great height. Wheeling down in graceful spirals, the machine reached a lower altitude, flew half way between the Victoria and Central Piers, then turned and dropped to earth with perfect precision."

No time was lost, and joy-riding at a guinea a head began on the following Monday, 12 May. During that weekend the *Mauritania* had sailed into Halifax, Nova Scotia with returning soldiers and two airmen named John Alcock and Arthur Whitten Brown, while the two US Navy Curtiss NC flying boats NC-1 and NC-3 were preparing to leave Halifax for Trepassey Bay, Newfoundland.

At Southport the sole rights to joy-riding from the foreshore went to the Sopwith Company, and in this case the scales may have been tipped in the opposite direction by the promise of a visit by Harry Hawker if successful in crossing the Atlantic. On Saturday 17 May the late-starting NC-4 reached Horta in the Azores, both NC-1 and NC-3 having fallen by the wayside, and the following day Hawker and Kenneth Mackenzie-Grieve took off in their Sopwith Atlantic biplane from St John's, Newfoundland but failed to reach the other side. The Avro Transport Company had to make do with the shore at Birkdale, a mile or so to the south of Southport, and about 100 acres of sand was enclosed to make a landing ground in front of the Birkdale Palace Hydro Hotel. It was one minute's walk from the Cheshire Lines Committee railway station, five minutes from the Lancashire and Yorkshire Railway station, and accessible by tram from Lord Street.

The hotel acted as agents and adopted quite a proprietorial air: "the Birkdale Palace Hydro Hotel has

RIGHT: On 4 August 1919, 504K E1663 was ditched in the Channel at Southsea. After recovery it became G-EACW.

arranged with the Avro Company of Manchester to inaugurate an air service of flights with the object of conveying guests to and from the hotel, and also for a series of pleasure civilian flights... For short flights a guinea will be charged, whilst an air trip to Blackpool will cost two guineas for a single and three guineas for a return journey..."

The stage was now set for Britain's first regular air service which, "beginning on Monday next (May 26th) will leave Alexandra Park aerodrome at 10 am, returning from Blackpool and Southport about 8 pm". The fare for a single journey was £5 5s 0d, and for a return £9 9s 0d, to either Blackpool or Southport. Joy-riding started at Birkdale on 20 May, when Hawker and Mackenzie-Grieve were still missing, and soon they had been given up for lost, except by Mrs Hawker. Therefore the national headlines on the morning of 26 May were filled with the sensational news that a Danish steamer, the *Mary*, had closed the Butt of Lewis flying the signal "SAVED HANDS SOPWITH AEROPLANE".

However, the new service did receive a brief mention in the *Manchester Guardian* of 27 May: "A civilian service between Manchester and the Lancashire coast had a formal beginning a few weeks ago... Nothing that might be considered as a regular service existed until yesterday morning. Two Avro machines carrying three fare-paying passengers then left the aerodrome near Alexandra Park and arrived at Blackpool... Nothing at the aerodrome before the departure gave the first flight any remarkable significance, the general public was represented by the Lord Mayor of Manchester (Alderman Kay) and the Lady Mayoress. The passengers arriving separately were quite casually provided with goggles and leather caps, took their seats,

> ***"The airline was overshadowed by demand for joy-rides"***

and the machine, after flying once round the aerodrome made course for Blackpool."

Actually there were four passengers: Mr F. A. Makin of Victoria Park, Manchester, a colonial civil servant on leave, Mr D. G. Miles, a superintendent in the Manchester GPO, Mr T. Longworth, a newspaper publisher, and Mr F. T. Curson, a *Daily Sketch* photographer, presumably travelling free and carefully ignored by the *Guardian*. None had flown before, but Makin said he had "just been living for this moment", and Miles was hoping to return that night. "There was only a gentle breeze blowing at the time, but haze and mist was in evidence at a comparatively low altitude making low flying advisable", said the report. At about 10.45, "the two planes 'took-off' within minutes of each other without any hitch, and, quickly attaining a height of about 1,000 feet made off in a due westerly direction and were soon lost to view. The route was via Southport: "If they did fly 'via Southport' it may have been to familiarize themselves with the regular route and a straight line from Didsbury to Birkdale did avoid the high ground north-west of Wigan and have the benefit of the Wigan-Southport railway line as a convenient aid to navigation."

However, the airline was wholly overshadowed by the enormous demand for joy-rides, and more sites were being opened up all over the country. By the end of June in excess of 5,000 passengers had been 'flipped' at Blackpool alone. For two guineas the pilot would loop, and for three carry out "a series of evolutions". One woman had completed 15 'stunt' flights in a week, and in all seriousness a Dr Bentall, when asked after his flight if he would recommend flying for patients, replied, "in the later convalescent stage it might be beneficial". According to

ABOVE: An unusual angle on a 504L, still bearing roundels on its wings and an indecipherable military serial on its rudder, as it taxies out for take-off at an undetermined location in 1919.

ABOVE: A spot of 'stunting' in the course of an Avro joy-ride out of Hounslow with 504K E4222, flying four-up! KEY COLLECTION

Commercial Aviation, a short-lived weekly, the Blackpool lady's comment upon her husband's return to earth was, "Hah, then, I hape tha' art satisfied: tha's been nearer heaven than iver tha'll be agin". *The Aeroplane* joked that the spectators were becoming so knowledgeable they were able to tell enquiring old ladies that the function of the propeller was to keep the engine cool, and reported that coalminers "think nothing of paying large sums of money for a really long flight..."

A special 'Night-Extra' edition of the *Sunday Evening Telegram* for 15 June secured the greatest scoop with the news that Alcock and Brown had landed at Clifden, Galway, shortly before 10.00 that morning after a 16-hour flight. Although Alcock was Manchester-born, and Whitten-Brown a Mancunian by residence, the *Guardian* was less than hysterical about the feat, which proved, "not for the first time, that they are very gallant men, [but] does not [...] prove much else. As far as can be foreseen, the future of air transport over the Atlantic is not for the aeroplane". Meanwhile the trans-Lancashire airway was "running like clockwork" with the following times: depart Blackpool noon, depart Southport 12.15, arrive Manchester 12.45; depart Manchester 14.00, arrive Southport 14.30, arrive Blackpool 14.45. This timetable was retained until the service ended.

Flying between England and France was permitted during the peace celebrations of 13-20 July, and on the 14th the first foreign civilian pilot to land in Britain since the war, Etienne Poulet, landed at Hounslow in his Caudron. The inaugural British flight took place the very next day, when Capt 'Jerry' Shaw and a DH9 of Aircraft Transport & Travel were chartered by Maj Pilkington of the St Helens glass firm to take him from Hendon to Paris. By the end of the month Avro 504Ks were joy-riding at Hounslow, Manston, Southsea, Weston-super-Mare, Brighton, Swansea, Fleetwood, Morecambe, Rhyl, and Waterloo near Liverpool, while 504L seaplanes were operating from Paignton and various Isle of Wight resorts. An extra service was being advertised as leaving Southport daily for Blackpool at 10.00 for £2 2s 0d single, £4 4s 0d return, and by the beginning of August the 10,000th passenger had been flown at Blackpool.

On 1 August Mr Bracegirdle, a Manchester fishmonger, sent 12 stone of fresh Fleetwood fish to Manchester by the Avro service, probably the first fish to travel by air — apart from flying fish. To mark the event, Bracegirdle presented the lady mayoress with two turbot. "It is believed they had not survived the journey", added *The Aeroplane* facetiously. Howard Pixton, winner of the 1914 Monaco Schneider Trophy race flew three hundredweight of *Daily News* from Windermere to Douglas Bay, Isle of Man, on 4 August in an Avro 504L seaplane. He made several trips a week thereafter until 3 September, usually when there was no midnight boat sailing from Liverpool. With the aid of the new four-passenger Avro 536 flying at Blackpool from mid-

RIGHT: The Avro 536 was created by widening the fuselage of the 504 to enable four passengers to be accommodated in the rear cockpit. It was evidently a very cosy arrangement.

LEFT: A typical period postcard, posted in August 1919, depicting 504 fleet number 5, D6229/ G-EABV, flying past Fred Oliver's Star Inn at Blackpool.

August, 500 passengers were taken up in a day, and one evening a man went out to Birkdale at about 9pm when it was blowing half a gale with cloud right down to the ground and offered £200 to be flown to the Isle of Man. He wanted to surprise his wife, he said, but in what circumstances one can only speculate.

At Swansea, Capts Bruce and Dalton were joy-riding from Brynmill, near Black Pill station on the Mumbles Railway, and on 11 August Bruce began a daily service to Llanwrtyd Wells, taking passengers up during the day from the grounds of the Abernant Hotel and returning to Swansea at night. Obviously this was just a positioning flight and the 'service' probably petered out after a week or so. A well-known event took place on 25 August when commercial flying between England and France was finally sanctioned, and Lt 'Bill' Lawford inaugurated the first daily international air service by flying an Aircraft Transport & Travel DH4A from Hounslow to Paris with journalist George Stevenson-Reece as passenger.

> **"The airway was 'running like clockwork'"**

September began with storms and continuous rain. One account describes how "an extra-ordinary storm sprang up one night about 12 o'clock increasing in violence", getting up to 65-85mph. "The Avros pegged down on the sands at Blackpool, Southport and Rhyl suffered considerable damage, the machines complete with sandbags and pegging-down gear being carried away". By the middle of the month the Avro 'Northern Stations' — Birkdale, Manchester, Fleetwood, Morecambe, Rhyl, Waterloo, Douglas and Windermere, of which Blackpool was the parent — had carried more than 20,000 passengers.

On the last day of September the regular daily service ended. The only untoward incident recorded during the whole period of operation was the arrival of Capt Pownall at Blackpool when the high tide had brought the sea right up to the

BELOW: In the early period these rather nice souvenir cards were given to passengers, this one being issued on 9 August 1919 to Arthur Butler, who had a 10-mile flight in Avro 536 K161 (later G-EAGM), for which he paid a guinea.

£1 1s. 0d. No. 463

AVRO JOYRIDES.

THE SANDS AERODROME, WESTON-SUPER-MARE.

Mr., Mrs., or Miss Dr Butler

Date 9/8/19.

Avro No. K161

Pilot's Name Captain A. N. APPLEFORD. Late R.A.F.

For Conditions of Flight see back

A.V.RO

SOUVENIR of a FLIGHT in an AVRO BIPLANE at WESTON-SUPER-MARE.

Date Aug 9th 1919 [illegible] 10 miles

Pilot [illegible]

Passenger Arthur J Butler

A. V. ROE & CO., LTD. NEWTON HEATH, MANCHESTER

ABOVE: 504L K145, subsequently G-EAFF, distracts holidaymakers in 1919. This aircraft was based at Hayling Island, Isle of Wight. In July 1921 it was sold to the Belgian Air Force.

BELOW: A very low pass at Blackpool by D6239, fleet number 9, later G-EADX, which was based at Southport.

barriers on the sand, and he landed on a road down to the beach.

According to figures published by the Avro Transport Company, of 222 flights scheduled, 194 were accomplished, 28 being prevented by weather and none interrupted by mechanical trouble. It said it had flown 8,730 miles between 24 May and 30 September. In fact, the correct date for the opening should have been 26 May and therefore the number of scheduled flights must have been 220, which agrees with 18 weeks of six days — there was no service on Sundays — plus the last two days of September. Either the flights accomplished or those prevented by weather should be reduced accordingly, but if the 'miles flown' figure is divided by the 'flights accomplished' figure of 194 the distance is exactly 45 miles, which would amount to about 12 miles from Blackpool to Southport, and 33 miles from Southport to Manchester.

Other firms claimed to have operated air services of various kinds, but they were usually just positioning flights. The closest rival to the Avro Transport Company for the honour of starting Britain's first airline was the North Sea Aerial Navigation Company, a subsidiary of the Blackburn Aeroplane & Motor Company. *The Aeroplane* reported, "A passenger and commercial service between Hull and Hartlepool was inaugurated by the arrival of a Blackburn Kangaroo biplane piloted by R. W. Kenworthy at Hull at 5pm on May 26th". The flight took about an hour, so the Avro machines were in the air long before their Yorkshire rival. Little can be found about this service in the local papers, but as Blackburn repurchased a number of Kangaroos from the government and most of them were with No 246 Squadron based at Seaton Carew near Hartlepool, very likely it was just ferrying these machines to its own aerodrome at Brough and offering seats to anyone willing to pay. Short-lived it may have been, the company ceasing to exist in 1920, but the Avro operation's place in the annals is assured.

Typhoon Ib RB396 looking ever more complete, with the rear fuselage newly finished and the project's cockpit section and tail positioned fore and aft. STEVE COMBER/COAP

BREWING UP A STORM

Any major restoration is a marathon, rather than a sprint — and that goes especially for when the subject is an aircraft never rebuilt to flying condition before. That's certainly the case for the Hawker Typhoon Preservation Group, making the latest milestone along that long road all the more of an achievement **WORDS:** BEN DUNNELL

LEFT: Mervyn 'Gerry' Blow, seated at front left, and colleagues on No 137 Squadron with a Typhoon in 1944 or '45. BNPS

Even at the age of 100, placing a rivet was pretty small beer for Mervyn 'Gerry' Blow, and especially on a Hawker Typhoon. The former RAF engine fitter worked on the potent fighter-bombers in service with No 137 Squadron, and then their Tempest successors on No 274 Squadron. But this one had a broader significance. It helped bring to completion the first fuselage section of the type to be made flyable since the war years, awaiting the point at which the rest of the aircraft is ready to join it in the air.

'Gerry' was an honoured guest of the Hawker Typhoon Preservation Group, as on 30 October it held a ceremony for supporters and other invitees to mark the latest milestone in its project. The rear fuselage of Typhoon Ib RB396/G-TIFY is now finished, and some of those present at Airframe Assemblies' premises at Sandown on the Isle of Wight had the distinction of adding those final rivets to conclude the job. But this section, while substantial, is only the first part of the rebuild process.

That story can truly be said to have started in 2016, when the HTPG was established. It followed the return to the UK four years earlier of RB396's wreckage, previously displayed in a small Dutch museum. This veteran of more than 35 operational sorties was on the strength of No 174 Squadron when it was shot down by flak on 1 April 1945, this while attacking mechanised transportation targets near Hengelo in the Netherlands. A successful forced landing followed. Its resurrection ranks among the most ambitious returns-to-flight currently under way, and inevitably there have been ups and downs. The rear fuselage, though, represents a tangible statement of intent.

As with any such rebuild, this has not proved straightforward. "It's been there on the Isle of Wight with Airframe Assemblies for five-and-a-half years, which is quite a long time", says project director and trustee Sam Worthington-Leese. "It went over in May 2019 following a successful crowd-funder, when we raised enough money to start the rebuild. There was no guarantee that we'd have the rest — we'd have to raise every penny. It was all going fairly well until COVID came along. The first year of COVID actually didn't really impact us, but then it was the second year when it really bit and peoples' finances started to feel the pinch. The rebuild had to be paused due to funding, and that lasted about 18 months. In December 2023 it restarted again, just before Christmas. The funding was all assured; we wanted to make sure we had that before we restarted.

> ***"The engineers are learning these things from scratch"***

"From an engineering point of view, there have been a few troublesome things. With something that is effectively unique, the engineers are learning these things from scratch. They're coming across problems they don't see in Spitfires, Hurricanes, Mustangs and Buchóns, which are most of their trade. There was a lot of head-scratching, a lot of standing around looking at drawings, a lot of trying to find new drawings — there

LEFT: Having celebrated his centenary not long before, 'Gerry' Blow secures one of the last rivets in RB396's rear fuselage. STEVE COMBER/COAP

VIA HTPG

THIS PAGE AND OPPOSITE: The progress made in restoring the rear fuselage section, illustrated in four images: above, at the HTPG's premises in Uckfield, East Sussex, before it went to Airframe Assemblies, still showing the wartime No 174 Squadron markings; then, top to bottom on the page opposite, the first rivets being removed following arrival on the Isle of Wight in May 2019; in the jig during September 2020; and just a few weeks before the ceremonial completion, with only a few skins still to be added.

were some gaps in the amount of drawings we have. Some decisions we took collaboratively caused slight changes of path along the way: this is what we're facing, what shall we do about it?

"There are some really interesting engineering elements to it. One is the foot-step. It's very similar to a Hurricane, in that you open a hand-hold and the bottom bit pops down, but it's very complicated and there's quite a lack of drawings of that area. The RAF Museum was very helpful to us with that. Andrew Boakes, our research guy who's a volunteer on the team, paid a number of visits to the museum with access to the step, photographing all the angles for the guys at Airframe Assemblies so they could work with what they've got. That was solved, and it's working, which is great.

"Andrew has been invaluable... he lives in Kent, the museum is in London, Airframe Assemblies are on the Isle of Wight, the rest of the rebuild's at Duxford [with the Aircraft Restoration Company], and he's been going up and down, up and down. I think this section alone would have easily cost 20 per cent more, £100,000, if we were having to pay an engineer by the hour to do all this, which means it wouldn't be finished yet.

> ***"There are some really interesting engineering elements to it"***

"We wanted to use as much original material from RB396 as possible. The original skins, obviously, couldn't be used but the frames and the stringers could. We're waiting for the final figure, but approximately 80 per cent of the frames and stringers are original material. The stringers could not be used in their single sections — there were areas within that were not good enough to use — so there have been some elements that have been created from new.

"In the pictures you can see irregularities, if you like, in the riveting and you can see certain areas where there are patches where the rivets are much more densely spaced than the others, which are quite uniform. That has been taken from an authentic Hawker battlefield repair technique to enable this original material to be reused, rather than just creating full new lengths of stringer.

"The tail joint is always an interesting topic when the Typhoon comes up, because of the failures in the early Typhoons. Hawker redesigned the tail transport joint, although it wasn't actually the joint that was the problem. The problem was traced to [...] the mass balance causing flutter, and effectively any

VIA HTPG

VIA HTPG

BNPS

joint would have failed. Anyway, they still redesigned the joint for the Tempest, but once the production of Tempests started, because the rear fuselage is exactly the same they built all rear fuselages from that point onwards with the new joint. Even though there's nothing that says that explicitly in their drawings, there have been modifications made to the drawings which it's reasonable to assume are these modifications. There was an article published in a magazine at the time talking about this new joint, so the evidence suggests that from the point the new tail joint was used, they were all of that design.

"Our aircraft, RB396, was built quite late in the war, in November 1944... that was after the time they started building Tempest tails, so the decision was taken that our aircraft would have the later joint. It'll still feature the 'fishplates', which were added to all Typhoons just as a mod [in an early attempt to cure the tail failures], but they didn't really do anything other than make people feel better.

❖

"The interior paint is obviously a special type of paint [...] and the colour was found to not be what you might call the normal interior green that you see on all the warbirds today. It was quite a different shade. As we are building this aeroplane as authentically as possible, we thought we'd get it matched. A company offered to help match it, and they came down to collect samples and take them away. They came up with the colour shade, and then another company, Indestructible Paints, offered to cover the cost of making that paint specially for us.

"Lots of little things like that take a bit more time and, obviously, cost a lot more money. Using original material in the frames, for example: they have to be heat-treated, in and out of the oven, reshaped. Obviously, everything that's going to be reused has to be tested, whereas if you make it from scratch you kind of don't need to do those things. But we wanted to go down this route from the early days."

Access to a Tempest airframe, specifically that of MkV JN768/G-TMPV which was acquired by the project in 2018, has been very important too. "The two rear frames of the rear fuselage were missing from our rear fuselage. But we have a Tempest rear fuselage, which, up until the point it was designated as a Tempest on the production line, could have gone in either 'pile'. That provided all the material for the rear two frames, including the joint. We've been able to make patterns for the canopy rails off the canopy rails that came from the Tempest, because they were the same. And, of course, if there's a piece of material on our aircraft — a frame, a stringer or so on — that can't be used but the same piece in another original airframe can be, we've taken the decision to use that rather than make the piece from new. It's not just RB396 in there.

"And that's going to go for the whole aeroplane as well, we have decided. It will cost more, there's no two ways about it, but where we have an original piece — even down to a bracket — that can be used, we will, because we want the aircraft to be a memorial to the Typhoon and, more importantly, to the air and groundcrews that operated them. If we can include a piece from an aircraft, that aircraft has a history, and more often than not that history will have a personal story that goes with it. When the time comes that this aeroplane flies, it might have 10, 20, 30, 50 or more personal stories woven into it. We think that's really important."

RIGHT: Sam Worthington-Leese, the project director, addresses the audience at Sandown on 30 October. His grandfather, Plt Off Roy Worthington was a wartime Typhoon pilot with No 184 Squadron.
STEVE COMBER/COAP

What now for the rear fuselage and the next section to be rebuilt? "It's quite a big piece, and Airframe Assemblies are quite keen for the space to start other projects, so we'll go to collect it. The plan is that, ultimately, it'll probably move back to the Aircraft Restoration Company at Duxford and go into storage. There's nothing for it to do now — it is a piece, it's ready. We're waiting on quotes from Airframe Assemblies, from the Aircraft Restoration Company and others as to whether or not we go with the cockpit next or the tail. Really, it comes down to funding. The tail will likely be less expensive than the cockpit, so it's likely we're going to do the tail next, but it just depends on quotes and the availability of the workshops. These guys are really busy."

The airframe is far from the only enormous challenge, for the Napier Sabre IIa engine is another. Just like the Typhoon itself, of course, no example of the 24-litre monster has ever been put back into the skies. In 2017 the HTPG acquired one that had been owned by Cranfield University and latterly kept with the Rolls-Royce Heritage Trust in Derby, but as yet it's still on the back-burner.

"We have the engine, it's in storage and it's in as good a condition as it was the day we got it, if not slightly better", says Sam Worthington-Leese. "And we've got approximately half an engine's worth of spares. But no internal work has been done because the clock starts ticking, and that costs money. To do the engine, we need to have the money for that section absolutely guaranteed, because if you stop half-way through with that, it's a bit different from a piece of a fuselage which can just sit in a workshop and wait. Once you open an engine up, it starts deteriorating a bit unless the correct procedures are followed in the

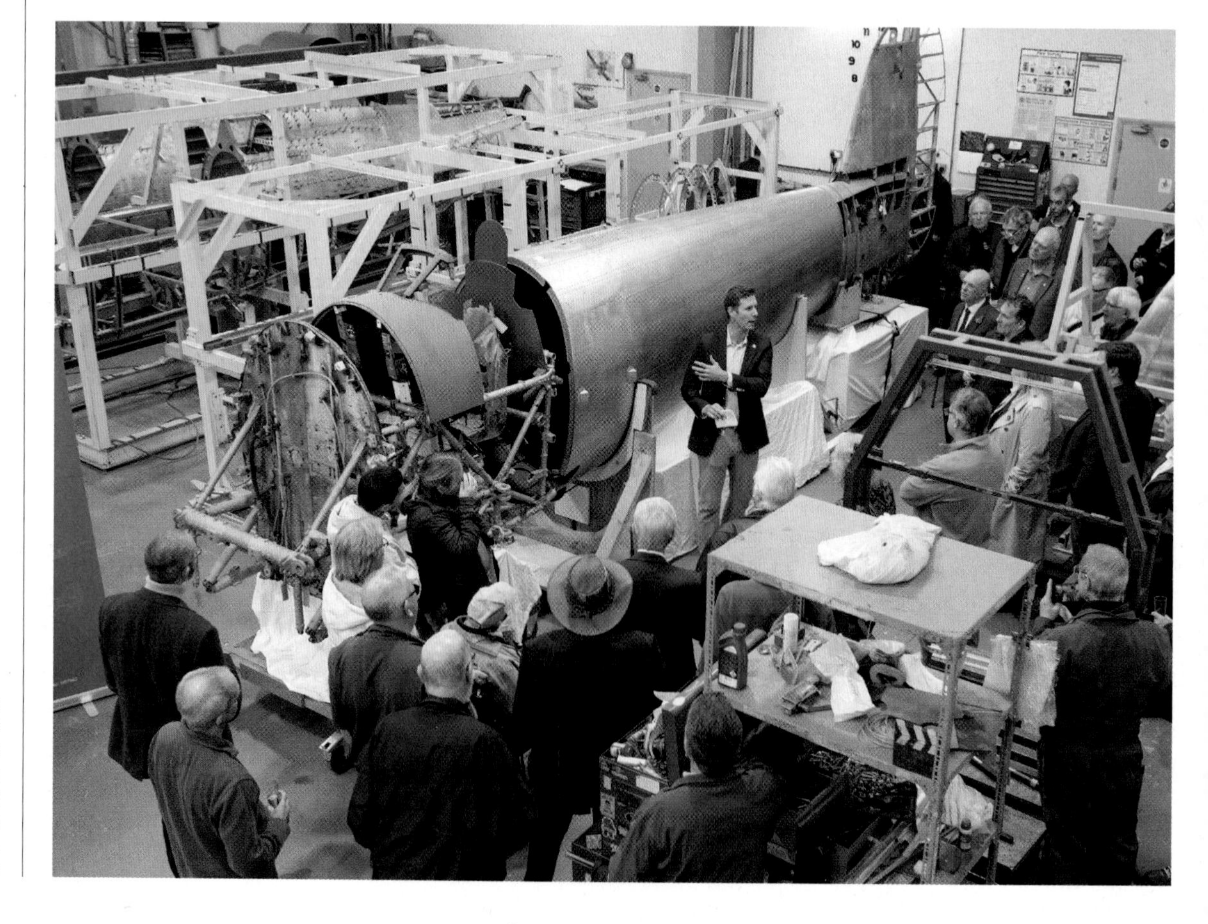

RIGHT: The event at the Airframe Assemblies workshop was attended by a strong contingent of HTPG supporters.
STEVE COMBER/COAP

LEFT: **Around 80 per cent of the original frames and stringers from RB396 have been reused in the rear fuselage.**
VIA HTPG

correct time. It's going to be very expensive, we know that. Quite how expensive we don't really know. We've estimated half a million-plus — it'll be 'plus,' for sure, easily."

Kermit Weeks is also having a Sabre-engined Hawker fighter-bomber restored for his collection, in the shape of Tempest V EJ693, and discussions have been instigated with him. In that effort Air Leasing at Sywell is playing a leading role, and Sam pays tribute to its late managing director Richard Grace, who died in October. "It was a big blow to all of us, because he's helped our project out an awful lot, personally and providing parts. All the Tempest parts we have came from Richard, and he's provided information and jigs". In turn, the RB396 team has provided a header tank for analysis and to make a pattern for EJ693, and hopefully there will be scope for further co-operation regarding both the airframe and engine as time goes on.

Exactly how long it takes will, it need hardly be said, depend on funding. "It's a little bit off a lot of people that's got us to this stage, with a few larger amounts that have come in from individuals and one or two companies on a smaller scale. We're seeking larger backing from companies, from industry, but we have been trying for nearly a decade and none really has been forthcoming yet. We're hoping that the fact that this first section is complete shows that this is no longer something we are hoping to do — it's now something that is being done. It gives some certainty that it's going to happen, because it is happening.

❖

"This section has cost £0.5 million, which is a lot, but there's been some extra work carried out; as I say, using original material, the to-ing and fro-ing, and the fact that it's brand-new for the companies that are building it are largely the reasons. It's taken a lot longer than we expected, and when you have to stop, you have to start again. That then costs a bit more, and it's subject to market forces for longer. That's just economics — the longer it takes, the more it costs. But again, the hope is that a few thousand people contributing modest amounts a month, a year or whatever from a couple of pounds upwards makes a big difference when it's added together, and it allows this progress. We're not waiting doing nothing, but while we wait to find some larger corporate interest, it really is down to the people who want to see it fly. If we all club together and chip in, then we can make it fly."

LEFT: **It has yet to be determined whether the cockpit or the tail will be tackled next.**
STEVE COMBER/COAP

That 'we' is, above all, a reference to the HTPG team. "Everybody is a volunteer. The composition has changed over the years; people have come, people have gone, and sadly a couple have passed away. But the team has stuck at it, and if it wasn't for them going out there trying to find the money, running the charity, organising the project, this would not have happened". Now, it's time to look ahead, push forward and take the next steps in getting a Typhoon flying.

For more information and to support the project, visit hawkertyphoon.com

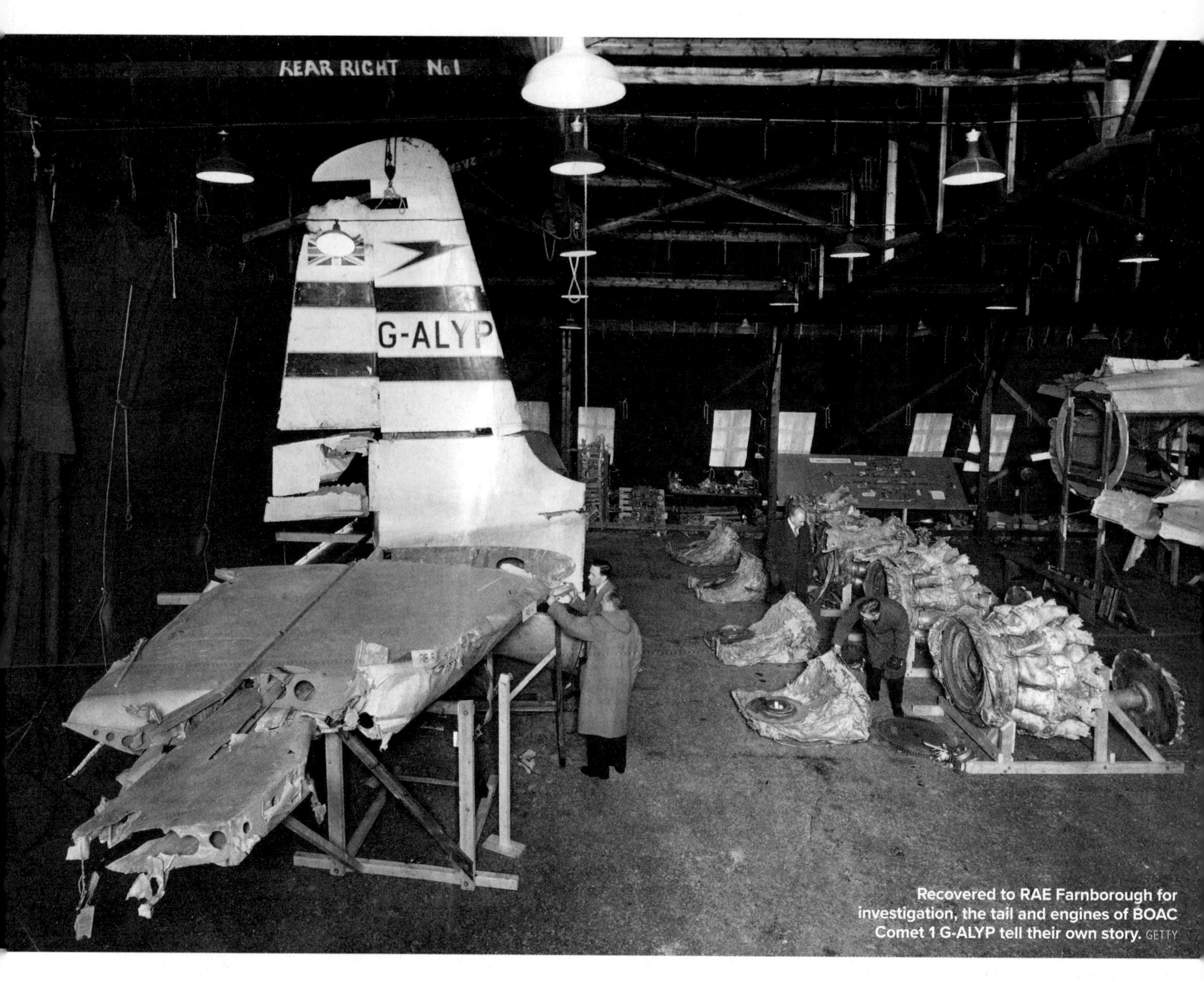

Recovered to RAE Farnborough for investigation, the tail and engines of BOAC Comet 1 G-ALYP tell their own story. GETTY

SEARCH FOR THE TRUTH

Seventy years ago, in January 1954, the latest in a series of accidents to befall the de Havilland Comet 1 occurred off the Italian island of Elba. The loss of BOAC's G-ALYP claimed 35 lives. Now, documents from de Havilland's archives shed new light on the story of the operation to recover the wreckage, and thus build as complete a picture as possible of what happened to 'Yoke Peter' **WORDS:** BEN DUNNELL

The senior de Havilland staff from Hatfield had, no doubt, looked forward to a quiet Sunday afternoon. Instead, they were to become embroiled in the aftermath of a terrible tragedy. One of them, his identity no longer known, had probably not long finished lunch on 10 January 1954 when, at 1.44pm, he received a call. It was from his employer's telephone operator, saying Reuters had been on the line asking for the company publicity manager, stating "a Comet had crashed and asking for details". At once he returned to the Hatfield works, just a few minutes away. Disaster had once more befallen the world-beating jet airliner.

Very soon this individual was talking to de Havilland's engineers at London Airport, where the DH106 Comet 1 had entered revenue-raising operation with the British Overseas Airways Corporation in May 1952. When the duty engineer, a Mr Dones, rang him back at two o'clock, there came news that the aircraft involved was the very machine which had operated the first commercial jet airliner service. BOAC Comet G-ALYP, known as 'Yoke Peter' in the phonetic alphabet of the day, was overdue in London. In the hands of 31-year-old Capt Alan Gibson, it had been operating flight 781 from Rome with 31 passengers and four crew on board, and was last heard of 67 miles out of Ciampino airport. Four fishermen had reported an air crash off the island of Montecristo, south of Elba, while the Italian air-sea rescue service "confirmed they had found wreckage."

Senior management at de Havilland now had to be put in the picture. Contact was made with public relations boss Martin Sharp, who undertook to inform sales director Francis St Barbe. Soon chief designer R. E. Bishop was aware. He in turn agreed that Peter Detmold, a senior engineer from the company's servicing organisation, should join the accident investigation. Within a few minutes, Detmold was booked onto an evening flight to Rome. On went the calls for much of the afternoon, Bishop speaking to BOAC deputy chairman Sir Miles Thomas, and being charged with briefing both Sir Geoffrey de Havilland and chief test pilot John Cunningham. By then, the extent of the calamity was becoming clear. News came in that bodies had been seen floating on the water's surface.

All this we know because a detailed, contemporaneous note was kept of that day. It forms part of a file of correspondence from, to and between key de Havilland figures, covering the early weeks of the 'Yoke Peter' investigation. This record has now passed into the hands of de Havilland Support Ltd at Duxford, and provides a unique insight into a very specific point of the Comet tragedy timeline.

> ***"Reuters had been on the line to Hatfield, stating 'a Comet had crashed and asking for details'"***

Of course, this wasn't the first DH106 hull loss. As early as 26 October 1952, G-ALYZ of BOAC over-ran the Ciampino runway having failed to get airborne, the airframe being declared a write-off. A Comet 1A, CF-CUN, of Canadian Pacific Airlines suffered another failed take-off on 3 March 1953, the 11-strong complement of crew and passengers losing their lives. Not two months later, BOAC's G-ALYV crashed soon after departure from Calcutta on 2 May, the death toll numbering 43. Eyewitnesses recalled, to quote the Indian investigation, seeing "the aircraft coming down in a blaze of fire through severe thunderstorm and rain". Structural failure was cited, specifically, "primary failure of the elevator spar in bending due to a heavy down-load imposed on a 'pull-up' by the pilot when the aircraft encountered a sudden down-gust". All three of those accidents were attributed in some degree to pilot handling. What happened to G-ALYP, it quickly emerged, could not be explained away in the same manner.

Peter Detmold arrived in Italy, eventually taking up what turned out to be a lengthy residence in Elba's Belmare Hotel. The Anglo-Mediterranean Salvage Company was engaged to locate the wreckage, and the Royal Navy provided a Royal Fleet Auxiliary salvage ship, the RFA *Sea Salvor*, to raise anything that was found. There followed a painstaking effort, undertaken in often inhospitable conditions — and one that suddenly assumed still greater importance just a few weeks in, when any hopes of an early resolution to the Comet saga were so comprehensively dashed.

11 January 1954

BOAC's operations director, Sir Victor Tait, called a meeting at London Airport, "to hear all that is known at present of the circumstances of the accident and to consider what action should be taken". In attendance were representatives of the airline and both the aircraft and engine divisions of de Havilland, as well as the Air Registration Board. Especially with the benefit of hindsight, the minutes make fascinating reading.

ABOVE: Original cables from de Havilland's Peter Detmold, on-scene in Italy, to his colleagues at Hatfield record the progress of the wreckage search.

TOP: G-ALYP was the first Comet 1 to enter service with BOAC, having made its maiden flight on 9 January 1951. AEROPLANE

ABOVE: 'Yoke Peter' was engaged in the Comet route-proving effort. KEY COLLECTION

Tait put to R. E. Bishop the Royal Aircraft Establishment's view that the earlier loss of G-ALYV had seen the aeroplane's break-up precede any fire. Bishop disagreed. He felt "something catastrophic had occurred", maybe "fire or explosion". The ARB man present, Robert Hardingham, noted how fatigue testing at Farnborough of the first prototype Comet had revealed cracks in the aircraft's skin, aft of the wheel wells. Other theories, of course, could not yet be ruled out. Whatever had happened, the top brass at BOAC felt it necessary to ground the Comet fleet, "pending thorough examination". No further passengers would be embarked on Comets as of midnight, and those aircraft overseas "would be flown home light". The line for public consumption would be that the decision was "a matter of prudence."

> ***"R. E. Bishop was inclined to the theory of an engine fire"***

13 January 1954

With Peter Detmold in position, Bob McCoy of the de Havilland service department cabled him a short questionnaire to ascertain the basic facts. The bodies found to that point were not burnt, but showed some scalding; evidence as to how the aircraft fell was still inconclusive, but pointed to a shower of debris; and a "ball of flame" was reported falling into the sea after the loudest of "several explosions", but witness evidence was "indefinite and unreliable."

17 January 1954

Detmold sent his first 'on location' report back to de Havilland. In it he summarised the known circumstances of the accident as they stood, the history of G-ALYP — including snags discovered on previous flights — and written evidence from a BOAC Argonaut captain who had been flying in the vicinity, the pilot of an Italian Air Force CANT Z506 rescue seaplane who overflew the wreckage three hours later, several Italian fishermen witnesses, and a pathologist. "All had suffered severe damage to internal organs", Detmold said of the passengers, "suggesting great violence."

19 January 1954

The ARB, BOAC and de Havilland debated mandatory modifications to the Comet fleet which could allow the type to resume flying in short order. It took in a long list of points, but — with little of substance to go on at this juncture, bar eyewitness statements — there was a notable focus on possible causes of an in-flight fire. However, the first pieces of wreckage had been found, including the secondary heat exchanger and its ducting, and tailplane sections of the front and rear spars.

20 January 1954

Further discussion involving the ARB, BOAC and de Havilland was more explicit about considering why G-ALYP might have crashed. The attendees of what became known as the Abell Committee after its chairman, BOAC's deputy operations director for engineering Charles Abell, covered six main areas: flutter, primary structural failure, flying control malfunction, structural fatigue, explosive decompression and engines. Abell, in the words of the final court of inquiry report, "said that the possibility of fatigue in the wing structure due to gusts was believed to be much more likely than fatigue in the pressure cabin, since this is subject to much less frequent changes of load."

A separate, specific investigation examined the possibilities of the Comet's autopilot "causing dangerous conditions", but found "nothing [...] that could cause the autopilot to endanger the aircraft, which had not already been foreseen and catered for."

21 January 1954

Pathological findings appeared to show that the Comet initially 'bunted', "flinging the passengers violently into the roof". Then, "Another severe load flung them to the floor", which was why the occupants sustained scalding, either from disrupted hydraulic pipes or the air conditioning system. Lastly, the aircraft broke up. "There is no evidence at all", Detmold stressed, "of a bomb explosion in the rear luggage hold."

25 January 1954

Two trawlers engaged in the search, *Favilla* and *Carmelina*, came to a sudden stop. They were sailing half a mile apart when their trawl wires fouled some large objects. Aboard the supporting Royal Navy frigate HMS *Wrangler*, Detmold watched as the ship's echo sounder was used to search the area. "Some indication", he said, "was found in either position of an object on the sea bed". It was in the vicinity of where the passengers' bodies had earlier been located.

ABOVE: Having been sighted by the vessel's underwater TV camera, a section of the Comet's fuselage wall is hauled aboard the RFA *Sea Salvor* on 26 February 1954. ALAMY

26 January 1954

Detmold was now on *Sea Salvor*, observing the trial employment of an underwater camera linked to Pye television equipment. It worked well, showing up several possible contacts, until the wind and sea swell became too much. As time went on, this became a useful tool, with a de Havilland representative sitting at the screen, ready to indicate what had been found and suggest how it might best be lifted.

2 February 1954

By now, Detmold had been living aboard the *Sea Salvor* for several days, but the recovery operation was proving frustrating. "Our news is simply this: since my last letter we have had just one fine day on which we laid four point moorings about a likely contact. We were unable to view our results that day as the moorings had disturbed the sea bed, clouding the water. During the night a gale developed, and though we rode it out until morning, it was then observed that we were shifting the moorings..." It was decided to shelter in a nearby bay and await better conditions.

3 February 1954

Air France managing director Henri Ziegler visited Hatfield for talks. Afterwards, in a letter to Francis St Barbe — then visiting de Havilland Canada — Bob McCoy recorded how R. E. Bishop had said in his and Ziegler's presence "that he was now more inclined to the theory that the Elba and Calcutta accidents were caused by a fire in or near No 3 engine."

4 February 1954

de Havilland wrote to the French operators of Comets, Air France and UAT (Union Aéromaritime de Transport), explaining the actions it planned to take following the discussions with the ARB and BOAC. It stressed that without having yet found any meaningful items of wreckage from G-ALYP or completed certain inspections and tests on the surviving BOAC aircraft, the list was subject to change on the basis of information thus gained. Precautionary modifications numbered 49 in all, covering a wide variety of items. A further

RIGHT: A crane transfers the largest piece of the aircraft yet to be found at this stage, on 16 March 1954, from the *Sea Salvor* to a barge. ALAMY

inspection schedule involved a host of components: for example, operators were instructed to check the flying control surfaces for loss of movement, all skins for distortion or cracks, and "especially" for damage around the crew, passenger and luggage bay doors. But these were very early days.

Even so, notions were developing. McCoy told Detmold, "The theory holding the lead at the present time is that the accident was caused by a fire in the starboard inner wing. You will recall that the heat exchanger photograph which you sent to me showed quite clearly that there had been a fire outside the aircraft. The theory is that a burner pipe on the lower part of the engine failed and caught fire. The Flight Engineer, seeing an increase in the fuel flow to No 3 engine would have isolated, thus increasing the fuel flow to the burner pipe which had failed. An explosion similar to that which occurred on a BOAC aircraft at Beirut would follow, blowing off the engine doors. It is suggested that none of this would necessarily have been noticed by the crew or passengers. The broken burner pipe would then direct the flame underneath the lower surfaces of the wing and this flame impinged on the air conditioning scoop which was in the closed position which is clearly shown in your photograph and more especially by an examination of the parts which are now at London Airport that the skin covering the scoop was burnt away from the outside. The fire would then be in Zone 3, assuming that it built its way through the end surface of the wing as it did in the case of the airscoop. From Zone three there is little protection of the centre section tank and the heat generated by the fire might well cause an explosion of this tank. This would cause a splitting of the fuselage, resulting in a violent decompression and a bunt of the aircraft. This would seem to line up with the medical evidence that the passengers were killed by a violent decompression and that the broken bones were caused by their being thrown into the roof of the aircraft."

> ***"The underwater search for parts of 'Yoke Peter' was a laborious business. It could be haphazard, too"***

The search for parts of 'Yoke Peter' was a laborious business. Finding each contact on the sea bed was, wrote Detmold, "a matter of several days' steaming". It could be haphazard, too. "Unless completely calm, handling the ship to within a few feet either side to ensure that unsearched gaps do not exist between the strips examined is not possible". It was hard work for the sailors and the ship, which had to move backwards and forwards on cables "for hours on end."

The latest frigate to join in was HMS *Wakeful*. Detmold didn't mind being on board. "There is a reasonable amount of comfort in this ship — bottles of it, in fact..." *Sea Salvor* was a different matter. "It is very overcrowded and at times eight people have lived and slept in a room not much more than 15ft square. This is mainly because there seems no control on the number of pressmen allowed on board. They are a nuisance as it is difficult for 24 hours a day to avoid a chance remark which may be quoted (I hope the Company will bear with me when I occasionally appear in the press)."

LEFT: The initials BOAC are visible on a section of fuselage skin brought up from the sea bed on 28 February. ALAMY

8 February 1954

The structural test house at Hatfield issued a report on Comet windscreen panels. "On a number of aircraft in service", it said, "it has been discovered that the windscreen panel 'B' has been cracking in the acute corners of the inner glass", while there was also "distortion of the frame". Tests under pressurisation showed the panel to be "satisfactory for strength".

16 February 1954

As Bishop's modification list for the aircraft reached 55 items, some at de Havilland were becoming doubtful as to their potential links with the accident cause. Another letter from McCoy to St Barbe made plain a degree of irritation. "The picture is I am afraid a depressing one", he said, "and I hope we will reach the end of the modifications which all and sundry seem to be thinking up. I have scrutinised these modifications very carefully as I was afraid that people were taking this opportunity of improving the Comet 1 and may have forgotten that the original idea was to attempt to produce modifications which would prevent a circumstance or combination of circumstances which might result in a catastrophic accident such as occurred at Elba. Unfortunately my scrutiny has not resulted in cutting down the number of modifications because they all appear to have some bearing on what we imagine might have occurred to the BOAC Comet."

22 February 1954

McCoy's latest missive to St Barbe revealed, "An interesting point which emerges [from the items recovered to that point] is that there is no sign of fire on any part of the aircraft except the starboard inner wing root. Unfortunately we have not yet recovered very much of this portion of the aircraft but when we do it may well tell us the whole story."

In separate correspondence, Detmold was reminded that all modifications being advised to Comet operators were advisory, rather than mandatory. "As you know", McCoy told him, "there

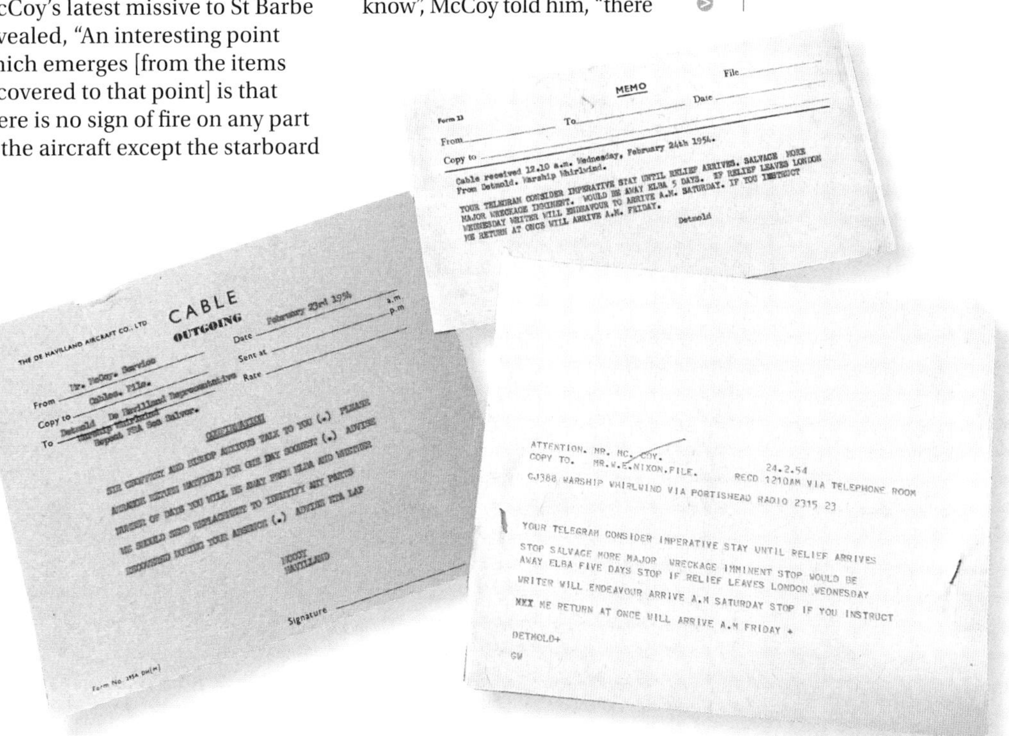

MEMO

Form 13 From To Date File Copy to

Cable received 12.10 a.m. Wednesday, February 24th 1954.
From Detmold. Warship Whirlwind.

YOUR TELEGRAM CONSIDER IMPERATIVE STAY UNTIL RELIEF ARRIVES. SALVAGE MORE MAJOR WRECKAGE IMMINENT. WOULD BE AWAY ELBA 5 DAYS. IF RELIEF LEAVES LONDON WEDNESDAY WRITER WILL ENDEAVOUR TO ARRIVE A.M. SATURDAY. IF YOU INSTRUCT ME RETURN AT ONCE WILL ARRIVE A.M. FRIDAY.

Detmold

THE DE HAVILLAND AIRCRAFT CO., LTD

CABLE OUTGOING

Date February 23rd 1954 a.m. p.m.
Sent at
Rate
From Mr. McCoy. Service
Copy to Cables. File.
To Detmold De Havilland Representative Warship Whirlwind Repeat FIA Sea Salvor.

CONFIRMATION

SIR GEOFFREY AND BISHOP ANXIOUS TALK TO YOU (.) PLEASE ARRANGE RETURN HATFIELD FOR ONE DAY SOONEST (.) ADVISE NUMBER OF DAYS YOU WILL BE AWAY FROM ELBA AND WHETHER WE SHOULD SEND REPLACEMENT TO IDENTIFY ANY PARTS RECOVERED DURING YOUR ABSENCE (.) ADVISE ETA LAP

MCCOY HAVILLAND

Signature

Form No. 1954 DH(M)

ATTENTION. MR. MC. COY.
COPY TO. MR.W.E.NIXON.FILE. 24.2.54
RECD 1210AM VIA TELEPHONE ROOM
CJ388 WARSHIP WHIRLWIND VIA PORTISHEAD RADIO 2315 23

YOUR TELEGRAM CONSIDER IMPERATIVE STAY UNTIL RELIEF ARRIVES
STOP SALVAGE MORE MAJOR WRECKAGE IMMINENT STOP WOULD BE
AWAY ELBA FIVE DAYS STOP IF RELIEF LEAVES LONDON WEDNESDAY
WRITER WILL ENDEAVOUR ARRIVE A.M SATURDAY STOP IF YOU INSTRUCT
XXX ME RETURN AT ONCE WILL ARRIVE A.M FRIDAY +
DETMOLD+
GW

will be a Public Court of Inquiry into the Comet accident in due course and there is always the possibility that [counsel] will say that de Havilland's knew that the Comet was defective and, as proof of this, they introduced Mandatory modifications."

5 March 1954

Tensions had developed on Elba. While some "very promising" contacts had been found, with hopes of recovering more significant airframe sections imminently, Detmold reported back to Hatfield that the on-scene representative of the Accidents Investigation Branch, a man named Goulding, was obstructing progress. Some salvaged pieces were left "lying around in *Sea Salvor* for three days", while others had been taken to Malta in a tug returning there from the Elba operation. The de Havilland personnel prepared some recovered servodynes for air-freight to Farnborough, but they were put back on a tug "at his orders". Hardly ideal. Thankfully, Goulding was soon to be replaced.

8 March 1954

Were notions of a major conflagration wide of the mark? Detmold thought so. "I am inclined to mistrust the evidence value of the various signs of fire", he wrote to McCoy. "It is incredible to suppose that a fire which scorched parts as far apart as the port centre flap and starboard undercarriage did not touch several pieces between. I am inclined to consider that at least some of the parts were burned by fire on the water, and am anxious to find fire evidence on a part sufficiently heavy to sink". With the prospect of better weather, Detmold had "high hopes of achieving much in the next two weeks."

17 March 1954

Two of the Rolls-Royce Ghost engines were raised and another two sighted. Detmold's examination of airframe parts elicited signs of an "intense" fire on the outside under-skin of the centre section, and smaller evidence of fire damage elsewhere. The condition of the skin under the fuel tanks and the rear spar web, he opined, "indicates possibility of outward explosion".

18 March 1954

With three engines having been salvaged, Detmold noted how one had a missing turbine, and that "severe tearing" of its tail pipe suggested "failure under power". He concluded, "plot thickens".

20 March 1954

"I am writing this letter in a trawler", said Detmold, "and the shakiness of the writing is entirely due to engine vibration and in no way to any excesses on the part of the writer". It was impossible, he wrote, to provide a comprehensive report on the wreckage recovered recently, as it was "stowed in a coal barge which is now so overcrowded that one cannot get at a large percentage of it". However, it was hoped to transport it to the UK during late March/early April, and he estimated around 55 per cent of the aircraft had been found. Operations were due to cease on or around 9 April.

23 March 1954

The Comet 1 was returned to service by BOAC on the Johannesburg route.

31 March 1954

Detmold cabled about a significant find: a "large piece" of the fuselage from the nose to bulkhead 17. Conditions had so far prevented detailed examination, but, crucially, he said, "no fire apparent".

BELOW: Some 70 per cent of the airframe by weight was salvaged and laid out at Farnborough. KEY COLLECTION

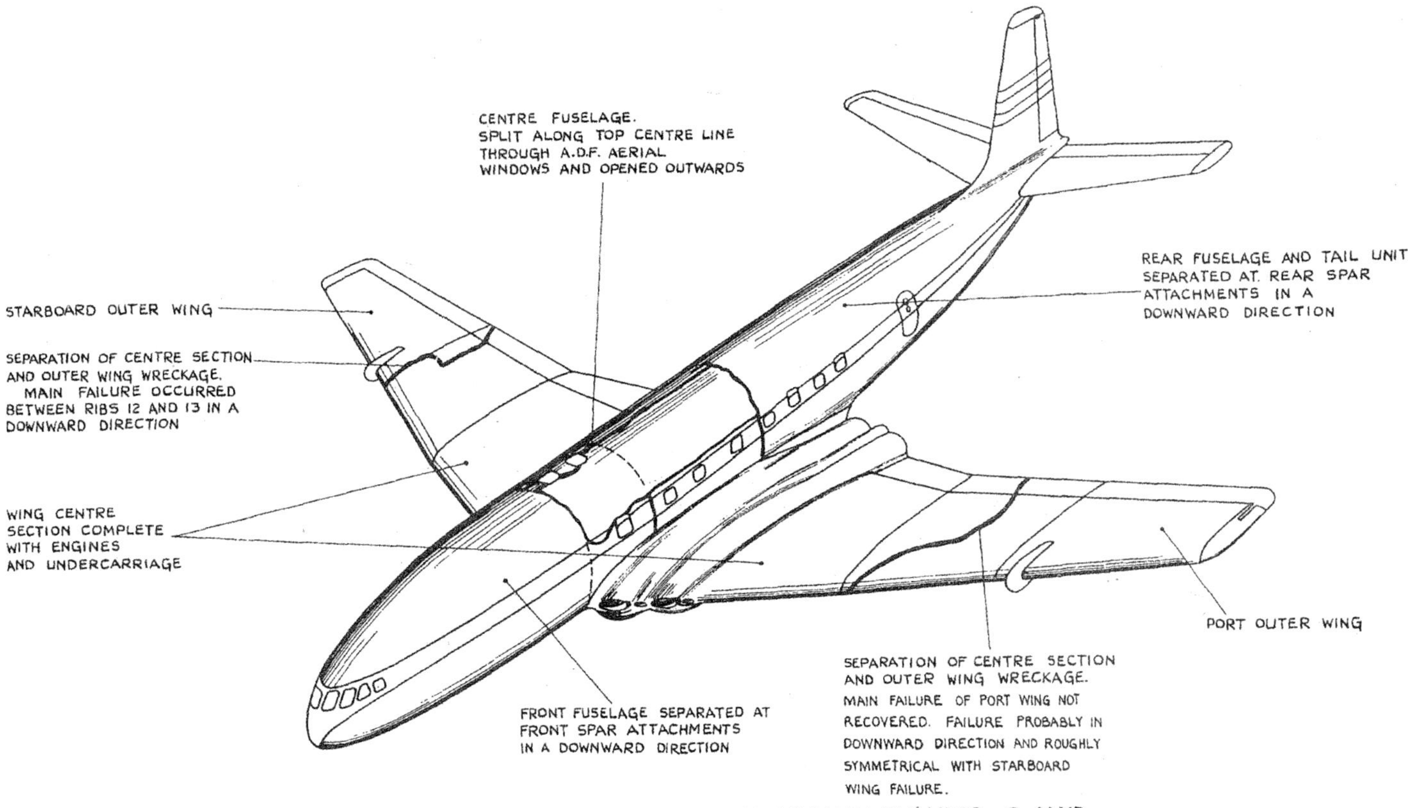

FIG. 11. LOCATION AND DIRECTION OF MAIN FAILURES—G-ALYP.

ABOVE: **A diagram from the court of inquiry's final report, showing where the primary failures on G-ALYP occurred.**

8 April 1954

BOAC Comet G-ALYY, being operated by South African Airways, came down in the Mediterranean near Naples. All 22 passengers and crew were killed.

With this new tragedy, the picture changed again. The UK's Air Registration Board withdrew the Comet 1's certificate of airworthiness, and its French equivalent likewise. From leading the world, de Havilland's pioneering jet found itself ignominiously grounded. In a letter to Detmold on the 14th, McCoy outlined how further investigation was planned to proceed, including the use of a BOAC machine by the Royal Aircraft Establishment at Farnborough for an exhaustive test of its structure and systems. This, of course, was the famous water tank test on G-ALYU, involving a cycle of pressurisations and depressurisations.

The wreckage recovered from G-ALYP was instrumental too. McCoy instructed Detmold to stay in Italy until he was convinced nothing more was to be found, and on 7 May the extension bore fruit in the form of numerous further items, including the starboard front fuselage from frames 10-16, complete with the galley, frame 18 with the starboard half of the bulkhead, and the main emergency exit with its surrounding structure. Detmold offered the view that, perhaps, "the port wing failed before the tailplane, and caused its failure by debris flying back or whether the port tail was struck first". By the time salvage efforts finally concluded in September, it was estimated that — according to the court of inquiry's report — "about 70 per cent of the structure, 80 per cent of the powerplant and 50 per cent of the equipment" had been brought up. Given the nature of the methods used, it had been an impressive effort.

> *"The substantial reconstruction of G-ALYP underlined what happened"*

The RAE's water tank test, to cut a very long story short, showed metal fatigue to be the cause of the Comet's fatal woes. A total of 3,057 flight cycles had been completed by G-ALYU — the majority of them simulated in the tank — when, on 24 June 1954, its fuselage burst open at the port-side forward escape hatch. The substantial reconstruction of G-ALYP's airframe at Farnborough underlined what had happened. A fatigue crack had probably developed "near the starboard aft corner" of the rearmost of two apertures containing the ADF (automatic direction-finding) equipment, "approximately over the front spar of the wing", and "spread fore and aft from it". "It is my opinion", wrote inquiry chairman Lord Cohen, "that the fundamental cause of the failure of the cabin structure was that there existed around the corners of the windows" — the ADF 'windows', it should be emphasised, not the cabin windows — "and other cut-outs a level of stress higher than is consistent with a long life of the cabin..."

With this revolutionary aeroplane, de Havilland stole a march on the rest of the world. But it had come at a terrible cost. In discovering the reasons why, and as such contributing to the advancement of aviation safety, the hard graft undertaken by the small team that found and recovered 'Yoke Peter's' remains is deserving of recognition 70 years on. A

With thanks to Mark Miller of de Havilland Support Ltd.

The TIGERS *of* TENGAH

No 74 'Tiger' Squadron had many firsts to its name during the Lightning era. When it flew its Lightning F6s to a new home at RAF Tengah in Singapore, it made the type's longest deployment to date — and some memorable years in the Far East were to follow WORDS: BEN DUNNELL

Lightning F6 XR768 was among the aircraft with which No 74 Squadron deployed to Singapore. KEY COLLECTION

Thirteen Lightning F6s, 17 Victor K1 tankers, more than 6,700 miles. Operation 'Hydraulic' was, when it took place in June 1967, the longest fighter deployment the RAF had ever carried out, not to mention its largest-scale, most complex use of air-to-air refuelling. The objective was to transfer No 74 Squadron from Leuchars, Fife to its new home at Tengah, Singapore, significantly upgrading the air defence capability of the Far East Air Force. And, across three waves, they did it, underlining Britain's commitment to a theatre recently wracked by conflict.

How different things had become. "Effectively, we appeared to be on a permanent holiday", remembers Dave Roome, one of 74's Lightning pilots. "Most of the time it was a very pleasant, quiet environment. We had no requirement for similarly fast reaction times on alert as in the UK, except during exercises". The Indonesian Confrontation had ended peacefully in August 1966, following the overthrow of President Sukarno and the signing of a peace treaty with Malaysia. A considerable British military presence remained — "the chief of the Indonesian Air Force was invited to Singapore and taken round the bases", says Roome, "effectively to wag fingers and say, 'Don't even think about it'" — but the fighting had ended. And within months of the Lightnings' arrival, their days with FEAF became numbered.

Stationing the type at Tengah, and in its new, longer-range F6 form, could be seen to represent the zenith of the Lightning force. A ninth front-line squadron had just formed, the aircraft was defending the airspace of West Germany and Cyprus as well as Singapore, and the fleet was about to reach its numerical height. Operation 'Hydraulic' was the ultimate demonstration of Lightning deployment capability to date. It took three waves of aircraft on successive days, the first leaving Leuchars on 4 June, the last arriving at Tengah a week later.

Part of the initial wave was Trevor MacDonald Bennett, who had joined 74 as a first-tourist the previous July. "We got to Cyprus", he recalls, "and the following day [5 June] we were due to fly to Masirah, off the eastern coast of Oman, but — unknown to us — it was the very first day of the 1967 Arab-Israeli war. We initially went north from Cyprus and were due to come down through Iran. The Victor tanker navigator leader was the one responsible for all the comms for the combined formation, giving all the appropriate international position reports. Tehran denied us entry into Iranian airspace, but he was a smart chap and said, 'Your RT is strength one and garbled, but thank you for clearing us through...' Our look-out became rather intense from that point, but we just flew through and landed uneventfully at Masirah. Then we were delayed for a few days because all our authorisation sheets had to be presented publicly to prove who we were. We were accused of being fighter escorts for RAF bombers supporting the Israelis."

> ***We were accused of being fighter escorts for RAF bombers***

In Singapore, the end of the Indonesian Confrontation had not diminished RAF Tengah's importance. It still hosted regular Vulcan and Victor deployments, and no other FEAF flying station boasted such a variety of based units. As Dave Roome says, "No 60 Squadron still had the Javelin, No 20 Squadron the Hunter, Nos 45 and 81 Squadrons had the Canberra, and then there was 74, which was there replacing No 64 Squadron on the Javelin. Royal New Zealand Air Force Canberra B(I)12s from 14 Squadron at RNZAF Ohakea were also regular visitors. The original plan for the Far East was that a second Lightning squadron would take over from 60, which disbanded at the end of April 1968. It would have been No 11 Squadron coming out to take over."

By then the bombshell had been dropped. In January 1968, with the economy in strife, Prime Minister Harold Wilson declared that British forces would withdraw from bases 'east of Suez' by the end of 1971. There would be no second Lightning squadron in Singapore. It would be left to 74 to hold the line as the last air defence unit in FEAF, not that the threat was too great.

ABOVE: The alphabetically ordered No 74 Squadron line at Tengah — code letters A, B, C and so on — with deployed Vulcan B2s and Victors beyond. TREVOR MACDONALD BENNETT

ABOVE: XR771 provides a platform for a 'Tigers' group shot. The black tail fins were applied to the Lightnings in defiance of official orders, 74 having been told to remove them during its days on the F3 model.
TREVOR MACDONALD BENNETT

"The Indonesian Air Force was very basic and quite old", Dave Roome notes. "Its fighter aircraft originated from the Soviet Union, consisting of the MiG-15 'Fagot', MiG-17 'Fresco' and MiG-19 'Farmer', though very few were serviceable, and their medium bombers such as the Il-28 'Beagle' were in much the same state, as was the pride of their bomber force, the Tu-16 'Badger'. We would have expected to see nothing more than the occasional high-level bomber, which, of course, was exactly what the Lightning was excellent against". Come 1967-68, Indonesia "wasn't really considered a valid threat."

But there was still a lot of good flying in a fascinating environment. "Being an air defence and an all-weather squadron", says Roome, "we worked with a first take-off usually at nine in the morning and a last landing at 11 at night, with one flight of the squadron — there were two flights — working 'days' and the other 'nights'. If you were on days, you worked effectively from a met brief at eight o'clock until about four o'clock. The night shift came in by four and worked through to 11.

"When we were required to mount any form of alert we'd do it on the squadron line, out in the open. That, of course, was a problem during the day in Singapore. It was a squadron rule that if we were called to cockpit readiness, which was effectively five-minute readiness, during the day we were only allowed to sit there for 20 minutes before somebody came out with two pints of water or squash. You downed that lot, and after 40 minutes, if you hadn't been scrambled, you were replaced by somebody else.

> *We held alert for 20 minutes before someone brought water or squash*

"But the Lightning had the most incredibly rapid scramble. We used to hold two-minute readiness from our flightline, and from there we could often be airborne within one minute. There was a gang-bar down on the right-hand side which turned on 11 switches; you stuffed the throttles forward to open the high-pressure fuel cocks, hit two starter buttons and began to motor the canopy down. You were almost going before the starter system finished firing.

"For our own practice, every now and again we would simulate the alert requirement. Somebody would go out and strap in, the telebrief would be plugged in and checked, and eventually a scramble would come, probably against another Lightning which had taken off 40 minutes earlier and was some way up Malaysia. It was good training, because we didn't do it all the time."

Practice intercepts of one sort or another were 74's bread and butter. "Either low-level or subsonic flying was concentrated in the Malacca Strait, very close to Sumatra", recounts Trevor MacDonald Bennett. "Supersonic flying would be out in the South China Sea to the north-east, which involved crossing an airway. That's why we had a particular departure known as 'Tiger's Leap', doing a full-reheat climb, whizzing over the top of the airway to get well clear of any civilian traffic. As the airspace above the Malacca Strait is not very wide we had to be careful not to infringe other territory, but the probability of being seen by the Indonesians at low level was very remote. We were given a fairly free hand."

Mostly the practice targets were other Lightnings, but there were several exceptions. Deployed Vulcans were among them, as MacDonald Bennett relates: "They could cruise round about 50,000ft and still manoeuvre — and quite substantially as well, so were a very difficult target. It would usually involve quite a significant tailchase, obviously requiring us to be well and truly supersonic to get up to the levels they were at and hope they wouldn't out-manoeuvre us, because they could do very easily. At the indicated air speeds they were flying at, we couldn't do much at all. It was a one-shot attack, really."

Preparing for Concorde operations in the Far East, not least by Singapore Airlines, October 1968 saw Project 'Cold CAT', researching clear-air turbulence in the low temperatures found at high altitudes in the tropics. "Two aircraft came out", Roome recalls, "a prototype Canberra PR7/9 from Bedford [WH793] and a USAF RB-57F, which spent a couple of weeks at Tengah and provided a high-level target for us on occasion. They were quite surprised when they did runs for us at around 60-65,000ft and the Lightning would go past above them. They were not used to that, so they would take a bit more time and come back a bit further up, and a bit further up, and eventually we wouldn't go past above them."

A more familiar presence was the Royal Navy. Twice during 74's time in Singapore there occurred carrier deployments, by HMS *Hermes* in 1968 and *Eagle* in 1970. "Then", says Roome, "of course >

A pairs take-off by XR761 (left) and XS927. Different training areas were used for subsonic and supersonic flying, the latter requiring a full-reheat climb to get clear of an airway. TREVOR MACDONALD BENNETT

The squadron's Lightning T5, XV329, being flown over a Chinese junk by Tengah station commander Gp Capt Philip Lagesen. PETER R. MARCH

TENGAH'S TWO-SEATER

Just one Lightning T5 was allocated to No 74 Squadron at Tengah. Since the trainer couldn't be fitted with overwing tanks, XV329 was unable to fly to Singapore with its single-seat brethren, so instead it was shipped across from Belfast docks. Once in situ, being officially assigned to 74 from 1 July 1967, the aircraft was used for a variety of tasks. There were local familiarisation flights with newly arrived pilots, and check rides alongside the squadron instrument rating examiner, qualified flying instructor and interceptor weapons instructor.

Many would agree it was a shame the RAF never bought an aircraft akin to the export Lightning T55, which was the trainer equivalent of the longer-ranged F6 and had more of an operational capability. On the F3-derived T5, says Dave Roome, "The ventral tank had a problem with leakage now and again, and very often we would find the T5 out on the line without the ventral tank on it. Now it was *seriously* short of fuel". The squadron used it during those periods for passenger rides with station personnel, lasting about 20 minutes. "You got rid of all the fuel in that time..."

When 74 disbanded and its aircraft were reassigned, there was again no practical option other than for XV329 to make the journey back to Britain by sea. This was to prove its undoing. Acid from its batteries leaked en route, and there was other corrosion damage. Arriving back in Belfast, the aeroplane was eventually deemed to be beyond economic repair. It was moved to the Leconfield-based No 60 Maintenance Unit, stripped for spares and scrapped.

'Buddy' refuelling with Sea Vixen FAW2 XP920, operated by 893 Naval Air Squadron from HMS *Hermes*. No formal clearance had been obtained for Lightnings to refuel from Sea Vixens before No 74 Squadron went ahead and did it. Ordinarily, approval might have required a Boscombe Down trial lasting several months...
TREVOR MACDONALD BENNETT

we would find ourselves up against the Sea Vixen, which was a very effective aircraft, capable of acting both as fighter and bomber. They could also work with us — as they did now and again — and even be tankers, because the Vixen could carry a 'buddy' refuelling pack.

"It worked fine, but the Vixen had no means to limit how much fuel the receiver could take. When you tanked off the normal tankers like the Victor, they would decide how much they were going to give you, and when you'd had your lot the fuel stopped feeding, but the Vixen fed fuel if you were plugged in. When I was offered the chance, I plugged into this Vixen and, almost immediately, the pilot said, 'Right, you've had 200lb... You've had 300lb, clear to break... You've had 400lb, *get out!*' You had this feeling you could see the Vixen's ribs starting to show as it became emaciated as you sucked it dry."

According to MacDonald Bennett, "The only aircraft I'd tanked from prior to this was a Victor, and it was a very formal process: having to come alongside on the port side and be seen by the crew, who'd clear you astern, and the chap through the periscope would then clear you for contact and so on. I came whizzing up alongside this Sea Vixen, sat on the left and said, 'I'm on the port side.' He replied, 'I can see that, the hose is out the back!' I thought, I can see where this is going. Luckily a bit of face was saved when I managed to make contact straight away. I then had the issue of this other Sea Vixen barrel-rolling around. He explained, 'I'm just letting my man have a look', but the observer was actually taking some very nice photographs."

It was with the Royal Australian Air Force that the most frequent affiliation occurred. There were two deployments to Australia itself, one to Darwin in June 1969 and another in April 1971 to Adelaide and Melbourne — the furthest from the UK the Lightning ever went — but more often these opportunities involved the RAAF fighters stationed at Butterworth, Malaysia. "When we got out there", says Roome, "the Australians still had a Sabre squadron, but also a Mirage III squadron, 75 Squadron. Later in 1968 a second Mirage squadron came up from Australia, 3 Squadron, both based at Butterworth. We did a regular exchange with one

GOING BALLISTIC

During the course of his tour at Tengah on No 74 Squadron, Dave Roome achieved a notable feat in Lightning history: the highest altitude attained by the type. "A Victor tanker was coming back from Hong Kong", he remembers, "and we had a signal in Singapore saying it was willing to give away some fuel. I was given the task of going up and taking some fuel, just as a straightforward bit of refuelling. I met him right up by the Thai border, on the east coast of Malaysia, near Kota Bharu. Now, we were restricted in supersonic flight to east of Malaysia, over the sea, while we did subsonic work in the Strait of Malacca, on the west coast. I picked up the tanker and filled to full. I was now left with full fuel and 400 miles or so to come back to Tengah, so I thought I'd try and see how high it would go.

"The Lightning was not very good at climbing subsonic — its subsonic service ceiling was just under 50,000ft — but I plugged the 'burners in, I accelerated to Mach 2 and climbed from 50,000. I levelled at about 65,000ft, reaccelerated, and to be honest I let it go faster than Mach 2. I went up to about 2.2 or 2.25 and zoom-climbed again. The accepted way was you selected 16° of climb and just held it, and as you went higher and higher the lack of downwash over the tailplane meant the stick came further and further back in the cockpit to hold that 16° climb, until eventually the stick reached the back-stop and the aircraft slowly went over the top. I topped at 87,800ft.

"When I got back we talked about it generally, and it was thought that [English Electric/British Aircraft Corporation test pilot] Jimmy Dell had been to 93,000ft. Some time later, Jimmy Dell came out with BAC and I had a chance to talk to him. I asked, 'How did you get to 93,000ft?' He said, '93,000ft? I never went to 93,000ft. 75, I think'. I told him I'd made 87.8, and he said, 'You've got the world record'... I don't think anybody beat 87.8."

flight of each squadron detaching to the other base, from Tengah to Butterworth or vice versa, for a week or 10 days of operating together. The detachments were known as 'Tiger Rags,' and were extremely good.

"There was a long-standing record for time between the Tengah and Butterworth air traffic towers. Tengah to Butterworth is 330 miles, and the Hunter squadron, 20, and the RAAF Sabre squadron had each vied for the fastest time. Then, when the Mirages arrived, they cut the time down quite markedly. It had been up at about 35 minutes, but it then came down to about the 30-minute mark. Eventually our boss, Ken Goodwin, decided we needed to have a go. We did it so well that we brought the time down to just over 24 minutes, and all four aircraft went past the Butterworth tower just about supersonic, leaving a lot of red faces in the RAAF. Unfortunately, it had also left a trail of noise all the way up Malaysia, because most of them were doing Mach 2, so it was banned after that. But we had the trophy, and we then put it to bed.

"The Mirage and Lightning had very similar performance. One area where we did have an advantage was that the Lightning could be mishandled at slow speed and remain remarkably docile. You had to really be quite silly to make it depart. With the Mirage they were scared about slow speeds because of the delta configuration. They could have a big problem there."

> ***"I told the Vixen pilot, 'I'm on the port side.' He said, 'I can see that'"***

For much of the time both the Mirage and Lightning were restricted to rear-hemisphere attacks, the Mirage with the AIM-9B and the Lightning with the Firestreak, another stern-only missile. Trevor MacDonald Bennett says, "One of our training intercept requirements was on a target doing in excess of Mach 1.6, so you were looking at a 1,000mph target coming towards you and you had to go round the back, which meant you had to be flying faster than that. Quite a demanding exercise. If we had the Red Top, which later took over from the Firestreak — although not completely, because we always maintained both types — we could make the attack from the front hemisphere, and for that you effectively had no need to be supersonic. That was much easier. You could be subsonic against a supersonic target coming towards you and get a good acquisition."

The largest exercise in which 74's Lightnings participated during their time in Singapore was 'Bersatu Padu,' meaning 'Complete Unity' >

ABOVE: 1970's multi-national 'Bersatu Padu' exercise saw Royal Australian Navy carrier HMAS *Melbourne* in attendance, allowing this formation of three Lightnings with an 805 Squadron A-4G Skyhawk.
TREVOR MACDONALD BENNETT

in Malay, from April-June 1970. As Roome states, "It was the first time the RAF sent a Phantom squadron out to Singapore — No 54 Squadron came out, and in fact set a world record on the way, because the first four aircraft did it non-stop in just over 14 hours. There were Vulcans and Victor tankers detached for that, the RNZAF brought its 14 Squadron Canberras, the Australians their Mirages, and there were forces on the ground and at sea."

Among the latter was the Royal Australian Navy's HMAS *Melbourne*, with the A-4G Skyhawks of 805 Squadron embarked. "It had been involved in so many incidents and accidents I think it had to sail about a mile behind the rest of the fleet!" laughs MacDonald Bennett. "We did some dissimilar ACM [air combat manoeuvring] against them as well, and it was extremely difficult. With the Lightning, it was absolutely hopeless to go at low speed and turn against any subsonic-type aircraft. Against, say, a Hunter, a Sea Vixen, a Skyhawk or whatever it might be, we used the vertical. The Skyhawk guys were pretty punchy pilots as well, and it was a very manoeuvrable, small, fighter. You'd think, 'I'm in just about the right position here', and suddenly realise you were looking at the wrong end of it."

Inevitably, 74 experienced several incidents during its FEAF sojourn. Four Lightnings were written off, two of them in fatal accidents within the space of just over two months during 1970. There were other issues, too. "You got rather blasé about fires", says Dave Roome, "because the Lightning had a dreadful record for fires in the air. Some were hot gas leaks [causing a warning], but there were several real fires out there too. I was sent off to do an air test one day because the aircraft had come back with a fire warning. The work had been done, and I said jokingly, 'I'll tell you what height the fire light comes on'. I came back and said, '28,000ft'."

Trevor MacDonald Bennett, meanwhile, was fortunate to complete his tour after sustaining serious hip injuries in a road accident. It was through the support of his CO, Ken Goodwin — whom he calls "an absolutely marvellous man" — that he returned to flying with 74 after six months convalescing in the UK. His first trip

> ***"The reality was that we were very poorly armed, quite frankly"***

back in an F6, involving a practice diversion to Changi, nearly added to the Lightning's accident statistics. "Just as I started my final approach to Changi's runway I felt a bit of a rumble, just a momentary one, and then there was an almighty bang. The number one engine seized solid, with lots of flames and smoke.

"I made a quick mayday call and flew down the approach, ready to grab the handle at any moment because we still had the alloy control runs to the tail at that point and they had a reputation for burning through very quickly. Thankfully I managed to get it on the ground, but it was very heavy, and of course there was no drag 'chute because the number one engine supplied the hydraulics to the tail 'chute doors. I just managed to turn off at the end, by which time it was well and truly on fire."

The draw-down of assets at Tengah was indicative of the change that swept through British foreign and defence policy. "Come July 1971", says Dave Roome, "we were the only RAF squadron left there. 60 had gone back in April 1968, 20 went in February 1970, as did 45, and 81 shortly afterwards. We did our final big parade and flypast on 25 August and then ferried the aircraft out of Singapore to Cyprus, where we gave our Lightning F6s to No 56 Squadron, which at that time was still operating the shorter-range Lightning F3s. Two of us went out each day with Victors through to Gan, and a day later from Gan direct all the way to Cyprus, which was a long leg — nearly eight-and-a-half hours.

"The boss [by now Dennis Caldwell] had gone on day one; day two was much the same. Several people said, 'No-one's done a flypast. Anyone going to do one?' I said I'd ask the Victors if they could cope with it. The Victor guy told me, 'We've got stacks of fuel. No problem with that'. I asked the permission of my supervisors at Tengah, my flight commander and OC ops, who was Erik Bennett [future commander of the Sultan of Oman's Air Force]. They came to the brief, and so did the station commander, Gp Capt Peter Latham of 'Treble-One' Squadron fame.

"There were three of us on that wave, including an airborne spare. I said we would get airborne, go round to the north to Johor Bahru, and then run through after the tankers got airborne. No high speed, because we'd have the overwing tanks on. We were spaced laterally, with my number two, Roger Pope, and Nigel Holder as number three in wide line-abreast by 200 yards. What I didn't say was the height I'd be at.

"Erik Bennett and the station commander were both up in the tower, and a friend of mine who was one of the air traffic controllers said they lost sight of me as I disappeared over the TACAN aerial, and went down past the tower... Peter Latham did not like this at all, and initially he suggested I should be recalled and court-martialled, but Erik Bennett said, 'That might not be a good idea, because we were both at the briefing

BELOW: XS769 is towed to the squadron flightline during August 1968. PETER R. MARCH

and we didn't ask him what height he was going to be at. Leave it to me — I'll punish him'. Peter Latham agreed to that.

"I went on to Gan, but a signal had got there before me saying I'd breached flying discipline leaving Tengah and removing my authorising status on No 74 Squadron. Well, the flight from Gan to Akrotiri was my last flight on No 74 Squadron, so removal of my authorising status had no effect whatsoever. I saw Erik several years later in Oman, when I was a CFS 'trapper' and we'd gone out there to examine SOAF. I said, 'I think I owe you a beer'. He replied, 'You owe me more than a beer, Dave...'"

The Far East was not a theatre for which the Lightning had been intended. An aircraft originally earmarked solely as a high-altitude bomber destroyer for European operations, lacking range and, even in F6 form, with little in the way of a multi-role capability could be seen as less-than-ideally suited to FEAF. Incidentally, it is interesting to speculate how a true multi-role Lightning might have performed in Vietnam, had such an aeroplane been procured by the Australians and engaged in that conflict. What were the shortcomings experienced by 74's pilots in Singapore?

"Although we knew they were going to retrofit the guns into the ventral tank — very British, to put guns in the fuel tank — that hadn't happened, so we were strictly missile-armed", says Trevor MacDonald Bennett. "The reality was that we were very poorly armed, quite frankly. The other major thing was the radar, which was, I suppose, pretty good for its vintage, but it was a pulse radar with all the problems of ground returns when looking down. The Phantoms, when they came out, really did make the point well and truly with their ability to pick up low-level moving targets against all the ground clutter with their pulse-doppler radars. Performance-wise, of course, the Lightning was superlative, but armament would certainly have been the main issue."

Yet despite these and other limitations, No 74 (Tiger) Squadron discharged its duties at Tengah with great efficiency and professionalism. Such an outstanding fighter unit, the first on the front line to operate the Lightning F1, F3 and full-standard F6, deserved better than disbandment after its stint with FEAF. Above all, MacDonald Bennett comments, "The squadron spirit there was just outstanding". That was the ethos underpinning all 74 did in Singapore.

With thanks to Rick Peacock-Edwards.

ABOVE: Over Singapore shortly after their arrival, Lightning F6s XR771, XS895 and XS896 fly with the overwing tanks that were so important for FEAF operations. Training sorties to check the tanks worked saw 74's aircraft going up the Malaysian coast at high level, letting down and returning at low level.
ADRIAN M. BALCH COLLECTION

THE BIG PICTURE

As of 1960, aircraft belonging to France's Institut Géographique National had reputedly performed photo-mapping of more than 60 per cent of the world. A fleet of B-17 Flying Fortresses contributed much to this impressive feat, and the IGN kept them operating until the eighties, from the North Pole to deepest Africa

WORDS: JEAN-CHRISTOPHE CARBONEL

While it started to make more commemorative and display appearances during the mid-1980s, as here at La Ferté-Alais in 1986, B-17G F-BEEA was still very much an operational IGN asset. DENIS J. CALVERT

ABOVE: The first quartet of B-17s acquired by the French state for the IGN in 1948, probably at their Creil base. From left to right are F-BEED, 'BEEB, 'BEEA and 'BEEC. R. LYONNET VIA RÉGIS BIAUX COLLECTION

In the turmoil following the fall of France, an administrative change might seem a minor affair. But it was hardly unimportant when, on 27 June 1940, the Institut Géographique National was set up to replace the military Service Géographique de l'Armée. Turning its management over to civilians was intended to keep the organisation's work and its assets from capture by the German occupation authorities, while also allowing, as hostilities continued, participation in resistance efforts and co-operation with the Allies. None of this saved it from the ravages of war, and in 1947 it needed to be completely re-equipped. The French government tasked the IGN with providing new, up-to-date maps of France and its colonies, and it was calculated that to do so 12 million square kilometres (6.18 million square miles) must be photographed, equating to eight per cent of the world's dry land.

With which aircraft would it go about this job? A few Lioré et Olivier LeO 45s, a French medium bomber whose design had emerged pre-war, and Nord NC701 Martinets, the French-produced version of the German Siebel Si 204 trainer, were impressed into photographic service but had neither the range nor the endurance necessary for the coverage of some areas, notably in French Africa. Then, in 1947, an opportunity arose to procure a number of Boeing B-17 Flying Fortresses. Gén Michel Ladouce was air attaché at the French embassy in Washington when he was approached by two businessmen who had many B-17s for sale. Most of these machines were fresh out of the factory, but with the end of the war were no longer of any use to the US Army Air Forces. They were kept in storage at Walnut Ridge, Arkansas.

Michel Ladouce told *Pégase* magazine, "I went to Walnut Ridge where I saw more than a thousand warplanes of all kinds — multi-engine bombers, single-engine fighters, all stored tail-up to save space. I selected four brand-new B-17s. To be certain the engines were in a good state, we ran them. When a spark plug failed, we moved on to the next aeroplane. Having definitively selected four B-17s, in addition I was able to get 16 spare engines and additional parts."

> ***"In 1947, the chance arose to procure a number of B-17s"***

The four Fortresses were transferred to France by an American, William P. 'Bill' Odom, a former AAF pilot who was accustomed to operating heavy aircraft in rough condition after a period with Ferry Command and a tour with the Chinese National Aviation Corporation flying 'over the Hump'. The whole effort received little publicity, as flying a B-17 across the Atlantic single-handed broke a few safety regulations even in 1947.

It should be noted that none of the B-17s, neither the first quartet acquired in December 1947 and January 1948 nor the subsequent ones, were IGN property. Rather, they were bought by the French state and loaned to the IGN. According to Ladouce, the Institut turned to him six months later to buy four more, but by this time the examples in question had been scrapped or sold off. Two further B-17s were acquired in 1950, and another two during 1952. An additional quartet followed in 1954, and the last in 1956.

On arrival in France, all the aircraft had to be converted from bomber configuration. The exceptions were 44-85594, which was already a photographic platform, and 44-83728 and 44-83735 with their plush executive interiors. This was undertaken by SNCAC (Aérocentre) in its Villacoublay workshops. First to be modified was 44-83729, registered F-BEED. No drawings of the modifications involved have survived, but a detailed textual description exists. First came

LEFT: The interior of an IGN B-17 configured for photo-mapping, with a photographer at work behind the large camera drums. IGN

RIGHT: Several of the Fortress airframes saw the scrapman's attentions at Creil. The building behind — which appears in a number of these images — is the 19th-century Château Boncompagne, named after the owner who had it built. Swallowed up by the expanding air base, it was used by the Germans during wartime, but latterly fell into disrepair and has now been demolished. JOËL MESNARD

removal of all military equipment: the nose, upper, lower and tail turrets, ammunition cases, armour plating, the rear gunner's seat, bomb sight mount, side machine-gun mounts, bomb racks and bomb bay fuel tanks. The total weight of all this amounted to 1,500kg (3,306lb).

The navigator's, pilot's and radio operator's positions now had to be adapted to the new mission. The hole left by removal of the chin turret was blanked off, a reinforced floor installed, new side windows fitted and a panel for navigation instruments placed in the nose, together with a seat for the navigator. The upper turret hole was filled in and new radios installed.

The bomb bay was first modified along the instructions provided by Boeing in a field service bulletin to turn a B-17 into a cargo transport, including the incorporation of a reinforced floor. The control lines were covered by a sheet metal casing.

Provision of a new position for the photographer in the rear fuselage saw the belly turret hole being blanked off by a panel incorporating two mechanically operated sighting windows for the cameras. Supports for cameras and film cases were added, and a beam with a sliding hoist — dubbed a 'monorail' — attached to the ceiling of the fuselage to handle the heavy photographic equipment. Naturally, this section too was given a reinforced floor, and seats for two photographers were put in. The whole electrical system was refurbished, with a new intercom between the different positions, and a 40-volt/25-amp electrical circuit fed the cameras. The gyropilot — which probably relates to the Sperry autopilot installed in the bomber version — removed from the pilot's console was relocated in the navigator's station.

After all this work, the empty weight of each aeroplane was about 15,000kg (33,000lb). Michel Bélikian, a former IGN photographer who flew his first B-17 mission over Libya in 1979, recalled to the Société Française de Photogrammétrie et de Télédétection that the aircraft were able to carry up to 3,000kg (6,600lb) of photographic material to an altitude of 10,000m (32,800ft)

A RARE 'CHRISTMAS TREE'

In 1953, the IGN received B-17F-90-BO 42-30177, a very historic aircraft that had flown operational missions with the 388th Bomb Group during World War Two and later been allocated to the commander-in-chief of French occupation forces in Germany, Gén Marie-Pierre Kœnig, as a staff transport named *Bir-Hakeim*. Taken on by the IGN in a damaged state, it was repaired to allow a ferry flight from Cologne-Wahn to Creil. While it was registered F-BGSG, the B-17F never flew again. It ended its days as a source of spare parts for the B-17Gs.

B-17F F-BGSG, named *Bir-Hakeim*, was allocated to the IGN but never flew with it and was scrapped.

for up to 16 hours of flight. The Wright R-1820 Cyclone engines were replaced often, roughly once a year in the case of most aircraft, as were the transparencies, mostly the nose bubble.

Remembering some of the operations in which he took part, Michel Bélikian said, "My flight bag included my flight suit, fur-lined boots, a leather vest, a flying helmet with intercom earphones, an oxygen mask, a microphone, a soldering iron, a Metrix [a brand of tool for testing electrical circuits], a few tools and the electrical blueprints for the on-board cameras. It was out of the question to have to go back because of a faulty camera! We climbed up to 30,000ft to take our photographs. We used negative film in 24 x 24cm (9.44 x 9.44in) format. The 120° angular field of our 88mm-focal length lens allowed us to cover a field 23km (14.29 miles) wide.

"The outside temperature was around -40°C, while the cabin heating was mostly used on the cameras. Flights usually lasted 10 hours while the aircraft gulped 10,000 litres of fuel and the crew used up the oxygen bottles stored in the ex-rear gunner position. The crew was made up of a captain, a navigator, a flight engineer and an in-flight photographer. A radio operator was not required, as Morse transmissions were no longer used...

"The SOM Poivilliers cameras consisted of a chamber to which were attached the lens and a removable cartridge containing 90 sensitive glass plates. Each cartridge weighted 70kg (154lb). The cartridges were stored in the former bomb bay. There were two cameras: one was in action while the other was being prepared. They were fitted onto damped turrets, the vertical position of which could be verified through a spirit level. They could also be rotated 30° to the left or to the right to compensate for in-flight drift. Drift was continually controlled by the photographer and checked by the navigator...

"You can easily imagine the appearance of the photographer with his fur coat, and his oxygen mask, communicating with the crew through a hand-held microphone for hours on end while the four engines were roaring around him. But what an atmosphere of friendship, of solidarity! This was unforgettable."

According to Bélikian, "the B-17 was not easy to fly, especially during take-off. With a crosswind, it became quite difficult. The pilot, with the stick pulled back into his belly, was juggling with the pedals to keep the machine in a straight line while rolling. The flight engineer was, during that time, adjusting the fuel mixture on the four engines. When the right speed was reached, the pilot pushed the stick forward to lift the tail. Acceleration took over at that moment and the aircraft took to the air. As if by magic, the wheels left the ground, a peaceful calm infiltrated the cabin and the B-17 displayed its obedience and its submission. It was like the taming of a thoroughbred horse."

"It was out of the question to go back because of a faulty camera"

There was a day when one of the machines embarked a stowaway, in the form of a crew member's terrier. The dog used to climb aboard the aircraft during pre-flight preparations, and Bélikian patted it while prepping the cameras. It was one of his first sorties, and he forgot to deplane the animal before closing the rear door. Bélikian recounted the story in his memoirs: "The aircraft took off, and as soon as my cameras were readied for the mission, while we passed 3,000ft during our climb, I went to the flight deck with the dog in my arms. The pilot looked briefly at me and went red with anger. I never saw anyone so angry: 'What do you want to do with this dog? We are going under oxygen in five minutes. There is no question of returning to base because of this dog!' I understood I had made a beginner's mistake.

"I quickly adapted a face mask to fit the dog's nose, while I donned mine. We reached 30,000ft. I wrapped the little dog in a warm garment as it was beginning to fall asleep through freezing. From time to time, I checked its heart but it was holding up. Eight hours later we landed at Creil — the dog was safe, but I had to buy a round of drinks at the airfield mess."

That was far from a typical incident in the lives of the IGN B-17s. Operating the world over, often in challenging climates, these veteran aircraft generally held up very well, even when far more modern platforms might have replaced them. Time gradually caught up with the Flying Fortresses, along with factors such as operating economics, but not before another string had been added to the legendary bomber's already considerable bow.

LEFT TOP TO BOTTOM: The changing face of the IGN fleet at the Creil base in the 1970s: from left to right, a B-17, Hurel-Dubois HD34 F-BICQ, Aero Commander 680F F-ZBAP and Dassault Falcon 20C F-BMSS. IGN

Creil on 10 February 1970, with F-BGSR (foreground) and F-BGSQ awaiting activity. PHILIPPE RICCO

LIVES OF THE FRENCH 'FORTS'

ABOVE: Two American classics in very different modes of operation from their designers' intention: F-BEEC parked at Ivato Airport in Antananarivo, Madagascar, alongside 'Super Cat'-configured PBY-5A Catalina N609FF of Canadian survey operator Geoterrex. The French geosciences company CGG was engaged in survey work in Madagascar and used aircraft such as the B-17; it part-owned Geoterrex, hence the employment of the Catalina too. PHILIPPE RICCO

B-17G-105-VE 44-85718/F-BEEC

Purchased by the French state for the IGN on 10 December 1947, the Lockheed-Vega-built 44-85718 was registered F-BEEC and arrived at Villacoublay on 13 July 1948. The following year, it operated in Africa, a first incident occurring on 17 February when the nose bubble was damaged by a bird strike. On an unknown date that October in Élisabethville, Congo, the tailwheel was torn away on landing and had to be replaced. Much of 1950 was spent at Creil, but at the year's end it went to Dakar, and the aircraft operated from Africa throughout 1951.

An aerial survey of Algeria in 1953-54 brought a curious incident on 17 May 1954: the rescue dinghy self-inflated, ripping away the door of its stowage bay. The whole bay had to be repaired and a wider investigation carried out to ensure other dinghies would not cause the same problem. Another adventure occurred at Agadir, Morocco, in 1956 when a tyre exploded on take-off. The machine landed without damage at Creil a few hours later.

Like many other IGN B-17s, during 1959 F-BEEC participated in the testing of a flight profile recorder, which may have been an early type of 'black box' flight data recorder. Operations from Abidjan, Ivory Coast took place in the early part of 1960. At Ouésso, Congo on 6 January 1962, the propellers and undercarriage suffered damage for reasons unknown, repairs being completed there. Tests of an ionospheric probe took place on 29 January 1964. Although the aircraft was prepared in 1965 for an operation to South Africa, temporarily registered ZS-EEC, its flight logs do not tally with the mileage expected from such a long journey. Assignments for 1966 were to the island of La Réunion and Madagascar; 1967 took the aeroplane to Kuwait and Iran, and on 27 December that year it was recorded as having an oil leak in Izmir, Turkey. A lengthy deployment, from 1971-73, was undertaken on behalf of the CNES, the French space agency, to support the Kourou spaceport in French Guiana — a regular haunt for F-BEEC.

> *"Many IGN B-17s took part in trials of a flight profile recorder"*

Having recently been to Algeria and Morocco, the Fortress's last flight in IGN service occurred on 25 August 1975, by which point it had amassed 7,471 flying hours. It was put into storage at Creil.

Resurrection came after 21 February 1984, when F-BEEC was sold to Warbirds of Great Britain. Registered G-FORT, it flew to Blackbushe that June, eventually passing from there via Stephen Grey at Duxford to the Lone Star Flight Museum in Galveston, Texas during 1987.

Today: owned by Mid America Flight Museum at Mount Pleasant, Texas, but stored at Madras, Oregon, awaiting return to flying condition.

B-17G-105-VE 44-85643/F-BEEA

Of all the IGN B-17s, this one had perhaps the most interesting CV. Bought on 12 December 1947, it arrived for its refit at Villacoublay on 19 March 1948. This was complete by early December, when it left for French Africa and what seems like a lengthy mission there, for the aeroplane was still in Cameroon during the first quarter of 1949, followed by Madagascar. Not until early 1950 did it return to Creil, but soon it was heading back to Madagascar. The beginning of 1951 found F-BEEA in Lomé, Togo, and the end of it in Brazzaville, Congo.

While 1952-59 largely saw the machine at Creil, there were a few African escapades, one of which led to wingtip damage in Algiers when a service truck drove into it. Back home there were tests of the flight profile recorder. A higher-profile role in the early part of 1963 was as a camera aircraft for the filming of Stanley Kubrick's *Dr Strangelove*, the B-17's shadow unfortunately showing up when it 'doubled' for a B-52. During its time in Greenland with Kubrick's crew, *Dr Strangelove* was applied above the access door.

Back on regular duties by May, F-BEEA took part in testing of the Breguet 'flying bomb' — actually a device for magnetometric recording, shaped like a bomb and suspended on a wire beneath the aircraft. This went on during 1965, for which a trip was made to Toulouse. Another bout of filming that year involved the aircraft being seen in the Gérard Oury movie *La Grande Vadrouille*. Approval was given in May 1967 for a mission to Australia, which required removal from the French registry and a temporary period with an Australian identity. There is no proof in the French files that it ever went there, though — still as F-BEEA — the B-17 visited Port Moresby, Papua New Guinea, in both June and July. Commitments in more familiar areas took in periods at Benghazi, Libya, in 1968, and Niger and Chad during 1969-70. Most of 1971 was taken up in Africa.

With 8,309 flying hours in the books, a figure way beyond anything Boeing had ever foreseen for a B-17, on 25 August 1972 the aeroplane was dismantled and placed in storage at Creil. Yet in 1974 it was reassembled and sent to N'Djamena, Chad, returning to base in mid-1975.

For 12 months from June 1978, F-BEEA was engaged in tests of the Vigie side-looking airborne radar (SLAR), developed by Thomson-CSF in conjunction with the CNES, over the Les Vans area in the Ardèche region of central France. The outcomes were highly positive: "As far as mineral exploitation is concerned", reported the IGN, "SLAR opens the way to photogeological-type interpretation in cloudy areas, and for that reason can be considered as a technique which makes it possible to select targets for prospecting ores". Those good results were reason to proceed further: on 5 October 1979, authorisation was given to mount a 4.5m (14.73ft)-long beam antenna under the belly of the B-17.

In June 1984, another Thomson-CSF system, the VARAN-S side-looking synthetic aperture radar, was fitted for a trial in the Molloy Deep area — the deepest point in the Arctic Ocean, north-east of Greenland — to determine whether sea ice concentrations could be accurately measured using radar. Claimed to be the first synthetic aperture airborne radar designed in Europe, VARAN-S obviously relegated Vigie to the status of a mere experiment. Three aircraft were used: a Convair CV-990 Coronado, a Convair CV-580 and F-BEEA. These experiments continued until April 1987, and a study in the Bothnian Sea off Finland called BEPERS (Bothnian Experiment in Preparation for ERS-1, the latter being a European remote sensing satellite launched in 1991). It required the B-17's airworthiness certificate to be extended by a few months.

F-BEEA also had a role in tests preceding the launch in 1986 of the French earth-imaging satellite SPOT 1 (Satellite pour l'Observation

LEFT TOP TO BOTTOM: At Yaoundé, Cameroon in December 1969, F-BEEA exhibits a sabre-type antenna on the nose, indicating a new avionics fit. The fuselage titles read Service des Activités Aériennes, the name given to the IGN's aviation element. R. LYONNET VIA RÉGIS BIAUX COLLECTION

Bright anti-collision markings were applied to F-BEEA and other B-17s for tests with the Breguet 'flying bomb' intended for geophysical prospection. PHILIPPE RICCO

Parked at Dublin in July 1986, F-BEEA was engaged in a survey of County Tipperary. It has a large under-fuselage sensor pannier and shows the revised nose glazing fitted for the photographic mission. LIAM BYRNE

The long, open panel beneath F-BEEA's rear fuselage was related to the side-looking airborne radar trials with which this aircraft was involved from the late 1970s. PHILIPPE RICCO

ABOVE: The 'white-top' livery helped cool F-BEEA and its occupants when operating under the harsh African sun. PHILIPPE RICCO

de la Terre). Michel Bélikian remembered, "from 1978 to 1986, each year I was involved in the 'SPOT simulation' campaigns [we did] for the CNES. The objective was to develop the multi-spectral digital cameras to be fitted to the SPOT satellite and to supply the photo labs which were to work on the satellite data with pictures to exploit. The data recorded by the satellite was compared to the photographic films taken simultaneously by the IGN. Those missions were mostly flown over French territory, but they could sometimes overfly neighbouring territories."

So it could have continued, but in 1989 F-BEEA was made available for the filming in the UK of *Memphis Belle*, joining two other ex-IGN Fortresses, the former F-BGSP and 'BGSR, among the fleet of five. On 25 July it crashed on take-off from RAF Binbrook, thankfully without fatalities, although the airframe was destroyed. It had been intended to use the aircraft for an exercise called HAREM (Halieutique et Radar, Expérimentation en Méditerranee — Fishing and Radar, Experiments in the Mediterranean), an effort to detect tuna with the VARAN-S radar. After the accident, a Dornier 228 replaced F-BEEA.

B-17G-105-DL 44-83729/F-BEED

Obtained for the IGN on 24 December 1947, this example arrived at Villacoublay on 3 May 1948 and was registered F-BEED. Its debut assignment in 1949 was to Madagascar, while 1950 saw it operating from Lomé in Togo as well as returning to Madagascar. 1951 was spent in Africa, and from 1955-59 it completed many more missions to African countries. The Fortress was grounded at Creil on 9 July 1959, with 4,189 flying hours. It was struck off the French registry on 21 October 1961, being used as a spares source and scrapped in 1973.

> *"It was intended to use F-BEEA to detect tuna"*

B-17G-105-VE 44-85733/F-BEEB

F-BEEB was bought on 12 January 1948 but had quite a short IGN life. It arrived in France during March with 36 hours in its logbook, and the "disarmed aircraft" — this wording in the reception documentation suggests it arrived with military equipment, turrets and so forth still in position, and just the weapons removed — remained at Villacoublay from 26 March until 10 May. It went to Orange-Caritat in August before returning to Villacoublay for its reception inspection in November. Note was taken that one of the engines had been replaced just before leaving the USA and its serial number did not match the aircraft's documentation.

Its IGN career proper began on 6 December 1948, being sent on a mission to Yaoundé, Cameroon. On 5 March 1949 it joined 'BEEA, 'BEEC and 'BEED on a joint detachment to Avironimamo, Madagascar, via Nairobi and Dar es Salaam. F-BEEB returned to Cameroon, but on a subsequent flight from Douala to Madagascar it crashed near Yaoundé on 11 March 1949, killing four of the five crew members.

B-17G-110-BO 43-39304/F-BDAT

Another short-lived machine, this B-17 arrived at Le Bourget on 17 March 1950 and was tasked with an assignment to Niger, reaching Niamey on 18 October. En route to Oran, Algeria at around 23.00hrs on 12 December it crashed for reasons unknown and was destroyed by fire — not surprisingly, as F-BDAT was carrying in excess of 10,000 litres of fuel and 560 litres of oil, it blew up immediately. The report was sketchy: "after taking off in a normal way, the aircraft flew horizontally at an altitude of about 400m before beginning to lose speed, maintaining a straight flight path until the impact". Three crew members died in the accident, three survived. The aircraft had logged 545 flying hours.

LEFT: **In Hanoi on 17 March 1953, F-BGOE nosed over into a small drainage ditch at the end of the runway. Little damage was done and the aircraft soon flew home.** VIA JEAN-CHRISTOPHE CARBONEL

B-17G-105-DL 44-83757/F-BDRR

Bought on 25 July 1950 and registered F-BDRR, this example opened its overseas mission tally by going to French Guiana. During 1956 it was in Guadeloupe, and it was resident for the whole of 1957 in Gabon. Having returned to Creil in the last quarter of 1958, it was back in Africa in 1960. Grounding took place the following year, with 2,883 flight hours, and by 21 October 1961 the aircraft was off the French registry. Briefly used as a source of spares, it was scrapped the following year.

B-17G-95-DL 44-83728/F-BGOE

Previously a VIP transport for the Shah of Iran, 44-83728 was acquired on 12 July 1952. It arrived at Le Bourget on 23 July and remained in the Aérocentre workshops until 17 October, being re-equipped as a photographic platform. Operated by the IGN as F-BGOE, its initial assignment from 1952-53 was in French Indochina. On 17 March 1953 it nosed over in Hanoi, damaging one engine and the glazed nose. Repairs were carried out locally and it returned home during 1954. Other overseas deployments from Creil were to Cameroon in late 1955, Gabon in 1957 — where it was damaged on 8 February 1958 when the port wing hit a tree on landing at Libreville — and Algiers in early 1959. A bird strike on 21 May 1964 necessitated replacement of the nose transparency.

During a flight to Clermont-Ferrand in central France on 15 June 1967, one of the Wright Cyclones failed. Continuing on three engines for two hours, F-BGOE managed to land safely at its destination. Its last flight, after 3,664 hours, was on 22 August 1967. Put into storage, the registration was cancelled on 27 May 1969. The B-17 was probably scrapped at Creil circa 1972.

B-17G-95-DL 44-83735/F-BDRS

It appears the inaugural IGN mission for this aircraft, acquired on 23 August 1952, was in French Indochina, then in the midst of conflict between France and the Viet Minh. On the brink of requisition by the army, the IGN crew flew back to France. Beside this anecdote, nothing else is known of its operations. By now dismantled, on 5 August 1974 it was sold to Euroworld as a spares source for F-BGSR, which it was to keep airworthy. Transported by road to Duxford, in 1978 the airframe was sold for £1,000 to the Imperial War Museum, which restored it for static display.

Today: on static display in American Air Museum, IWM Duxford.

B-17G-85-VE 44-8889/F-BGSO

This former RB-17G model was bought for the IGN on 12 August 1954, and registered as F-BGSO. No detail is known of its operations until it was grounded on 7 June ➔

BELOW: **The boxes in front of F-BGSQ are casings for glass plate photography.** IGN

ABOVE: One of the Breguet 'birds', or 'flying bombs', hangs beneath the fuselage of F-BGSO at Creil in 1969. In operation, these instrument casings would have been towed on a long line, so as to remain distant from the magnetic influence of the aircraft. PHILIPPE RICCO

1974. The aircraft's last flight was on 8 September 1976, on delivery to the Musée de l'Air after 6,534 flying hours. IGN photographer Michel Bélikian was on board and remembered, "after landing at Le Bourget, a big official party was held where I had the opportunity to meet Mrs [Jeanne] Fontaine, the first French flight attendant. She had flown on board Farman Goliaths during the twenties!"

Today: in storage at Musée de l'Air et de l'Espace, Le Bourget.

B-17G-105-VE 44-85784/F-BGSR

Purchased on 31 October 1954 and registered F-BGSR, this B-17 arrived at Le Bourget on 1 November 1954. After being in Oran during early 1955, detail of its use is hazy until it reappeared at Creil in December 1958 to be test a Mk5 model of the flight profile recorder. There were a couple of subsequent mishaps: at Antananarivo on 24 June 1968, an over-zealous firefighter clipped one of the Fortress's wingtips with his truck during an exercise, while on 6 March 1970 it made light contact with another aircraft when it slid on an icy taxiway. Later that year it was detached to Benghazi.

As the B-17 fleet grew gradually smaller, on 22 June 1973 F-BGSR was dismantled for storage. Then, however, it was sold to Euroworld on 5 August 1974, its French registry being cancelled on 17 September with 5,318 flying hours. After reassembly, it received approval to fly to Britain, landing at Biggin Hill on 15 March 1975 with the US registration N17TE. Soon it took up residence at Duxford and was named *Sally B*, and on 5 August 1976 the British registration G-BEDF was allocated. Still flying in the hands of Elly Sallingboe and her colleagues at B-17 Preservation, *Sally B* is now the sole airworthy example of the type in Europe.

Today: airworthy with B-17 Preservation at Duxford.

B-17G-85-VE 44-8846/F-BGSP

Delivered from the Lockheed-Vega factory in Burbank, California on 17 January 1945, 44-8846 was assigned to the 351st Bomb Group and flew six missions during World War Two. After hostilities, it was stationed in Germany with the 45th Reconnaissance Squadron until it returned to the USA. On 7 December 1954, the aircraft was acquired by the French state, and registered as F-BGSP. As far as is known, it carried most of its IGN missions from Creil except a late-1960 visit to Gabon. During December 1959, it was among the aircraft used for the flight profile recorder experiments. It joined F-BEEA in filming *La Grande Vadrouille*, and enjoyed another big-screen outing in 1968's *The Biggest Bundle of Them All* — or *Bande à César* as it was known in French — alongside the likes of Robert Wagner and Raquel Welch, transporting the booty from a train robbery. Notable later taskings were to Saudi Arabia for photography in 1976, flights over the wrecked crude oil tanker *Amoco Cadiz* after its 1978 grounding off Brittany to monitor the resulting spill using colour and infra-red cameras, and a 1979 remote sensing project in east Greenland with a view to future mineral exploration.

F-BGSP was grounded in 1979 and put in flyable storage, emerging to participate in the 1984 Bastille Day flypast over Paris — in the 40th anniversary year of D-Day, it was joined by two Douglas C-47s, with the Patrouille de France just in front. During 1985 it became F-AZDX in the French historic aircraft

RIGHT: The B-17 that's now *Sally B*, then F-BGSR, at its home base. PHILIPPE RICCO

registration series, still owned by the IGN, which obtained sponsorship from various sources for its operation at airshows. Handed over in 1987 to the Association Forteresse Toujours Volante with 9,483 flight hours, the aeroplane was eventually repainted into its wartime colours as *Pink Lady*. It was based successively at Orly and Melun, but ceased operation in March 2010.

Today: on static display, but in engine-running condition, with Association Forteresse Toujours Volante/Musée Volant Salis at La Ferté-Alais.

ABOVE: As the day's activities at Creil get under way, F-BGSP is towed to the flightline. PHILIPPE RICCO

B-17G-100-VE 44-85594/F-BGSQ

Unlike most of the IGN B-17s, this one had already been modified in the USA to become a photographic platform, the Middletown Air Materiel Area at Olmstead AFB, Pennsylvania doing the work. It was bought by France on 29 December 1954. In the summer of 1957 it arrived at Libreville, where it remained until the first quarter of 1958. F-BGSQ joined the group of B-17s testing the flight profile recorder through 1959, while in 1960-61 there were visits to various African countries, returning to Creil in early 1962. That November it was in Beirut; returns were made to Africa in 1963-64.

Occasional incidents punctuated these missions. On 5 March 1963, F-BGSQ had to land at Algiers on three engines after one failed. Another powerplant gave up the ghost on 20 December, while landing at Douala. Flying from Tunis to Creil on 19 March 1965, an unplanned diversion had to be made to Montpellier after an oil leak required the shut-down of engine number four. Operations thereafter were mostly from Creil, where the B-17 was grounded on 14 November 1969 with 4,971 hours logged. The date of deletion from the French registry is unknown. It appears to have been scrapped around 1972.

B-17G-35-BO 42-32076/F-BGSH

This aircraft was delivered to the AAF on 24 January 1944, operating as *Shoo Shoo Shoo Baby* with the 401st Bomb Squadron of the 91st Bomb Group. Damaged by flak on 29 May 1944, it landed at Bulltofta, Sweden and was interned. A transfer to Swedish ownership followed in 1945 and the B-17 was converted into a transport by Saab, serving with the airline SILA; later it was resold to Danish carrier Det Danske Luftfartselskab and then the Danish military.

Bought by the French state for the IGN in 1955, it was registered as F-BGSH and arrived at Creil on 21 February 1956 with 2,488 hours logged. Modifying the machine into a photographic platform took a week. During 1956-57 it operated in Lebanon, French Guiana and the Caribbean. Thereafter it remained at Creil, except in 1960 when it mapped the Congo. F-BGSH went into storage in 1962, at which point it had 3,364 hours. Disassembled for spare parts in 1964, it was removed from the French register on 13 February 1970. In June 1972, it was sold for a symbolic one franc to the US Air Force for exhibition in the Air Force Museum at Wright-Patterson AFB, again as *Shoo Shoo Shoo Baby.*

Today: on static display at the National Air and Space Museum's Udvar-Hazy Center, Dulles Airport, Virginia.

Thanks to Edouard Suilva at the DGAC, Régis Biaux, Henri Lacaze, David Legg and Philippe Ricco.

BELOW: Early days as a warbird for the former F-BGSP, as La Ferté-Alais witnesses a spectacular display in 1985. The aircraft is now based there, and regularly maintained such that it may fly again. DENIS J. CALVERT

SPECIAL RELATIONSHIP

Half a century has passed since the first visit by a Lockheed SR-71 to UK shores, and the start of a link between Britain and 'Blackbird' that came almost to define the height of the Anglo-American bond. But the road to US Air Force SR-71 operations from Mildenhall was not always a smooth one **WORDS:** BEN DUNNELL

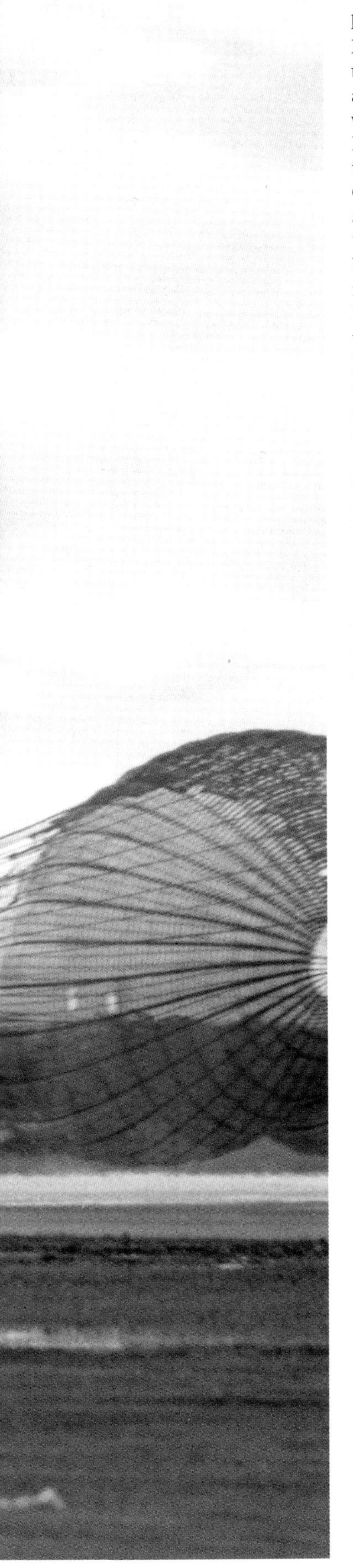

Just two years earlier, it wouldn't have been allowed. Well, almost. A US Air Force Lockheed SR-71A could still have set a speed record between New York and London, but ending the flight in a blaze of publicity at the Farnborough show: no way. Not British enough, you see. Even after a recent relaxation, the Society of British Aerospace Companies' myopic insistence that aircraft participating in its biennial 'shop window' have substantial UK content would have kept this most spectacular exhibit out. But in 1974, finally Farnborough went fully international, so 'Kelly' Johnson's unmistakeable shape settled onto the Hampshire aerodrome's wet tarmac, and entered the history books.

This was more than just a record flight for the sake of it. When pilot Maj James V. Sullivan and reconnaissance systems operator Maj Noel F. Widdifield touched down in SR-71A serial 61-7972 that September Sunday afternoon, they were completing what, for them, was a fairly standard sortie. In a sense, it was a belated one, for the 'Habu' — as the aircraft had been dubbed by locals in Okinawa when it was deployed to Kadena AB on the Japanese island — should have been seen on UK soil the previous year. But it was also an obvious precursor to a more regular presence, especially when '972 proceeded from Farnborough to RAF Mildenhall prior to heading home, and another record.

The broader background really begins in December 1971. Prime Minister Edward Heath was shortly to travel to Bermuda for talks with US President Richard Nixon, at which they were to have a wide-ranging discussion of the world situation. Just a few days earlier, the Foreign Office received a request from the Americans which demanded Heath's attention. They had, a memorandum to Heath by an unnamed Foreign Office minister outlined, asked for "occasional use of their base at RAF Mildenhall" by SR-71s engaged in reconnaissance operations. "As instances of its possible use the Americans have mentioned: monitoring an Arab-Israeli cease-fire; undertaking urgent reconnaissance during an Eastern European crisis. (They probably have in mind a possible Soviet invasion of Yugoslavia or Romania.) Although they have not said so, overflights of foreign territory could include the Soviet Union itself."

As described by type expert Paul Crickmore in the latest edition of his book *Lockheed Blackbird: Beyond the Secret Missions* (Osprey, 2024), Strategic Air Command's original April 1970 plan for SR-71 operations in Europe had involved a detachment at Torrejón AB, Spain. But the Spanish government refused, so Washington turned to London. It was stated there was no desire to base SR-71s permanently in Britain, "and they accept that the aircraft would not be deployed here or used on operations without our specific agreement on each occasion. They would make available to us all the intelligence gained". Each deployment would involve two SR-71s from the 9th Strategic Reconnaissance Wing at Beale AFB, California, plus their supporting KC-135Q Stratotanker air-to-air refuelling aircraft, while only "small and inconspicuous works" would be needed at Mildenhall to support the aircraft, these paid for by the Americans.

> **“*The Americans asked for occasional use of Mildenhall by SR-71s*”**

But the Foreign Office could see potential pitfalls. Memories of the need to conceal the nature of previous U-2 detachments to Britain may well still have loomed large, even if they had at the time been 'black world' Central Intelligence Agency affairs, whereas the SR-71 was a publicly acknowledged USAF asset. "It is possible", the memo said, that the presence of SR-71s at Mildenhall "would sooner or later become public knowledge", leading to "Parliamentary and press interest, and probably some speculation about the role of the aircraft in view of its known capabilities and the analogy of the U-2."

More seriously, "There could be serious diplomatic difficulties if the aircraft were detected, or even engaged, during overflights of foreign territory and it became apparent that they were operating from the UK. For example, the

LEFT: A very wet Farnborough welcomed Maj Jim Sullivan, Maj Noel Widdifield and SR-71A 61-7972 on 1 September 1974.

ABOVE: Among those who greeted Sullivan (left) and Widdifield (centre) as they descended the SR-71's steps was 15th Air Force commander Lt Gen William Pitts. VIA NOEL WIDDIFIELD

Egyptians could well object to flights over the Suez Canal area but the Americans might nevertheless wish to proceed. If the fact that such flights were being mounted from British bases then leaked out, this could involve us in a major row with the Egyptians and we might have to ask the Americans to desist. Our difficulties with the Egyptians could be exacerbated if the Americans were to transmit the results of these flights to the Israelis. Problems could similarly arise in connexion with any flights over Warsaw Pact territory, especially over the Soviet Union... Its operation from a UK base, with the use of British airspace, might not be easy for the countries concerned to substantiate, but the possibility cannot be ruled out, especially if the presence of SR-71 aircraft here has become public knowledge". Quite how it was proposed to operate SR-71s from Britain without the public being aware is open to speculation.

The 'top secret' document went on, "We can clearly give no advance assurance to the Americans that we would agree to operations (or even necessarily to a precautionary deployment) on each and every occasion; it is possible that there would be some occasions on which we should want to say no. Acceptance of the present American proposal would thus expose us to the possibility of tension between Governments on some future occasions; it would equally expose the Americans to the risk of being unable to undertake operations to which they attached importance and for which they had been counting on Mildenhall. As against these potential difficulties, there is the strong argument that our long-standing co-operation with the Americans in intelligence matters gives us access to a great deal of information which we have no other means of obtaining and that rejection of the American proposal would carry some risk of reducing this co-operation in the future (especially if there is any current disposition in the US Administration to believe that our entry into Europe may herald some weakening in Anglo-American collaborative arrangements generally). It is also likely that we should see strong advantages to ourselves and NATO in some of the operations which the Americans would wish to conduct with SR-71 aircraft based in the UK."

On balance, it was thought any problems with public or press attention could easily be dealt with, while the Foreign Office felt, "on balance, the risks of embarrassment should be taken, having in mind the importance which the Americans themselves attach to this proposal, the general desirability of maintaining our intelligence co-operation with them, and the Ministry of Defence's belief that SR-71 reconnaissance operations of the kind the Americans have in mind could well be of value to ourselves and NATO on some occasions". The recommendation, therefore, was to "agree to the American request, on the clear understanding that no SR-71 aircraft will be deployed here, and no individual SR-71 missions will be flown from a British base, without our prior agreement."

Heath concurred, and the Americans were duly informed. But not until the Arab-Israeli Yom Kippur war of October 1973 was a request

RIGHT: Facing the press, the two SR-71 crew members were accompanied by their wives, who had flown out to the UK — at their own expense — in advance. It was Ann Widdifield who set the wheels in motion for a flight in Concorde G-AXDN during Farnborough week. VIA NOEL WIDDIFIELD

made for British SR-71 basing. A US Joint Chiefs of Staff memo dated 8 October outlined the "immediate requirement" for intelligence on "military targets in Syria and Egypt", with "military dispositions and surface-to-air missile (SAM) sites in Egypt along the Suez Canal and in Syria near the Golan Heights" being afforded highest priority. The document is still heavily redacted to obscure any mention of the country and location involved, but the Joint Chiefs proposed the "immediate deployment" of an SR-71 to Mildenhall in order to provide, "Off shore peripheral coverage of targets in Syria and Egypt, including ports, coastal airfields and combat operations in the Sinai within 20 miles of the coast", and "Overhead coverage of all important target areas".

Lt Col James H. Shelton Jr and his RSO Maj Gary L. Coleman were the crew. "The reason the SR-71 got alerted in the October timeframe", Shelton recalled to the author in 2013, "was the fact that, during that war, the Russians were supporting the Egyptians, and of course we were very supportive of the Israelis. The Russians were launching satellites to find out where the battle lines were and what was happening in the war, but we couldn't take any of our satellites out of their Russian orbit because of the priority we attached to that area. It was asked whether the SR-71 could cover the Middle East. Well, naturally it could, but the original plan was to fly from Beale AFB in California through the Middle East and recover to RAF Mildenhall in England. It was going to be an eight-and-a-half-hour mission.

"We went down for the briefing on 10 October 1973, and in the meantime the maintenance recovery team was on board a tanker heading towards England. When the tanker landed, the British said, 'You cannot land the SR-71 here'. The argument was that Britain relied too heavily on Middle East oil and didn't want to be accused of supporting any sort of mission like that. So, they cancelled the mission. Gary and I went home. We came in the next morning, and they said, 'We've got a new plan'. Now we would fly from Griffiss AFB, New York, through to the Middle East and recover back to Griffiss". And that, on 13 October, was what Shelton and Coleman did. In 61-7979, they spent 11 hours 13 minutes in the air, a new SR-71 record, with 13 KC-135Qs in support.

ABOVE: Lockheed dominated Farnborough in 1974, the SR-71 being corralled with a C-5A Galaxy and, just visible at the top, a P-3C Orion.
VIA NOEL WIDDIFIELD

But the recollection of Britain's position, coming as it does from an American perspective, understandably repeats a misconception held in Washington. This was that the UK objected to the SR-71 sortie being flown from its soil. In fact, it merely had reservations, which were wrongly interpreted — and have been portrayed in some accounts — as a refusal.

> *"The UK merely had reservations about the SR-71 sortie"*

In a letter to Foreign Secretary Alec Douglas-Home, the British ambassador to Washington, Lord Cromer, noted a subsequent discussion he'd had with the US Defense Secretary, James Schlesinger. Cromer explained, "that we had (at considerable inconvenience to Ministers) gone out of our way to agree to the US request, subject to the usual reservation. Schlesinger replied that one of our reservations had been that material derived from the flight should not be passed to Israel. He was not sure this was either a standard or a helpful reservation. I replied that we had taken our policy of strict neutrality in the conflict very seriously. There would have been no conceivable advantage in risking a confrontation with the Arabs on this, had the information leaked out."

By late November 1973, the impasse had been ironed out. The Washington Special Actions Group was a task force of senior officials from across the US government and its agencies, set up and chaired by Secretary of State Henry Kissinger as a means of co-ordinating crisis responses. The minutes of its 9 November meeting on the Middle East include a discussion in which the possibility of landing an SR-71 in Greece was mooted, along with Iran. Deputy Defense Secretary William Clements said, "I don't think the Shah would let us", to which Joint Chiefs of Staff director of plans Admiral John P. Weinel replied, "Not even if we gave him an SR-71?" But on 29 November, Joint Chiefs chairman Admiral Thomas Moorer told Kissinger the JP-7 fuel used by the SR-71 would begin to arrive at Mildenhall from 1 January 1974. Kissinger added, "After January, we can fly out of the UK."

Even so, period reports describe the Anglo-American relationship as not then being at its height. A piece by Jack Anderson published in the *Washington Post* on 18 February described how President Richard Nixon had been weakened internationally by the burgeoning Watergate scandal, that Kissinger had frosty relations with Heath, Douglas-Home and Cromer, and that a British diplomat had described the US ambassador to London, Walter Annenberg, as "a disagreeable fool". "British sources", said Anderson, "also confirmed published reports that Kissinger angrily canceled a plan to fly SR-71 spy planes out of a base in England during the Middle East fighting. The stories claimed that Kissinger was angered by Heath's demand that British knowledge of the operation be kept strictly secret.

"According to our British sources, Heath merely insisted that the Israelis should not be shown the reconnaissance photos taken by the spy planes. In any event, Kissinger ordered the spy planes to bypass Britain, which resulted in costly mid-air refueling operations and delayed for three days some of the intelligence on Soviet deliveries to Egypt and Syria."

While denials came from both sides of the Atlantic, later accounts from within the British government support the assertion that it was Kissinger who decided not to fly the SR-71 from Mildenhall. James Callaghan, Foreign Secretary in the Labour government elected that year, wrote to Prime Minister Harold Wilson in November 1974, "in fact the Americans called off the flights, because of what they thought was 'the obvious deep concern in London', and we subsequently heard from Dr Kissinger that he had felt that the United States could not use Mildenhall because our agreement had been given 'so grudgingly and reluctantly', though this was not in fact the case."

> ***"We actually could have made the flight without having to refuel"***

Was the UK visit in September 1974 specifically intended as a lead-in to regular SR-71 operations from Britain? Speaking nearly 50 years after the record flight he undertook with James Sullivan, Noel Widdifield says, "I had no insight into what was planned for the future. The decision had been made for us to display the airplane at Farnborough. As a result of that, Barry Goldwater [Arizona senator and a recently retired Air National Guard major general] had suggested to then-President Ford that we try to set a record, and things moved forward from that. As events eventually turned out, obviously that wasn't a bad deal, because that got us to England with the airplane and probably made it easier later on, but that's speculation on my part.

"Jim and I were the senior crew, crew SO-1 — chief of stanboard [the standards and evaluation board] and chief of the navigation branch together. We were told, I guess, about three to four months before the event that it was going to happen, and that we were the crew selected because we were the senior crew. That's the first we knew about it. But then nothing happened for quite a while. We deployed to Okinawa, came back; I took some vacation, and at some point about a month before the wing commander came to us and said, 'It's a go', with us as the primary crew. But even before the wing commander talked to us, the local base paper there in California came out and my wife said, 'Hey, looks like you're gonna go!'

"First of all, it was a routine flight. It was no different than any other flight. Every single one of those required a considerable amount of time for planning. The route was planned and laid out by the navigation branch, which was a bunch of guys who did the mission planning. They developed all the documents needed, developed the program for the computer for the route, and worked to get FAA clearances through the United States and so on to make sure the route was approved ahead of time. The tankers had to be scheduled to meet us, because we needed tankers after take-off, just prior to arriving in New York, mid-way along and waiting for us in England in case we had a problem.

"It was a very early take-off. We flew night missions all the time, but it was still very early. The only thing we saw that was much different was that there was a little more activity as we got ready to fly — our suit-ups and so on. Our kids were able to come and watch us, and there were some other visitors..."

Once they were under way, "We accelerated through the Machs, up to Mach 3 at 80,000ft, and from there started on the route. We flew south over the southern part of the United States and up the east coast. All the route was programmed to

BELOW: The crew for the return flight: Capt Harold Adams (right) and Maj Bill Machorek. DENIS J. CALVERT

avoid populated areas. As we came towards New York, we told the tanker we were there and started our descent from 80,000ft down to 25,000ft. We took fuel and from there started our acceleration to cross over the 'gate' at New York. There were imaginary rings drawn around New York and London that we had to 'clip' in order to establish the distance. We climbed back to 80,000ft and made our way on.

"We actually could have made the flight without having to refuel, but we would have been below the minimums in case of an emergency in the London area. So, we had to descend for a tanker en route near Newfoundland. Same process: we descended down, hit the tanker, accelerated back up.

"After we got to 80,000ft, we were still not quite over the Atlantic when we had what was called an 'unstart' [a problem whereby, when the SR-71 was flying supersonically, the shockwave in the engine inlet throat could be rapidly ejected from the front of the inlet and the movable intake 'spike' on the Pratt & Whitney J58 would go into the subsonic position, suddenly stopping airflow and reducing thrust]. You knew which engine had unstarted when your head hit the windscreen on the opposite side of the cockpit... We didn't have any trouble restarting, and didn't really lose any altitude or speed. Then we continued on all the way to London.

"As we approached London, obviously we contacted air traffic control there. We came in, made our descent, did a flyby and landed at Farnborough after one hour 54 minutes and 56 seconds, to be exact. We taxied in to the place where we had to park, opened the cockpits and were greeted by our wing commander [Col Pat Halloran] and the FAI [Fédération Aéronautique Internationale] representative who then checked us to make sure we were the same people who'd got into the airplane at Beale. Kind of funny-sounding, but that had to be done! Climbing down the steps, we were greeted by several other people including our wives and 'Kelly' Johnson, who we were very happy to see."

❖

Johnson, the Lockheed 'Skunk Works' supremo and mastermind behind the SR-71, was just as happy to see them. "It has exceeded all my expectations", he said of the flight. Sullivan and Widdifield had set an average speed of 1,806.95mph for the 3,461.53 miles, and their time not just broke but smashed the previous New York-London record of four hours 46 minutes, set during 1969's *Daily Mail* Transatlantic Air Race by a Royal Navy Phantom FG1. It has never been bettered.

"Still in our pressure suits", continues Widdifield, "but with our helmets off, we were taken into a place where the media was gathered. They threw a lot of questions at us. At that time President Ford called us. He talked to Jim for about two or three minutes, and then talked to me for a couple of minutes. He wanted to know what my job was, because he didn't know what a reconnaissance systems officer did. So I told him about it, and I said the main job was to make sure it was a New York to London flight, not a New York to Paris flight."

The publicity coup had been achieved, and a successful flight made with, the 'unstart' aside, no technical problems. It wasn't a wholly happy day for the Americans at Farnborough, for while the SR-71 and its crew were being feted, the Sikorsky S-67 Blackhawk attack helicopter prototype crashed during its display in the afternoon flying programme, killing one of the two test pilots on board and putting the other in hospital, where he died nine days later. But the SR-71 remained the headline-grabber, present at the SBAC show all week, albeit static only — and not always on public view.

On 9 September, Widdifield recalls, "Jim and I took the airplane over to Mildenhall". It had been decided to go for a London to Los Angeles record on the return flight, this time with Capt Harold B. 'Buck' Adams as pilot and Maj William Machorek as RSO. They had been the supervisory crew for the

ABOVE: 61-7972 on the Mildenhall tarmac, being readied by its groundcrew. The first visit to the Suffolk base no doubt proved useful in preparation for future SR-71 operations.
DENIS J. CALVERT

ABOVE: Photographer Denis Calvert recalls well the events at Mildenhall on 12 September 1974: "After the press call, the ra-ra and the take-off, everyone went home. Less than an hour later, 17972 returned to Mildenhall after a snag and an illuminated caption, to make a final trans-Atlantic departure the next day."
DENIS J. CALVERT

outbound mission, deployed in advance to the Suffolk base. Again the attempt — mounted on 13 September — was successful, '972 covering the 5,463 miles in three hours 47 minutes and 39 seconds, equating to a 1,435mph average.

"We were just a flight crew", stresses Widdifield, "so we didn't understand all the machinations going on beyond, but it was clear among people from within the wing who were there, and a three-star from 15th Air Force, that they were happy we were able to make the thing happen, and I'm sure a lot of that was in their minds about future deployments if needed". More broadly, Gerald Ford had only assumed the presidency a few weeks earlier, following Richard Nixon's resignation over Watergate. "I think America needed a little bit of a political boost", Widdifield says with a smile. "I've heard people speculating that Goldwater and Ford wanted to do the flight for that very reason. They needed something positive that was happening about the US, and they thought it would gain a lot of publicity, which it did.

"And the thing I thought was really important was that it symbolised the long-term relationship between the US and Britain. It was a salute to that as well". The era of SR-71 operations from Mildenhall which would follow, and the intelligence they gathered, only served to cement that bond still further.

With thanks to Dr Kevin Wright.

RIGHT: The crews from the two record flights meet President Gerald Ford at the White House.
VIA NOEL WIDDIFIELD

With characteristic diamond afterburner shockwaves, SR-71A 61-7971 climbs out of Mildenhall on 2 February 1983. BOB ARCHER

BRITAIN'S 'BLACKBIRD' YEARS

1974

1 September
Arrival at Farnborough of 61-7972, breaking New York-London speed record

13 September
London-Los Angeles record set by 61-7972 on (eventual) departure from Mildenhall

1976

20 April
The return to Mildenhall of '972, accompanied by two of the 'Habu's' specialised KC-135Q tankers, for an eight-day deployment incorporating two training sorties over the North and Norwegian Seas and the English Channel

6 September
The second SR-71 to visit Mildenhall is 61-7962; as part of NATO training exercises 'Cold Fire' and 'Teamwork', it flies six sorties over the course of 19 days

1977

20 May
In the hands of pilot Maj Tom Alison and RSO Maj 'JT' Vida, 61-7958 flies the first operational sortie mounted from Britain by an SR-71, collecting electronic intelligence and high-resolution radar imagery of the Soviet submarine base at Murmansk

24 May
Another operational 'first': a mission over West Germany to cover the inner German border area, again by '958, with Maj 'Buz' Carpenter and Maj John Murphy as pilot and RSO

16 November
Inaugural 'Baltic Express' mission by Maj Bob Crowder and Capt John Morgan in 61-7976 en route from Mildenhall back to Beale

1979

16 March
A mission to the Middle East is flown from Mildenhall with '972, as tensions erupt between North and South Yemen, causing concern in neighbouring Saudi Arabia

31 March
Official establishment at Mildenhall of Detachment 4, 9th Strategic Reconnaissance Wing, then flying U-2s as well as SR-71s

1980

12 December
Start of the longest SR-71 deployment to Mildenhall yet, 61-7964 staying for four months due to concerns about the potential for Soviet military intervention against the Solidarity movement in Poland

1982

23 December
A second aircraft joins Det 4

1983

9 July
61-7955 arrives at Mildenhall, falsely marked as '17962', for a period of operational evaluation of the ASARS (Advanced Synthetic Aperture Radar System), before its integration into the whole SR-71 fleet

24 October
Det 4's first sortie to cover Lebanon, following the bombing by Islamic Jihad terrorists of a barracks used by US marines — this was a rarity in that the French government permitted an SR-71 overflight

1984

5 April
The British government agrees to the US request for permanent SR-71 basing at Mildenhall, putting Det 4 on a firmer footing

1986

16 April
The first of three Det 4 sorties to Tripoli and Benghazi, Libya, providing post-strike damage assessment following the 'Eldorado Canyon' raids; including the use of airborne spares, the small detachment generated an unprecedented six aircraft missions over three days

1989

20 November
Det 4 flies its last operational mission; the USAF's SR-71 programme ends the following day, its premature retirement caused by budget cuts

1990

20 January
Last SR-71 of Det 4, 61-7967, leaves Mildenhall

Mildenhall's annual Air Fetes provided Det 4 and its 'Habus' with some of their most prominent moments in the limelight. KEY

SQUADR ST

When the Fundacja Eskadra — meaning Squadron Foundation — acquired its first example, it had been a few years since a MiG-15 last took to Polish skies. Now it has two, and there are more classic Warsaw Pact-era jets to come **WORDS:** BEN DUNNELL

ON
RENGTH

An almost ethereal air-to-air capture of the Fundacja Eskadra's Lim-2 (right) and SB Lim-2 over a patchwork of Polish fields. FILIP MODRZEJEWSKI

ABOVE: Both the founders of the Fundacja Eskadra, Mateusz Strama and Bart Maciejczyk (right), are commercial airline pilots for a living. FILIP MODRZEJEWSKI

Need a piston-engined warbird for your European airshow? Take your pick. Want a classic jet? The choice is, to put it mildly, somewhat more limited. All around, for the past decade operators have been folding and aircraft grounded, the underlying reasons myriad. In Switzerland, what was a healthy scene has all but disappeared in little more than the twinkling of an eye. Barring a few very welcome stalwarts with training and lighter combat types, the UK has witnessed a similar, if more drawn-out process. The Nordic nations aside, better news has been decidedly lacking. It's a brave move to go into vintage jets, so to find a new organisation not only doing so but actively expanding comes as a welcome tonic.

About 25 miles north-west of Warsaw, Modlin Airport is, in many respects, your typical low-cost carrier hub. A functional, modern terminal building, a decent stone's throw from the capital, a steady bustle of Boeing 737s — you know the kind of place. But how many other Ryanair bases boast a pair of privately owned MiG-15s on their patch? This is where the Fundacja Eskadra has set up shop, its Polish-built single-seat WSK-Mielec Lim-2 and two-seat SB Lim-2 now featuring prominently at Europe's major air displays, and bringing a nostalgic shape back to local skies. In an age long before the budget travel takeover, Modlin was home to the Polish Air Force's 45. Lotnicza Eskadra Doswiadczalna (45th Experimental Aviation Squadron), and specimens of both were on its strength. What's more, when the country's last Lim-5, the locally manufactured version of the MiG-17F, was retired in 1993, it happened here. The foundation is now restoring just such a machine to join its flying fleet. Even in the 21st century, Modlin and MiGs are a very suitable fit.

The story really starts in the village of Góraszka, once a centre of vintage aviation in Poland. At its grass airstrip, not far east of the capital, businessman and pilot Zbigniew Niemczycki established the Fundacja Polskie Orły (Polish Eagles Foundation) during 1997. Soon it became the country's foremost 'flying museum', as well as hosting the annual Góraszka International Air Picnic, an airshow of considerable renown.

> ***"The two-seater only needed a few days to be made airworthy"***

A Polikarpov Po-2, more correctly a Polish-produced CSS-13, and a Yak-18 started its airworthy fleet; a Messerschmitt Bf 109 G-6, recovered from a lake, was restored to static standard. But its ambitions didn't end there, and when in 2000 a Lim-2 (MiG-15bis) and SB Lim-2 (MiG-15UTI) were donated by Jerzy Lewandowski, who had exhibited them in his aviation museum at Łódz-Lublinek, plans were set in train to put them back into the air. These are the same two aircraft now based at Modlin.

Since the 1955-vintage Lim-2, serial 602, was in the best external condition, it was brought up to taxiing standard by the 2007 Góraszka show, Niemczycki duly parading it around the aerodrome. Parked outdoors, the SB Lim-2, serial 006, made a rather sorry sight with its faded paintwork. Yet it was actually in good nick, and the restoration to flight of this 1953-built machine began in earnest that same summer. The airframe, engine and systems posed so few problems that what might otherwise have been a long, demanding project concluded with a maiden flight from the Polish Air Force training base at Deblin on 26 May 2010.

For three seasons the SB Lim-2, registered SP-YNZ, was active on the display circuit. It had become the first MiG-15 to fly in Europe since the Old Flying Machine Company's similar ex-Polish two-seater more than a decade earlier. Then, though, the Fundacja Polskie Orły ceased operation. SP-YNZ was grounded at Biała Podlaska, while the future of the Lim-2 project and other aircraft — among them a second SB Lim-2 and a Lim-5 obtained from Lewandowski with airworthy restoration in mind — became uncertain. Góraszka airfield, sadly, was built on.

While airline pilot Mateusz Strama was getting into historic aviation, buying a Boeing Stearman N2S-3 in the US and bringing it to Warsaw in 2014, the idea of flying anything like a MiG was nowhere near his agenda. But having displayed the biplane trainer for a few years, he hankered after something faster. With a friend, he acquired Pratt & Whitney R-2000-engined Yak-3U *Czech Ride*, a former Reno racer, from an owner in France. This very potent steed was his entry into heavier metal. Then came a message from another airline colleague, Bartosz Maciejczyk, which took things in a whole new direction.

"One afternoon", recalls Mateusz, "Bart texted me to say a Polish MiG-15UTI was for sale and we

"Break, break... go!" The two Polish MiGs split formation. FILIP MODRZEJEWSKI

RIGHT: Passenger rides are now available in the two-seat SB Lim-2 from the foundation's Modlin base near Warsaw. FILIP MODRZEJEWSKI

could get a good deal on it. Was I in? Of course I was. We went to Biała Podlaska, where the aircraft was based. It was in an old military hangar and hadn't flown for seven years. But a good thing was that Aleksander Daniluk, the mechanic who is now working for us, had been taking care of the aircraft even though he wasn't paid to do so. Every so often he would go and do an engine run, check all the systems and keep it in good condition. When we got the aircraft in 2019, it only needed a few days of work to make it airworthy for the ferry flight from there to Mielec. That flight was done by a Polish pilot who used to fly MiGs in the military, Sławomir Hetman, and then we started extensive work on it to prepare it for the season and for Polish CAA approval."

Thus was SP-YNZ resurrected, and the Fundacja Eskadra formed. Daniluk knew the aeroplane well, having been one of the two technicians who originally returned it to flying condition. The former aviation director of the Fundacja Polskie Orły, Mate Krasztel, has also come in to volunteer on the technical side for the new operator, which took up residence at Modlin in May 2020.

"Bart was the first one of us to solo the aircraft", Mateusz Strama continues. "At that point there was no other option to receive training, so he did all the practice with the gear and flaps and the emergency drills with the aircraft on jacks. Then he did taxi runs and take-off rolls to a stop. After that, he flew it. One or two months later, I started flying it here at Modlin. Once we'd gained enough experience flying circuits and aerobatic sorties, we began attending airshows.

> ***"There are enough spares for another five or 10 aircraft"***

"Our first season was 2020, which was also when reassembly of the Lim-2 started at Góraszka. The aircraft was basically dismantled, but the engine had been overhauled, which was nice. Part of the deal for buying it was that we would have access to the hangar there, with all the parts to finish the restoration. We had two guys working on it every day, Aleksander and Rafał Stolp, except for weekends when they would come to Modlin to take care of the flying aircraft. That season we flew something like 30 hours, or 50 sorties, each.

"The next year we finally came to an agreement with the Polish CAA to do our own training. We designed a syllabus based on a military one, and we flew two-and-a-half hours each with the Polish test pilot and chief examiner, Mirosław Obrebski, including simulated engine-out approaches, aerobatics, stalls, go-arounds — all that kind of thing. It finished up with the sign-off in our logbooks that it was recognised by the Polish CAA that we were fully approved to fly this aircraft and train on it. That was a big step for us. There were no longer any issues about whether it was OK to fly or not. We received special dispensations to fly at lower altitudes

BELOW: The cockpit of the Lim-2 shows the upgrades that make the aircraft easier to operate in the modern environment, such as the GPS moving map and the digital artificial horizon — and, very prominently, the original gunsight. KEY/BEN DUNNELL

at airshows, and had another good season including events in Poland, Slovakia and the Czech Republic.

"After almost two years the Lim-2 [registered SP-MIG] was ready, but we had to move it from Góraszka to Modlin by road. It didn't fit the trailer we prepared, so we fitted transportation wheels to the fuselage, and a towbar. We towed it at night behind a car for almost 100km, through downtown Warsaw. A police patrol came to take a look, but they thought it was something to do with the military, so they let us carry on.

"On 11 June 2021, Bart did the first test flight on it. There were no issues at all. We started flying in formation and going to airshows with the two aircraft, doing quite a nice tour of Poland and other countries. One excellent invitation for the Lim-2 was to AirPower 22 [at Zeltweg, Austria], which was our first really big airshow. Initially we were supposed to go for static only, but then they decided to go for the display. Lots of people were very happy about it. In 2023 we attended Melun-Villaroche near Paris, where we flew the historic formation with the Messerschmitt Me 262 and the Sabre [Frédéric Akary's Canadair-built example]". It attended the Melun show again in September 2024.

To make life easier for these and other activities, the aircraft must be as user-friendly as possible to operate. "We are approved, as per the flight manual, to fly full IFR [under instrument flight rules conditions], and we use this on ferry flights. Of course, we try not to go into bad weather because we're very limited on fuel, and we fly for pleasure so we don't want to get into situations where we're in cloud low on fuel, or anything like that, but it gives us the capability to fly over the clouds at higher flight levels. For this kind of aircraft it gives a much better true air speed and much less fuel burn. When Bart flew from Warsaw to Melun last year he did so at flight level 280 [28,000ft], IFR, with just one stop in Germany for fuel. You can get speeds of up to 800km/h ground speed. We could go even faster, but that's a good 'sweet spot' between economy and speed.

"We have modern avionics — basically a Garmin moving map, transponder and PFDs [primary flight displays] — to be able to fly legally in European airspace both VFR [under visual flight rules] and IFR. Usually we fly to big airports,

Before its paint was fully stripped, the Lim-5 still sported the North Vietnamese camouflage first applied by the Old Flying Machine Company in the 1990s. KEY/BEN DUNNELL

SWEET SEVENTEEN

In being bought by the Fundacja Eskadra, there's a definite sense of Lim-5 serial 1211 having come home. Now under restoration in the organisation's facility at Modlin, the fighter had become well-known in Britain as it led a peripatetic existence, even without flying. Prior to that, it rolled off the WSK-Mielec line in 1958 as one of more than 250 units of this MiG-17F derivative to serve with the Polish Air Force. Others went to Bulgaria, East Germany and Indonesia.

During the summer of 1995, as the late Ray and Mark Hanna's Old Flying Machine Company branched out ever further into jet warbirds, serial 1211 arrived by road at Duxford. It was put into North Vietnamese markings and registered G-BWUF, but the Lim-5 was never destined to fly in Britain. Acquired in 2002 by David Miles, it took up the new identity G-MIGG and was loaned to the Bournemouth Aviation Museum before moving to North Weald. There it attracted the attention of its now owners, who wanted a MiG-17.

"We found a Chinese-built one [a Shenyang J-5] in the US", recalls Mateusz Strama, "but it was really complicated to bring it here. There was also one in Poland that was in pretty good condition, and we negotiated to buy it, but then we found out that 1211 was available. It was a quick decision. Within a few days we went to North Weald with our mechanic, did some checks and agreed a purchase with the owner. It only took two or three weeks before the aircraft was here at Modlin.

"The aircraft is in very good condition. Its last flight was in, I think, 1991, and the engine had something like 15 hours on it since overhaul. For most of the time in the UK it was hangared, so there's no corrosion on it. The rubber hoses were replaced about 10 years ago, when the aircraft did some engine runs — including afterburner tests — at North Weald. Even the hydraulic fluid, the oil in the engine and the fuel in the tank were still nice and clean, and because they preserved the engine with all the fluids in, it was really good for the systems.

"Of course we are going to remove the tail, replace all the hoses, overhaul the engine, give it an updated cockpit and everything else. But it's still good it's not an aircraft that was sitting outside for 30 years as a monument. It was being prepared for flight and kept in a hangar.

"We have all the tooling and all the parts to make it happen. We've been collecting parts [...] and, actually, things like the generator, the pumps and the hydraulic accumulator are the same as in the MiG-15. It needs special jigs to remove and lift the wings, some specific tooling to remove the hoses and their connections from the fuselage, and transportation gear to be attached so we can move the fuselage around when the wing is removed. We'll do NDT [non-destructive testing] inspections on all the important components."

The Polish CAA has created a group to supervise the restoration. "They know which parts we have, what the facility is like, what the experience of the mechanics is... We have to report to them, and they will come and visit every so often to check on progress. If we use parts from external sources, who produced them, who overhauled them? We have to present proper certificates. At the end of the process they will be present at the final tests of the engine, of the controls, of all the systems. Then we'll do the test flights under their approval. When everything is ready, they will issue the final certificate."

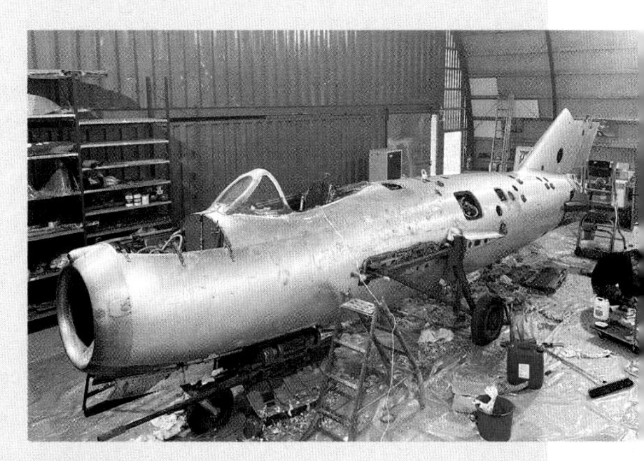
In the Modlin hangar, Lim-5 1211 sits on its transportation gear, which enables the fuselage to be moved around while the wing — and thus the regular mainwheels — are removed. FUNDACJA ESKADRA

ABOVE: Having a two-MiG fleet, with more to follow, has catapulted the Fundacja Eskadra into the top rank of European classic jet operators. FILIP MODRZEJEWSKI

so we don't want to have any issues. Each aeroplane is equipped with two radios, so there's always a back-up, and an IFR set-up for the instruments. We can communicate with each other on the second set if we have to. And we use modern civilian batteries."

Inside the foundation's facility, there's a veritable treasure-trove of spares holdings. "We've been collecting them since we bought the first aircraft, so for five years. Lots of them have come from Polish sources, but also Albania and some other countries. Since we've had our own hangar we've been able to have a self-contained storage area, where we have at least five, 10 or 15 pieces of each component, new or overhauled — pumps, generators, valves, hydraulic accumulators, everything. There are enough spares for another five or 10 aircraft."

The question of making the operation of aeroplanes such as these financially viable is another matter entirely. Airshow revenues cannot hope to cover costs, so all avenues need exploring. Here the flexibility shown by Poland's CAA has paid dividends, for an official regulation now permits passenger rides in the two-seat SB Lim-2, and there are hopefully further opportunities to come. "Usually", Mateusz describes, "the sortie is 20 minutes airborne from Modlin, which is just enough to do some aerobatics and some low passes. If the person has a pilot's licence, they can take the controls for a while.

"We operate under the Polish experimental category, which is a national category. Those rules were basically made for this kind of aircraft, covering ex-military types or highly modified ones, and they're pretty good... This year we should receive certification as a maintenance organisation for experimental aeroplanes of the MiG family. Once we have that, we will be a continued airworthiness maintenance organisation for the type of aircraft we operate, with approved mechanics, and we will be able to train new mechanics. We are planning to extend our certification to include aerial work and to set up a training organisation, so we can offer conversion courses on the MiG-15."

Already the foundation's expertise has been called on by other type operators. When the Norwegian Air Force Historical Squadron's SB Lim-2 was flown again after its 2020-21 grounding for the COVID-19 pandemic, pilot Kenneth Aarkvisla needed to do some refresher training. Having obtained temporary Norwegian CAA approval as a type rating examiner, Bart Maciejczyk supervised Kenneth as he did his recurrency flights. More recently, Maciejczyk's training of a new pilot allowed Argentina's Museo Nacional de Aeronáutica to get its revived example, LV-X216, back into the air at Morón in March 2024 after several years of inactivity.

On one of the foundation's patches are depicted four different MiG types. Naturally the MiG-15 is among them, together with the MiG-17 to represent the latest acquisition. Also shown are a MiG-21 and a MiG-23. Do they depict future ambitions? "That's the dream", says Mateusz. "It's a natural next step for us to get a MiG-21, and with what we know of today's regulations, it should be doable to make one airworthy and fly it. We are collecting parts already, and we've made contact with some mechanics who used to work on them. Those guys have pretty recent experience because the aircraft was retired by the Polish Air Force in 2003. Of course the systems are more complex, but they are similar in the nature of how they operate [...] and it should be possible to maintain them in the civilian world without a huge group of people."

Given the approval for passenger flying, a two-seat MiG-21UM would be an obvious choice. "We need to find a nice example that we can bring here and start work on. There's one that's already on the horizon. The long-term goal would be to offer 100 per cent legal supersonic flights and to have people coming from all over the world to take them. In the experimental category here, whatever you put in the flight manual and they certify you to do, you can do. If we could prove we could fly the aircraft at Mach 1.1 — of course, for a MiG-21 that's no problem — and they approve it, we could go and do it."

And what about the MiG-23? "Bart's father used to work on them in the Polish Air Force as an engineer at Słupsk-Redzikowo", Mateusz notes. "For Bart, ever since childhood, it's been a dream aircraft to fly. It's probably not easy to get one in good condition — probably we'd have to buy one in the States for lots and lots of dollars, and now, after the accident [at Thunder over Michigan in 2023], it's even harder. It's a complex aircraft with its swing-wing system, and it's huge, so I don't think one would fit in this hangar. But who knows?"

Who knows indeed. But one thing is certain: in bucking the trend of decline for classic jets, the two flying MiGs Poland has now are making a very significant contribution to Europe's aviation heritage. And that, alone, is well worth applauding. A

For contact details through which to book the Polish MiGs for airshows, visit fundacjaeskadra.pl

BELOW: The single-seat Lim-2 giving an excellent solo display during the Air Legend show at Melun-Villaroche in September 2023. Since the images with this article were taken, this aircraft has received red lightning flash markings on the fuselage sides.
BEN DUNNELL

"SIMPLY THE GREATEST"

That's how one of the pilots who flew Concorde G-BBDG describes this production test example of the supersonic airliner, 50 years on from its maiden flight **WORDS:** ALAN SMITH

Wednesday 13 February 1974 saw Britain's third Concorde, G-BBDG, slip unheralded into RAF Fairford at the end of its maiden flight from Filton, during which it had flown supersonic at Mach 1.3 in a quick dash down the Bristol Channel — proof indeed of confident progress. Almost unnoticed on a dull, cloudy day, it took its place alongside prototypes G-AXDN and G-BSST to complete the flight test programme that had been running for five years and was to see Concorde safely into airline service. In France, at Toulouse, three other prototypes were busy with their own areas of test responsibility. Concorde was the most tested civil aircraft of all time.

In fact 'DG's arrival was not quite unseen, as I was one of a small group of British Aircraft Corporation personnel who witnessed the event, accompanied in formation by Canberra WH793. Like everyone

watching I was immediately struck by the looks of the aircraft, the extra length of the production fuselage fining out the lines and making it, for me, simply the most beautiful aeroplane ever. I was privileged to fly her many times over the next four years, but as a relatively junior test pilot I had to wait my turn. We all had to: she was rightly in the hands of the engineers and flight test teams that would smooth her way through the programme to come.

My opportunity eventually came, and it was well worth the wait when John Cochrane and I flew 'DG from Fairford to abeam the Canaries and back on 17 July. My logbook entry records how we reached Mach 2.12 and flight level 570 during the three-hour 35-minute sortie, after which I noted, "simply the greatest". It was, without doubt it was, and a glimpse of things to come. I did not know then that I was destined over the next four years to fly eight of the 10 British Concordes, and some 130 hours on 'DG. Once I even flew 'DG three times in one day — heady stuff.

As a production-standard aircraft, 'DG was involved primarily in finalising development work to culminate in the granting of the all-important certificate of airworthiness. For my part, the most interesting flying I shared involved engine intake trials. In the main they took place from Casablanca and involved occasional fortnight-long detachments there, flying south to find the cold upper air that exists near the equator. On a typical flight we would head out to sea and be supersonic in about nine minutes from lift-off. Our route took us south, tracking between the Canary Islands and the African coast, levelling off the climb at 50,000ft and cruising at Mach 2.0.

The flight test would then involve the flight engineer taking manual control of the engine intake ramps and progressively inching them open until the engine surged. That point was noted and recorded by test engineers at their station in the cabin and the exercise repeated as the flight conditions changed, such as height, speed, air temperature, aircraft weight and so on. Eventually these points of a surge line were computed and used in the digital automatic control of the ramps.

"Concorde in the clear-blue upper air was visually magnificent"

An engine surge, although not pleasant, is really no big deal. However, when the aircraft yaws through loss of thrust, a sympathetic surge could be set off in the engine which shares the nacelle, and that was more noticeable. Now, if it wasn't your day and all four engines joined in, you had a truly focusing incident. I would be less than honest if I failed to confess it was rather frightening, if happily uncommon. Although we had no engines damaged, our French colleagues had a different experience when ramps were destroyed and an engine significantly harmed on one of their test flights.

Normally we would end our southerly track at about 14° north of the equator and then turn about on our return to Casablanca. The cold upper air we sought was certainly achieved; I personally saw -83°C and +118°C skin temperatures, all this in shirtsleeves. Caviar and champagne were quite absent on these flights, and in all my years testing the aircraft not a single in-flight cup ever passed my lips. The automatic operation of ramps that slowed down the intake air to below supersonic speed, while the aircraft was flying at or above Mach 2.0, was without doubt one of the great success stories of Concorde.

A truly memorable occurrence for me with 'DG was funnily enough not flying her, but being alongside in our Canberra, WH793, at some 30,000ft and Mach 0.75. I converted onto the Canberra at Boscombe Down in December 1973, the same month as my first flight in Concorde G-BSST. It was an unforgettable, awesome trip, Concorde in the clear-blue upper air being visually and audibly magnificent. With four

OPPOSITE PAGE: Concorde G-BBDG, built with constructor's number 202, powers into the air from Filton for its maiden flight on 13 February 1974. BAE SYSTEMS

BELOW: On the ground in Kuwait City, where high-temperature measured performance take-offs were carried out during 1974. KEY COLLECTION

RIGHT: The arrival of 'DG at Fairford, accompanied by Canberra PR7 WH793 in the overhead. ALAN SMITH

Olympus engines screaming at you and the delta wing drawing you into contact if you weren't very careful, concentration was imperative.

Incredibly, this high-tech and costly exercise was carried out simply to film the used water from the galley sink draining away and clearing any sensitive external areas on the aircraft. Sitting alongside me and filming all of this with a cine camera was Dick Storey, friend and flight test engineer. I had my camera with me and took my own photograph, showing the blackboard paint on the underside of 'DG to highlight the draining fluid.

Some testing was, of course, rather mundane — if you can call a Concorde flight by that name. Frankly, it never felt like that to my colleagues and I, who lived, breathed and coveted all the time we were lucky enough to experience, share and enjoy. I refer to cruise performance flights, air conditioning checks, long-range radio tests and the like. I remember two of our young lady secretaries when taken on a cruise performance test, their first flight ever, enjoying a quiet snooze. That speaks for the normality of the aircraft, I suppose, and all the time at Mach 2.0. I can hear Sir George Edwards perhaps saying, "Yes, that was the hard bit!"

> ***"I was given for the first time some personal training on the aircraft"***

Amazingly — well, I thought so — in June 1975, some two years after flying Concorde G-BSST, I was given for the first time some personal training on the aircraft, in 'DG. In the industry, you are just a bum on a seat sometimes. Over five flights, day and night, plus some tests on the new training simulator at Filton, I flew all that was necessary to have the aircraft listed on my airline transport pilot's licence. In the event, that was denied me, which hurt deeply. There was apparently some chance I might be included in the forthcoming route-proving trials alongside British Airways crews. Eventually I wasn't required, and they were flown by our more senior test pilots. But I was still needed to train BA's first course on the new simulator, and that was a challenge. One of my trainees was the delightful and very able Christopher Orlebar. A particular reward for me a short time later was to command G-BOAC on its delivery flight to Heathrow for those trials and have my wife sitting on the jump seat behind me, an ego trip if there ever was one.

With the introduction of Concorde into British Airways

RIGHT: A unique look for a Concorde, as 'DG conducts water drain trials with blackboard paint applied to its underside as a means of showing where the fluid went. ALAN SMITH

Otherwise liveried in the standard British Airways 'Negus' scheme despite not being owned by the carrier at this stage, 'DG also sported black-and-white flight test photographic calibration markings on the fuselage sides.
NATIONAL ARCHIVES AND RECORDS ADMINISTRATION

RIGHT: Parked outside Filton's enormous Brabazon Hangar, in which 'DG spent its early months in flyable storage. This rather anonymous scheme with 'Aérospatiale/British Aerospace' titles was the one in which the machine finished its test career. PETER R. MARCH

service, the Fairford flight test centre closed in 1976 and 'DG was flown to Filton to await its fate. However, new tasks were found for her with possible improvements to the engine intake, and I was lucky to be included in another detachment to Casablanca in 1978. By this time we were down from 11 test pilots to four. These tests resulted in the modification of the intake with a thin lip that gave a decided performance improvement, readily adopted by the airlines. On that detachment Brian Trubshaw and I flew at Mach 2.21 and 62,000ft, the second fastest Concorde flight ever. The accolade of the fastest, Mach 2.23, rests with G-AXDN under John Cochrane's command in March 1974.

My involvement with 'DG — indeed, with flying Concorde — ended after those flights. Later in 1978 I reverted to my role as senior training pilot at BAe, mainly on the BAC One-Eleven. However, as an instrument rating examiner I was able to maintain some degree of credibility as I checked the continuing instrument flying ability of some of my Concorde pilot colleagues, using the Concorde training simulator.

In some ways, rather like her arrival in 1974, 'DG slipped quietly into retirement at Filton on Christmas Eve 1981, with Peter Baker in command for her very last flight. I was the only person standing by the end of the runway to witness and photograph this rather emotional and signal event.

BELOW: Brooklands' most popular museum-piece basks in the sunshine. ALAMY

LEFT: **Emerging from its purpose-built hangar, which was not tall enough to accommodate the aircraft with its vertical tail attached.** PETER R. MARCH

With no further test work envisaged, the aircraft was parked almost out of sight, a rather forgotten, sad figure. Later its appearance was not enhanced when it was cocooned in a balloon-type fabric cover to fend off corrosion. But a new life turned up when she was bought in April 1984 by BA for spares and, during 1988, eased into a new, custom-made hangar, apparently never to be seen whole again. It could not be returned to flight and used for fare-paying passengers, because in certain areas the airframe wasn't quite suitable. This stymied an idea on BA's part of making the aeroplane airworthy again in the 1990s, to provide extra redundancy within its Concorde fleet when the other examples underwent maintenance. But it did play a useful role in the aftermath of the '9/11' attacks, being the subject of tests on the newly strengthened cockpit doors both BA and Air France were forced to introduce.

To my delight, 'DG eventually found a new home at the Brooklands Museum. She was disassembled and trundled down the M4 on suitable trailers in May-June 2004. Living close to the motorway, I witnessed her on the journey with mixed emotions, tempered by a real sense of joy that she was going home. A few days later, a few colleagues and I celebrated her arrival at Brooklands with a bottle of bubbly generously dispensed by the museum director Allan Winn. It was a more than just resting place, for a lot of Concorde structure had been manufactured there, and she could be preserved, loved and enjoyed for many generations.

The word 'enjoyed' needs qualification, really, because 'DG is now used for a wide variety of events, from a simple visit to a wedding with champagne, cream teas et al. Not everyone's cup of tea, you might think — I know some purists object to the 'media event' interior and would prefer a flight test scenario that reflected her original purpose. I suppose I am of that ilk, but fully recognise that commercial success will prolong her future for years to come, thereby enabling many people to admire and enjoy her elegance. Indeed, I here acknowledge that she was the finest and most beautiful aircraft of the 75 types I piloted in my flying career of 50 years. A

LEFT: **Once at Brooklands, it took a couple of years to undertake restoration and preparation for display. This was the scene in November 2005.** KEY/KEN ELLIS

THE 'BUCC' STOPS HERE

"It was a big beast of a British design", says former RAF Buccaneer S2B pilot Ned Cullen, 30 years after the mighty maritime strike jet was retired. And did it go out in style... **WORDS:** BEN DUNNELL

Buccaneer S2Bs of Nos 12 and 208 Squadrons airborne near Lossiemouth in September 1993. Two of the jets are among those repainted in grey towards the end of the type's life. KEY/DUNCAN CUBITT

For an aircraft the RAF hadn't originally wanted, it wasn't a bad way to bow out. In fact, it was as probably fond a farewell as the service has ever seen. The conclusion of Buccaneer operations brought with it a spectacular celebration, many memories, and more than a sprinkling of sadness at a great aeroplane going arguably before its time. At least it didn't happen with a whimper. No 208 Squadron's disbandment event at Lossiemouth towards the end of March 1994 gave the 'Bucc' the send-off it deserved, and then some.

The axe had been wielded several years before. Just before the House of Commons rose for its summer recess in July 1990, Secretary of State for Defence Tom King bore bad news. Behind the bland corporate title of the Thatcher government's 'Options for Change' defence review lay a series of swingeing cuts, from which the British military, some might argue, has never recovered. With the end of the Warsaw Pact threat, it contended, force structures and manpower could be substantially reduced. To say it was based on an optimistic assessment of the post-Cold War 'peace dividend' is to be wildly generous. Among King's announcements, he said, "We see the Buccaneer force in the anti-ship role being replaced by dual-capable Tornados redeployed from Germany and re-equipped with Sea Eagle missiles."

There was an irony in the events which began to unfold barely a week later. Iraq's invasion of Kuwait

ABOVE: XX885 still sported its *Sky Pirates* nose art in honour of the force's part in the 1991 Gulf conflict. CROWN COPYRIGHT

precipitated decades of coalition military involvement in the Middle East, and consigned belief in a 'peace dividend' to history. And as the RAF went to war in the Gulf during January 1991, the Buccaneer, its days numbered, found itself on the front line. Deployed at short notice to Muharraq, Bahrain, an initial six aircraft, soon increased to 12, flew 212 sorties without loss. Their crews from Nos 12 and 208 Squadrons, and No 237 Operational Conversion Unit, both laser-designated targets for Tornado GR1s using their Westinghouse AN/ASQ-153 Pave Spike pods and performed precision strike missions of their own with Paveway II laser-guided bombs. Using tactics honed over water at low level, but adapted to medium level over land, the contribution of the 'Buccs' was an outstanding success.

But the inevitable could not be staved off. The fleet started to be drawn down, and the disbandment of No 237 OCU on 1 October 1991 heralded what was to follow. Instead, crew conversion was to be conducted by a Buccaneer Training Flight within No 208 Squadron, not that there would be many neophytes to come. The last incoming officer commanding of a Buccaneer unit, 208's new 'boss' Nigel Huckins, was one. A little later, Ned Cullen had the honour of being the last first-tourist to transition to the type.

"I had been holding at Chivenor for the Tornado GR1 when this 'Bucc' slot came up", says Ned. "After speaking to a couple of 'Bucc' mates and stuff, I thought I'd go for it". That was in the summer of 1992, and he arrived on the training flight that October. "I had excellent instructors", he recalls, "and I would say I took to it fairly easily, although it was a pig in the circuit". Given the aircraft's impending retirement, Ned's was to be a short tour with 208, as he was made combat-ready on 12 March 1993. But it was to encompass some splendid experiences.

Underpinning those closing months was the need to remain operationally capable. "The basis of it was six-ship anti-shipping strike with BAe Sea Eagle missiles", says Nigel Huckins. "That was our bread and butter. It required that we deliver 24 missiles from two different directions, all arriving over the target ship at the same time. On exercises we'd have a Nimrod [or a P-3 Orion from another NATO country] to cue us, because the Sea Eagle had a range of about 60 miles and, obviously, you wouldn't be able to pick a target up on your own radar at that range — not at low level, anyway. A Nimrod up high somewhere would feed us the details, and the navs had to work out the geometry, taking the wind into account, to get the missiles to arrive 90° apart all at once. Our other maritime attack was to toss Paveways in from about three-and-a-half to four miles away, using the Pave Spike designator."

But there were more strings to the Buccaneer's bow. For Nigel, part of the role harked back to his days on the Jaguar with RAF Germany, as 'Bucc' crews still needed to do weapons system training for the nuclear strike role. If necessary, the force would have used some of the RAF's remaining stock of WE177s, and this carried on being the case until disbandment. "It was very much a 'back of the pocket' capability", Nigel comments. "We did no training for it, apart from the run-up for WST."

That was not the case with 'buddy-buddy' air-to-air refuelling, despite the gradually deteriorating

RIGHT: An old No 208 Squadron tradition revisited for one last time: over the pyramids on 19 July 1993. CROWN COPYRIGHT

serviceability of the fleet's ageing Flight Refuelling Mk20 pods, which were mounted on the starboard inboard pylon. As ex-No 208 Squadron pilot Neil Benson remembers, "You didn't learn it on the conversion unit; you learned it on the squadron. Some of the navs were designated as air-to-air refuelling instructors [...] and they could tell when things weren't quite right. If you were approaching it too fast, if you were in completely the wrong position, then they could say, 'Back off a bit', or whatever.

"Tanking speed was 280kt, which in a Buccaneer was as slow as you wanted to go without putting any flap down. The Speys were quite powerful, so to fly along at 280kt the throttles were quite far back. If you were slowly bringing the throttles back, they would get to a point where they would suddenly wind all the way back, and spool down. At 280kt you were right on the verge of that.

"The Buccaneer was quite difficult to tank off at times. It was fairly stable, but at night it was very difficult because you didn't have any reference to give yourself a horizon. If you tanked off a VC10 or a Victor at night, you could see the wings and you could see the lights on the extremities of it. You'd got some perspective of that aircraft's angle of bank, or if it was straight and level. With the Buccaneer you didn't. All you had if you were doing it tactically were some very dim red, amber and green lights on the hose-drum unit.

A graphic illustration of the challenge was given to Nigel Huckins when, as he puts it, "I did some night aerobatics. It was in the middle of my tour — I'd just qualified in night tanking, and we were doing a three-ship on a typical night profile, which was 'hi-lo', going high and letting down low. It was great. Close formation, at night, in cloud, no goggles, just on the nav lights. Let down, climb back up, and a quick 'prod' off the tanker.

> *"The next thing, we were spinning at night"*

"We [Huckins and navigator 'JJ' Parsons] were just coming up the Moray Firth and the tanker pilot said, 'I've got to turn 20°'. We were in a bank, and there were stars above and lights below. I got totally disorientated and shut the throttles to back out of the tanker, but I obviously had a bit of left drift on when we hit the jet wash. The next thing we knew, we'd flipped 270°, so we were spinning at night. I think it started off at about 16-17,000ft, and we got down to 10 or so before it came out. Looking out, the

ABOVE: Sqn Ldr Rick Phillips, one of the most experienced Buccaneer hands, leads the Queen's Birthday Flypast 16-ship. BAE SYSTEMS

Manston on 10 June 1993, and 'Buccs' as far as the eye can see. DENIS J. CALVERT

RIGHT: Out of Gibraltar in XV352 on 23 February 1994, Fg Off Ned Cullen and Flt Lt 'JJ' Parsons perform a MACEX (Maritime Co-ordination Exercise) with HMS *Liverpool* in the Mediterranean Sea. VIA NED CULLEN

Lossiemouth runway lights were about 12 miles away, so we did the longest straight-in approach without touching the controls, landed, shut it down and went to the bar. The next morning I told the station commander about it, and I had to requalify at night tanking.

"That was one of the three exciting things that happened to me during my tour. I had a crow fly down my intake on take-off when I had four 1,000lb bombs on board. By the time I aborted, it had managed to weld the wheels, and it took them a day to get it off the runway. Then one night we landed with normal aerodynamic braking, put the nosewheel down and tapped the brakes to check they were working. The right brake went on full, the left brake not at all and we swerved off the runway. We were the last one to land, and in the RAF when you were the last one to land while night-flying the visual controller in the tower was already half-way down the stairs... All of a sudden we saw the lights come back on: '28, are you all right?' 'No, we appear to have left the runway and are on the grass. Could you send a tow, please?' They never found out why it happened."

With the number of NATO exercises, training deployments and display commitments, it was rare for the entire Buccaneer force to be together for long during its final full year. The early months of 1993 alone saw Exercise 'Triplex', bombing targets at the Wiley Sike range in Cumbria in the face of Tornado F3 opposition, followed by a Joint Maritime Course, Exercise 'Northern Banner' and Tactical Leadership Training at St Mawgan. There was a trip to Norway for 208, practising short-range Paveway tactics against fast patrol boats, and an armament practice camp to Decimomannu, Sardinia, which took in air combat manoeuvring with Italian Air Force F-104 Starfighters as the opposition.

All of this ran up to the Queen's Birthday Flypast, and a special Buccaneer salute by both squadrons. They were designated to supply a 16-ship as the lead element, the last time such a large 'Bucc' formation could be mounted. No fewer than 20 jets detached to Manston in pretty much a whole-force effort, and on the day itself Rick Phillips duly led the diamond 16 over Buckingham Palace. Poor weather prevented their planned overflight of Coningsby's open day, but the primary duty had been carried out.

"There was great camaraderie on the outfit", says Neil Benson, "cemented by the role. The maritime strike/attack role wasn't well-understood on the outside — the

BELOW: A full suite of Buccaneer weaponry, including Sea Eagle anti-shipping missiles, GBU-12 Paveway II laser-guided bombs, the AS37 Martel anti-radiation missile and the AIM-9L Sidewinder air-to-air missile. KEY/DUNCAN CUBITT

ABOVE: A veteran of 12 Gulf War missions, XV352 storms over the Tain range on the Dornoch Firth, crewed by Flt Lts Dick Catterall and Mark Rodden. ANDREW BROOKS/ AVCOLLECT.COM

dedicated role was coming to an end now the Cold War was over. There was a lot of pride in the aeroplane. We knew it was old, but its capability was excellent, and we kept it to a really high standard right the way to the end. For me, that was the most important thing. There was no let-up of standards whatsoever."

That much was evidenced by some of 1993's subsequent activity. In what was now a rarity, provision of four AIM-9G Sidewinder missiles allowed 208 to make a successful deployment to Valley for live firing. Trials work saw an evaluation of the Sea Eagle's electronic counter-countermeasures and the Blue Parrot radar's ability to detect a Tornado. It was during the late 1980s that Ferranti's Blue Parrot was upgraded for the over-water role in conjunction with the Sea Eagle, while the Sky Guardian 200 digital radar warning receiver, FIN 1063 inertial navigation system — which, as Neil Benson describes, "could 'talk' to the Sea Eagle, so we could select and pre-program it as to where in a group of ships we wanted it to attack" — and ASR889 radio were added. Back then, the Buccaneer was slated to carry on until the new century. But even if that didn't happen, as an early-1990s maritime strike platform, it had very few equals.

"It was still a great jet at its role and had extremely long legs", remarks Ned Cullen. "You could go along all day at 540kt, at which a lot of other jets would run out of fuel, and it was superb at low level, very stable at 100ft over the sea". Neil Benson elaborates: "The radar warning receiver had a direct audio feed, so we could hear the audio signal before the processor in the display could work out what it was. That could be an advantage. You would hear a tinkling, like breaking glass. If you were on an exercise and you knew that, say, F-16s were against you, as soon as you heard this sound we would power up to at least 550-580kt, widen and split. We'd then get the signal on the receiver and it would come up 'F-16'.

"It was still a great jet at its role and had extremely long legs"

"Even if it was an F-16, a Tornado F3 or whatever, because we'd got the power up we could out-run them and disappear off. Yes, a Tornado F3 was very fast at low level, but it couldn't catch us because they'd run out of fuel. Exactly the same with an F-16. Some people might think they were faster and could just catch you and shoot you down, but not if we saw them first. The ability to sustain up to 580kt at low level without excessive fuel burn was an absolute godsend in the Buccaneer, tactically."

July 1993 was dominated by the last regular deployment to Akrotiri, Cyprus, to maintain night currency due to the lack of darkness hours at Lossiemouth. "We spent a month out there with both 12 and 208", Nigel Huckins remembers. "One squadron flew the aeroplanes out there; we swapped over after two weeks, and after another two weeks the other brought them back. There are many historical pictures of 208 flying past the pyramids, and while we were on our Cyprus detachment we managed to do that as well, with an RAF photographer, Rick Brewell.

"We negotiated through the embassy and the air attaché, and got permission, but as soon as we appeared in the Egyptian FIR [flight information region] they said, 'Who, what, why?' They had a route which went way down south of Cairo, through the desert, and it was a very murky, sand-blown day. All of a sudden I looked out and flashing past beneath us — bloody hell, it was an SA-3 [surface-to-air missile] site! They eventually said we could do an approach into Cairo International Airport, so I led a five-ship, four plus the photo-chase, on a formation ILS. It was the last time 208 flew past the pyramids."

But nobody could escape the fact that, as Nigel says, "There were some challenges, because the aeroplane was getting very old". Taking part in September 1993's Exercise 'Solid Stance', XV867 of No 208 Squadron made what turned out to be its last flight. "'Skids' Harrison's

THE BUCCANEER'S FINAL SHOWS

Neil Benson had arrived on No 237 OCU for training in April 1990, and was assigned to No 208 Squadron that October. He'd been a first-tourist qualified flying instructor on the Jet Provost, so the Buccaneer — to which he'd asked to be posted — was his second tour. "Normally a QFI joining a squadron on a second tour would become a squadron QFI", he says, "but as 208 was a very experienced outfit going towards the end of the life of the aeroplane, it already had a full cadre of QFIs. That was a little disappointing, but I understood why. So, to be chosen for the display was fantastic. I had to do a check-out with the station commander, John Ford, in a Hunter, so he could give me the thumbs-up. That all went very well. I was crewed with Gary Davies as my navigator, a pretty experienced Buccaneer chap.

"We started rehearsing at about 5,000ft, as all display pilots do, and worked through and brought it down eventually to 500ft for the aerobatic manoeuvres and 100ft for the passes. The sequence was fixed — No 18 Group, in my experience, was a bit of a risk-averse crowd. We were told, 'This is your display sequence, this is what you do'. It went all the way through to our approval by the AOC, which was at Kinloss in May 1993.

"The Buccaneer's not really an aerobatic aeroplane. It wasn't cleared for any looping manoeuvres, because once you got the nose down it was very easy to have trouble getting it back up. You couldn't sustain any negative g with it, so we couldn't turn it upside-down and leave it upside-down. And, like the Lightning, it suffered from roll-yaw coupling, so when you completed a snap aileron roll, because of the inertia and where the mass is in the aeroplane you got a tremendous amount of yaw. If you did more than one 360° roll, there was a high risk that you could enter a spin and depart the aeroplane, which would have been fatal at low level.

"But it was very fast and very stable at low level, so that's how we arrived — officially at 550kt and 100ft, although we pushed it up to 580, which was still legal. The massive split airbrake was unique, so to go from 580kt on arrival and then do a low and slow pass, that airbrake was out all the time. It really did slow us down markedly, so the next pass was with everything down: the gear, the flaps, the hook, the aileron droop, the tailplane flaps.

"The first display for us was, very fittingly, at Brough [the old Blackburn factory airfield] on 22 May. We based ourselves at Waddington to fly it. Chimneys, factories, you name it — it wasn't like an open airfield site or anything like that. As a debut, absolutely tremendous. I know for a fact we set all the car alarms off when we arrived, which caused chaos. That was our baptism of fire.

One of No 208 Squadron's 1993 show commitments was the Great Warbirds Air Display at Wroughton, on which weekend No 12 Squadron had obviously laid claim to the photo-reconnaissance flash crate they shared between them to fill the bomb bay for displays. ALAMY

"Our next one, the day after, was a bit unusual. It was at Eglinton in Derry, Londonderry as it was then. That had required a whole host of approvals, and they weren't going to let us do it. Eventually they decided we could do it, but we couldn't land there — and we had to carry a pre-programmed flare pack, because at the time there was an IRA threat, and some intelligence that the Stinger surface-to-air missile may have found its way into IRA hands."

Then came the year's first really big occasion, Air Fete '93 at Mildenhall. Accelerating, following a barrel roll, back towards the crowd and turning onto the display line in a vicious strong on-crowd crosswind brought a focusing moment. "I probably pulled a little bit too hard trying to line up. Flying the display, you did used to take it very carefully beyond the ideal angle of attack" — which would have been met by a change in the beep tone emitted by the Buccaneer's audible AoA indicator — "but doing it on this occasion I got into wing rock. That was a signal to back off a bit."

208's display crew for 1993: navigator Flt Lt Gary Davies (left) and pilot Flt Lt Neil Benson. VIA NEIL BENSON

As with many RAF aircraft back then, more than one display crew was allocated. In the case of the Buccaneer, that meant No 12 Squadron also maintained an airshow commitment, with the late Flt Lt Glenn Mason and his navigator Flt Lt Ian Donnelly. They ended up flying the last ever public Buccaneer display, at Cranfield's Dreamflight Airshow on 19 September. It wasn't supposed to have been that way, though. Benson and Davies were meant to perform the following Sunday at Bierset in Belgium, as part of a show bidding farewell to the Belgian Air Force's Mirage Vs, but the airbrake incident back at Lossiemouth mentioned in the main article caused a precautionary grounding.

Instead, their season had ended with the closing slot of the Leuchars Battle of Britain 'At Home' Day. "As a kid, I always wanted to be a pilot in the air force. My dad was a very good golfer, and used to golf at St Andrews a lot. I'd go up and stay there. In the evenings, we'd sit at the end of the runway at Leuchars, hoping a couple of Lightnings would scramble on QRA. We always went to the Battle of Britain days, so to do my final display there was very fitting for me."

ABOVE: **How splendid XX894 looked in the 809 Naval Air Squadron colours applied for the retirement do. This was the only one to feature the bomb bay door fuel tank, which gave an extra 450 gallons of JP4. Navy Buccaneers didn't carry it because it would have increased all-up weight beyond what was compatible with operation from British carriers.**
DENIS J. CALVERT

undercarriage lowered while we were many miles off the coast of Ireland, off to attack the American cruiser USS *Ticonderoga*. It was really stormy weather, and we were flying as a three-ship. He was doing about 480kt at the time, and of course it ripped the doors off and punctured his fuel tanks, so he lost a whole load of fuel. One of his undercarriage legs was stuck down, the other was up. Eventually we flew to Leeming, because everywhere in Scotland had an amber weather state. It all collapsed when he got there."

No 12 Squadron disbanded as a Buccaneer unit on 1 October 1993. As a Tornado GR1-equipped squadron, it immediately re-formed at Marham, taking over aircraft and personnel from No 27 Squadron straight after its own disbandment. 208 took on some of 12's Buccaneer crews, and entered its final phase. It was not without incident.

LEFT: **A proud moment for Ned Cullen at the disbandment festivities: meeting Roy Boot, the Buccaneer's chief designer at Blackburn.**
VIA NED CULLEN

Returning from the 'Solid Stance' debrief in the Netherlands, an otherwise uneventful trip ended with John Fraser and Stevie Tait breaking into the Lossiemouth circuit. Their CO remembers well what followed: "As 'Fraz' taxied in, the whole airbrake was sort of hanging on the hydraulic jack". It had been a major failure, and not how Tait — who had also been the navigator when XV867 had its undercarriage problem — would have wanted to end his valedictory Buccaneer flight.

More broadly, says Nigel Huckins, "Our biggest challenge was keeping the fatigue under control. The experienced pilots could come back off a trip with virtually no counts at all. The youngsters could use a month's g in one sortie. Of course, once the airframes ran out they had to go through checks, so there was a relatively high maintenance bill, and it didn't always give us the hours we wanted. But we still had plenty of spare bits."

"The whole airbrake was sort of hanging on the hydraulic jack"

The Hunters assigned to both squadrons helped ease the burden. Long employed as 'surrogate' trainers given the lack of dual-control Buccaneers, the T7As and T8Bs enjoyed gainful employment on six-monthly pilot checks by day and night, yearly instrument ratings, and as 'bounce' aircraft for simulated visual threats. Neil Benson believes he was the last in-service RAF pilot to qualify as first pilot on the Hunter, excluding the test world.

Overseas detachments had been a constant feature, and January 1994 continued the pattern. Volkel in the Netherlands was one destination, and Gibraltar, for so long a regular 'Bucc' haunt, another. Ned Cullen, who was crewed with Russ Hall, has good reason to remember the latter. "Everyone had told me the runway was short at 'Gib'. 'You need to put her down on the numbers to avoid a watery arrival at the other end of the strip'. With all this in mind, following our RV over the Bay of Biscay with a Victor tanker, I was determined not to screw up my first landing [there]. I think I was a tad over-eager on the brakes, burst the right tyre, and after we started slowly veering off the runway I just heard Russ over the intercom shout, 'Hook, hook, hook!' as we headed into the deep storm drain that ran parallel with the right side of the runway. The CHAG [chain arrester gear] saved our bacon that day". And, he adds, "an experienced nav in the back to call for the hook."

Nigel Huckins recalls, "The Sea Eagle was a very clever missile, a sea-skimmer with a pop-up capability, and a lot of electronic countermeasures. I think we had a very real capability against capital ships. We did practise against our own — we did one on the last detachment to Gibraltar, where we worked up the anti-air capability of the Type 42 [destroyer] HMS *Liverpool* going out on the Armilla patrol in the Gulf by 'playing' Sea Eagles, simulating a launch at 40 miles and then flying as low as we were supposed to be. It was Sea

ABOVE: A classic shot of No 208 Squadron on the Tain tower roof: shown left to right are Flt Lt Steve Reeves, Flt Lt Dick Catterall, Flt Lt Gary Bremmer, Flt Lt 'Skids' Harrison, Flt Lt 'JJ' Parsons, Flt Lt Neil Devine, Flt Lt John Green, Wg Cdr Nigel Huckins, Sqn Ldr Mike Scarffe and Fg Off Andrew 'Ned' Cullen, with Flt Lt Glenn Mason and Flt Lt Gary Davies making their presence felt in XX889. ANDREW BROOKS/AVCOLLECT.COM

Dart versus Sea Eagle with the Type 42s, and I think we could challenge that pretty well.

"The day after we'd flown against *Liverpool*, we went out to the ship to watch our guys doing their work. We were climbing round, and the top of the bridge house had a Union Jack on it. When we'd flown past it we'd never seen that Union Jack. I asked how high the top of the bridge house was: 35ft. That's how low we were flying. The Buccaneer, when you got down to 20-30ft, was just like it was on a cushion. It sat there, absolutely solid, as if it was on rails."

While the likes of a final Joint Maritime Course exercise in late February showed 208 remained very much operational, all eyes were now focused on the disbandment weekend. Knowing the Buccaneer draw-down would be under his leadership, Nigel Huckins recounts, "When I'd had my interview with the AOC to become CO, I stated that my aim was to do it safely. Knowing it was a very charismatic aircraft to its crews, that was going to be a challenge". He had the idea of painting six aircraft with the insignia of each RAF Buccaneer squadron, and a seventh in overall Royal Navy colours, specifically those of 809 Naval Air Squadron. Permissions gained, it was a delightful gesture.

The scene was set for 'the mother of all parties'. Buccaneer veterans came to Lossiemouth from far and wide for the 25-26 March festivities, among them Tom Eeles, by then station commander at Linton-on-Ouse. "After recovering from the inevitable hangover on Saturday morning", he says, "we gathered over at the No 208 Squadron site. All the aircraft started up, taxied out and got airborne, joining up in a diamond nine for a few flypasts, interspersed with a solo display [by Glenn Mason and Gary Davies]. At this point I think it was suggested to AOC No 18 Group that it might be a good idea for him to go into the crew room for a coffee, a suggestion he readily agreed to. Meanwhile, outside we were treated to the most spectacular beat-up of the airfield I have ever seen. Eventually the Buccaneers re-formed as a big echelon, the AOC emerged and we witnessed them all breaking into the circuit in sequence, landing in stream and taxiing in. They parked in a line, folded their wings, then all shut down together. There wasn't a dry eye to be seen."

> ***"It was the most spectacular airfield beat-up I have ever seen"***

The flying had lived up to the occasion. "I think we did her proud", reflects Ned Cullen, who as the most junior pilot was not in the diamond nine, but was allowed to join in the 11-aircraft beat-up. What's more, he and his colleagues had lived up to Nigel Huckins' long-stated aim of being safe with it. "By and large, they were all reasonable", Nigel says. "On the final weekend, I think 'Skids' Harrison did the lowest pass I'd seen. He went through the HAS site, and you couldn't even see the top of the fin..."

Formal disbandment of No 208 Squadron took place on 31 March, though the next day it returned in its new guise as a reserve squadron flying the Hawk within No 4 Flying Training School at Valley. The Buccaneer wasn't quite done, though. Several airframes needed ferrying to new homes, and crews

With thanks to Andrew Brooks, Denis J. Calvert and the Buccaneer Aircrew Association.

stayed at Lossiemouth to do the honours. Some became battle damage repair or fire trainers, others were destined for preservation. En route to Marham, and a career as a ground instructional airframe, XV332 diverted into Cottesmore with a hydraulic leak. Dick Catterall and 'JJ' Parsons completed its journey on 12 April, which might have been the type's last RAF activity. However, there was one more to come.

Sold to the Ulster Aviation Society, XV361 was flown to Aldergrove on 5 April, Nigel Huckins at the controls. The intention was to move it by road to the society's then base at Langford Lodge, but when this was found impractical there was only one answer. Martin Hopkinson and 'JJ' Parsons travelled over to Belfast and, as they had so many times before, crewed up. But this was to be a trip with a difference. Getting airborne out of Aldergrove, they kept the undercarriage down and headed the very short distance south-west to Langford Lodge. Only 92 seconds later, they were on the ground. Thus ended the final RAF Buccaneer flight.

It had provided the very definition of sterling service, but somehow there was a feeling the 'Bucc' had been undervalued despite its qualities. "I think", opines Nigel Huckins, "when the Buccaneers came back from RAF Germany and went into No 18 Group, they became a bit of a 'Cinderella' force, as much because they were consigned to the maritime role as anything". Neil Benson concurs: "The Buccaneer was never, shall we say, a popular aircraft with the higher ranks of the air force. It was a workhorse but it was never one to be put on a pedestal. I don't know if that went back to when TSR2 was cancelled, the F-111K was cancelled, and we had to make do with a navy aeroplane."

A last-ditch idea of retaining six Buccaneers as tactical tankers was rightly rejected, but there were better ideas as to how its career could have been perpetuated. Nigel Huckins' view? "Putting a decent navigation system in it — a Tornado-type system with an updated computer. We bought some GPSs which we stuck in the cockpit, and they did help. When I flew all the way back from Berlin [after the last open day at Gatow in June 1993] my navigator Russ Hall, who died recently, went on strike because I said I wanted the GPS in the front". A 'Bucc' with the Tornado GR1's nav equipment, Ned Cullen says, "would have made a formidable jet."

Neil Benson agrees. "On the aerodynamic side, superb. On the avionics side, we could have done an awful lot better, even with basic modern avionics. Mind you, looking back, while we might have wanted a new head-up display or whatever, an experienced navigator in a Buccaneer using the Blue Parrot radar could pick up ships at a quite incredible distance. You've got to be careful what you wish for..."

Perhaps the RAF hierarchy ended up thinking the same about the Tornado GR1B, the maritime strike conversion which equipped Nos 12 and 617 Squadrons, but not for long. The Sea Eagle was retired from both the Tornado and Sea Harrier fleets in April 1999, after which Armed Forces Minister John Spellar outlined why: "the Strategic Defence Review showed that we needed less capability in the field of open ocean anti-surface ship warfare". Truth be told, that capability had been diminished the moment the Buccaneer was retired.

ABOVE:
The stack of specially marked Buccaneers in the colours of the Royal Navy and all the type's RAF operating units: from bottom to top, Nos 12, XV, 16, 208 and 216 Squadrons, and No 237 OCU.
BAE SYSTEMS

LEFT:
Not the lowest flyby at Lossiemouth on 26 March 1994, but a good effort in XX899 nonetheless.
SIMON WATSON

AEROPLANE meets DAVE MACKAY

VIRGIN GALACTIC

He fulfilled a childhood ambition by becoming Scotland's first astronaut, but this ex-Harrier pilot is just as proud of his days flying for Shuttleworth

WORDS: BEN DUNNELL

Commercial, passenger-carrying spaceflight: for a long time, notwithstanding the enthusiasm of various proponents, it remained little more than a pipedream. But then, in 2023, the once unthinkable happened. Virgin Galactic's SpaceShipTwo went into orbit with paying customers on board, heralding nothing short of a new era in aerospace. Now, thanks to its efforts, space tourism has become almost routine. Last year alone, Virgin Galactic conducted half-a-dozen such missions, taking 14 private astronauts aloft — all of them making their first spaceflights — as well as five researchers.

This is the result of almost two decades' worth of development and testing, or more if one takes SpaceShipTwo's experimental predecessor into account. And in that, Virgin Galactic called on a man steeped in more traditional aviation. Dave Mackay became its chief pilot in 2011, his expertise having been honed in the crucible of British flight-testing, Boscombe Down. He also spent many years on the UK airshow circuit in a variety of historic aeroplanes, most notably with the Shuttleworth Collection. There is no-one else who can talk with equal authority about the flying characteristics of both a 1910 Blériot XI and a spacecraft.

Dave has now made three spaceflights, earning for himself on 22 February 2019 the title of Scotland's first astronaut. With it he fulfilled a childhood ambition. He lives in New Mexico now, but his gentle Scottish accent remains. It was from the Virgin Galactic headquarters at Spaceport America, not far from Las Cruces, that Dave joined me remotely, the Jornada del Muerto desert being a touch far to travel. But soon we'd rewound to those formative years in a very different environment.

"I was born on the north coast of Scotland", says Dave, "but my father was in the police force, and when I was six years old he was moved down to a village called Helmsdale, which was a natural geographic entry point to low-flying area 14T — T meaning tactical. It's a road and

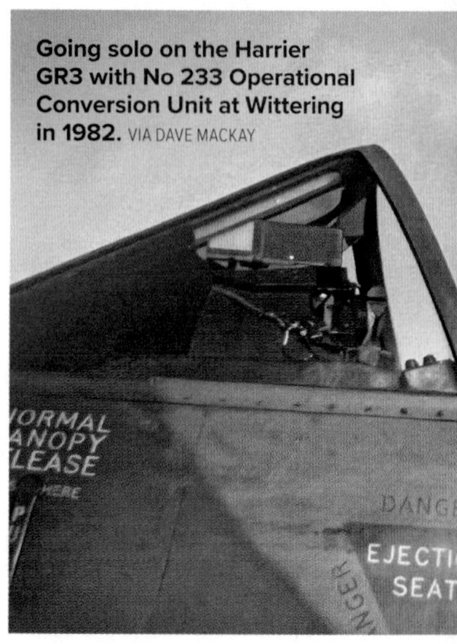

Going solo on the Harrier GR3 with No 233 Operational Conversion Unit at Wittering in 1982. VIA DAVE MACKAY

Happy days were spent as a Shuttleworth Collection pilot, here performing a practice display in the Sea Hurricane. DARREN HARBAR

Learning to fly on the Bulldog in 1977 with the Universities of Glasgow and Strathclyde Air Squadron. VIA DAVE MACKAY

ABOVE: While on No 3 Squadron in 1985, Dave took part in the regular pilot rotation to Stanley in the Falklands. VIA DAVE MACKAY

river valley on the eastern seaboard of Sutherland, and Helmsdale is a fishing village there. Just to the south is RAF Lossiemouth, or RNAS Lossiemouth as it was back in the day, and Buccaneers from there — and many other aircraft — would take off, fly across the Moray Firth and enter the low-flying area overhead Helmsdale. As a young kid, here were these military aircraft flying over our village [...] very fast, at very low altitude, making a lot of noise. I thought, 'Wow, that is amazing. How do you get to do that?' I wanted to be a pilot; my mother used to say that's all I ever talked about.

"Of course, the 1960s was also a time of the space race: Mercury, Gemini and Apollo. Apollo in particular was really well televised, even in the UK, so again I watched in real time these massive rockets, with the countdown process, going off into space. I vividly remember Apollo 8 flying around the moon, which was just incredible to think of, and of course Apollo 11 and the later explorations of the moon. Somewhere in that process I found that those astronauts were former military test pilots, so now I was thinking I could fly Buccaneers at very low level in Scotland, become a test pilot and then an astronaut, flying to the moon and then Mars, which was going to be next. This was the hugely ambitious dream I came up with.

"Many years later I read a story about [comedian] Eddie Izzard, who'd been to see his school careers advisor. They asked, 'So, what do you want to do when you grow up?' He said, 'I want to be an astronaut.' Now, Eddie Izzard is a really smart and clever person, and could well have been an astronaut if he'd wanted to. The careers advisor just laughed and said, 'Now come on, seriously, what do you want to do?' For similar sorts of reasons, I kept my ambitious plan to myself, because I didn't want to be laughed at.

"There were other, local inspirations. The Hawker test pilot Duncan Simpson came from Golspie, which is only about 17 miles down the coast. That gave me hope: it can be done. My family knew his family as well. I didn't meet Duncan for many years, but I met his brother, who was a local doctor, and his mother. I also met Duncan's uncle, Duncan Menzies, who was himself a test pilot. He was a farmer near Invergordon. They all listened to me and were very welcoming. I wrote a letter to Hawker Siddeley when I was 16 or 17, asking how you became a test pilot. Duncan Simpson replied to me, saying I should join the air force, go to test pilot's school and so on. There seemed to be a path.

"I always had an interest in mechanical things, pulling them apart, putting them together again, seeing how they worked and pretending I'd made them better. I went off to the University of Glasgow to do aeronautical engineering — I think I was realistic enough to realise I may fail at some point, and to think about what I'd do if I did fail and couldn't become a pilot. Aeronautical engineering would be a good alternative career, but it's also important for test pilots to have an engineering background, to be able to converse with other engineers and understand each other.

"University was also where I learned to fly, because I joined the University Air Squadron there. Those were some of the most enjoyable times I ever had in the air force, even though I wasn't yet in the air force! If there was ever any doubt in my mind, that's what made me think I wanted to do more of it. To be honest, I struggled to complete my degree because I was so infatuated with the flying. I did too much flying and not enough studying. But I got through, and then joined the RAF.

"I left university with just over 130 hours on the Bulldog. Included in that were aerobatics, low-flying, formation flying — all that kind of thing. That allowed me to go straight into the Jet Provost T5 at Cranwell,

RIGHT: Nineteen different types were on the agenda at EPNER, the French test pilots' school, including the Alpha Jet. VIA DAVE MACKAY

so I did officer training there and stayed for basic flying training. My first instructor was Jerry Bartlett... he was always happy with me and I was getting good marks, but he said, 'Dave, you need to be a bit more aggressive'. This was puzzling to me. If I was doing a 1g stall, how could I do that more aggressively? He'd say, 'You should go and look at so-and-so and see how he does it'. Well, he was a pretty cool, aggressive kind of guy, but later in training he washed out. Ultimately, you are who you are. That's your character. If I'd made myself more aggressive, it would have all been a pretence. But, apart from that, I thought he was a great instructor.

"When I went on to advanced flying training at Valley, the flying was much more exciting. Initially we learned to fly the Hawk, and then we got into more tactical flying at low altitude. We had nothing to drop at Valley, but they would tell us to fly over this bridge at this time. The Tactical Weapons Unit at Brawdy was where we started firing weapons and dropping practice bombs, and it was a lot of fun. The target-tug down there was 'Winston', the Meteor F8, and so we were very careful not to shoot 'Winston' down.

"All the way through flying training, when you finished each phase they gave you a form where you could put down your first, second and third choice [for an operational posting]. All the way along I put down 'Harrier, Harrier and Harrier'. I wanted to fly single-seat at low level, and the Harrier looked like an extraordinary aeroplane. At the end of TWU 'Jimbo' James, my instructor, looked at it and went, 'You can't do that'. I told him it was what I wanted to do. He said, 'You *cannot* do that. You *have* to change it'. We had this argument, and eventually I changed it. I wrote down, 'Harrier, Jaguar, Lightning'... I handed it over and stomped out of his room. I went into the crew room for about five minutes, and then went back, knocked on his door and told him, 'No, I want to change it back again'. He looked at me and said, 'Good man'.

> ***"As soon as I had the minimum hours, I applied for test-flying"***

"I was selected for Harriers, and almost simultaneously the Falklands War broke out, so there was a delay in me starting my course. Eventually I went to Wittering for Harrier training with [No 233 Operational Conversion Unit], and it was a long course, but it was everything I had ever dreamed of. Really exciting to fly, and, particularly at light weight, an amazing thrust-to-weight ratio. It was an aircraft you had to be very careful with, because it would bite if you didn't handle it properly, but I loved it.

"At the end of training I was meant to be going to No 1 Squadron, but at the last minute it was changed, and I went out to Germany with No 3 Squadron. It was tough, flying in Germany at that time. We were at Gütersloh on the North German Plain, the weather was often really bad, and in the rules we had a minimum of 5km visibility, but often it seemed to me that 5km in Germany was a lot less than it was in other parts of the world". Dave experienced some of those places, deploying as part of the regular rotation of Harrier pilots to Belize and the Falklands. But his dream of test-flying was still on the horizon.

"As soon as I had the minimum number of hours, I applied. I went for interview, and at the end of it they said they had exchange postings, sending students to America — to Patuxent River or Edwards — and to France. I thought, wow, I'd love to go to Edwards, the home of test-flying, so I said I'd be happy to do that. But I was selected for EPNER [the École du Personnel Navigant d'Essais et de Réception], the French test pilots' school at Istres. I think there were a couple of reasons they did that. I reckon a lot of people said 'no way', and didn't want to do it in France, but I actually had quite a good qualification in French from school, a Scottish Higher.

"Each pilot was teamed up with an engineer and a technician. My engineer had been to the École Polytechnique and was an exceptionally clever, very highly

ABOVE: Carrier trials of the new Sea Harrier FRS2 — later known as the FA2 — aboard HMS *Ark Royal* in 1990. ALAMY

Evaluating the Super Étendard from Landivisiau during the EPNER syllabus. VIA DAVE MACKAY

The 1990 Middle Wallop show brought a display in P-51D *Susy* from the late Charles Church's fleet. PETER R. MARCH

Another Harrier variation to sample was the Vectored-thrust Aircraft Advanced Control (VAAC) T4, then on the strength of RAE Bedford. VIA DAVE MACKAY

qualified guy. In ground school, typically the lectures were 40 minutes. I would cope with it for about 20 minutes and then start to lose it. But when we went back into our little office, I would ask this engineer and he would explain things really, really well — actually, better than a lot of the staff". During the EPNER course, Dave flew 19 different types, the Super Étendard and Mirage 2000 included.

It was as a fully-fledged test pilot that Dave returned to the UK, being posted to the Fast Jet Test Flight — of which he later became commanding officer — within what was still the Aeroplane and Armament Experimental Establishment (A&AEE) at Boscombe Down. There, he says, "I got involved mainly in new Harrier and Sea Harrier projects. That was the time when we were getting the Harrier GR5, so we had a GR5A version and the GR7, and on the Sea Harrier side there was the FRS2. I was really busy at Boscombe Down, with a lot of Harrier and Sea Harrier flying, and a lot of Buccaneer flying, the Buccaneer having been my inspiration.

"There was plenty of time up at West Freugh near Stranraer doing weapons testing, including a lot of fuse proof-testing for the navy, which was always quite extraordinary because they tested their fuses by dropping bombs. We had to do that every six months, I think it was — a great little detachment. West Freugh is on the coast, and the range was just off the coast. We used to take off and turn downwind into the range for a calibration run. If that went well, there were two more runs to drop your bombs and you were done. You could be done in 15-20 minutes. The Buccaneer carried a lot of fuel and could go a long way, so you had an hour-plus of fuel you could go and fly with.

"On one occasion I did a 'hi-lo-hi' from the south of Scotland to the north, and called my mum and dad up to say I'd be overhead at 12 o'clock, or whenever it was. I ended up flying over my village in the same way as I'd seen Buccaneers do many years before. My mother was on the doorstep waving a towel. By that time my father had retired from the police force and become a 'gillie' on the river, and when I flew up the river valley I didn't see him but I saw his car. When I called that night, he was laughing and he said he'd been helping an 80-year-old guy across the river when I flew overhead… This old boy nearly fell over, with my dad holding onto him. He said to my dad, 'What the bloody hell was that?' My father told him, 'That was my son…'

"I ended up extending at Boscombe Down a couple of times, so I finished my RAF career there. I flew the whole way through — I never did a ground tour. But I knew what was coming, because I'd been told. I just couldn't work behind a desk. I didn't want to do it, and I didn't know that I'd be good at it. So, I decided to leave the air force. It was a big step, because I'd loved it. It wasn't a great time to leave, timing-wise. There weren't many airlines recruiting, but suddenly Virgin Atlantic said they were looking for some pilots. I applied, and I got in."

With Virgin, Dave flew first the Boeing 747 'Classic', largely meaning the -200 model, and then the Airbus A340-300. That job led directly to the one he has now. But, to go back a little, it was while he was still a test pilot that warbirds entered his story. Having previously had no taildragger time at all, at EPNER Dave flew the CAP 10 a lot. He subsequently converted onto the two Harvards the A&AEE used as photo-chase platforms. So, when property developer Charles Church was looking for more pilots to fly his warbird fleet, based very close to Boscombe Down at Roundwood Farm near Micheldever, the circumstances were ideal.

"I knew some of the people involved", says Dave, "because [fellow Boscombe test pilots] Dave Southwood and Reg Hallam were both flying there. I went along to meet Charles for an interview. We sat in his beautiful home, and we actually ended up talking about fishing… Anyway, I passed the interview and started flying for him, initially in the Pilatus P2, which is a lovely aeroplane". But by the time he flew his first display, in the P2 at Barton in August 1989, Church had tragically been killed in the crash of his Spitfire V, 'EE606'. Under the leadership of chief engineer Dick Melton, the collection carried on operating, and Dave worked his way through all of it.

> ***"I called my mum and dad to say I'd be overhead at 12 o'clock"***

"The next aircraft I flew was the two-seat Spitfire IX, PT462. Reg Hallam did my check-out — he was a lovely guy. We went to Blackbushe, and he gave me an excellent brief, telling me how tricky it was to land. He was absolutely right. I ended up floating way down the runway, but it all worked out fine". Dave went on to display it at three venues on one busy weekend in June 1990 — Fleetlands, Dunsfold and Biggin Hill — and at Wittering for a No 1 Squadron reunion the following year.

In due course he added P-51D Mustang G-SUSY, HA-1112 Buchón G-HUNN and Hurricane XII G-ORGI, though he never flew the latter pair at any shows. Indeed, the Hurricane was only ever test-flown in Britain before being exported to the USA. "It didn't turn out the way we expected it", Dave recalls. "It wasn't nearly as nice as the books from World War Two would have you believe about this nice, stable platform. It had some very interesting lateral and directional control characteristics, and we were scratching our heads about it for quite a while. When we looked into it, there were multiple changes made to the back end, so there had clearly been issues with it right from the get-go.

"Those four, the Spitfire, Hurricane, 109 and P-51, were very interesting aeroplanes for me to compare. For a long time I thought the P-51 was the bee's knees, but then I came back eventually to the Spitfire. The P-51's wing is amazing up to the point where the airflow starts to break down, and you can get a very nasty wing drop with very little warning of it. As a pilot, what you want is an aircraft that talks to you, that tells you where it is while you're looking out in combat. In the P-51, that was really hard.

"The Spitfire wing talks to you, and you can feel it. As you're approaching the limit of what the wing's going to give you in terms of lift, you get into buffet, and

LEFT: A 1992 detachment to West Freugh for weapons testing on the Harrier GR7. VIA DAVE MACKAY

RIGHT: The debut public display for the Source Classic Jet Flight was the Empire Test Pilots' School 50th anniversary event at Boscombe Down in 1993, Dave flying one of the Vampire T55s led by the Venom FB50. PETER R. MARCH

the buffet gradually increases in intensity up to the point where it stalls. And when it stalls, it just mushes. It doesn't drop a wing or anything. The field of view from the Spitfire is excellent and the flight controls are very light. In the P-51, and the 109 in particular, the control forces are huge. If I was to pick any of them for 1-v-1 air-to-air combat, I would go for the Spitfire every time."

Gradually the Church fleet was sold off, but by then Plane Sailing's Paul Warren Wilson, an old acquaintance from Harrier days in Germany, had been in touch. "Out of the blue, he rang me up and asked me if I'd like to fly the Tigercat. A wonderful aeroplane, with its tiny, narrow cockpit, the two massive engines, tremendous performance and beautiful flying characteristics. Grumman did a great job with it — the controls were really well-harmonised, and it was light in roll. A few times we went from place to place as a pair with the Catalina, on which my wife was a hostess, making the tea. She landed on water in it, which I never did, and I'm still a bit jealous."

Fittingly, Dave's first Tigercat demonstrations were in Scotland, at Glasgow's 1991 World Yacht Grand Prix. The 1992 season saw him performing 16 times in the machine, appearances at some of the major historic aircraft displays — the North Weald Fighter Meet, La Ferté-Alais and the Great Warbirds Air Display at Wroughton — among them. Then it, too, was sold to the USA. But the advent of the Source Classic Jet Flight, set up by Don Wood, in 1993 saw Dave moving on to the vintage jet scene. Over the next three years he participated in mixed Vampire and Venom formations up to a six-ship, largely alongside fellow names from the test-flying community.

And it was through that world that the chance to fly for the Shuttleworth Collection arose. Once the then chief pilot, John Lewis, had given his approval, Dave began serving his Old Warden apprenticeship. "I was a little unusual in that I arrived with quite a bit of warbird type experience, but nevertheless I had to work in the tower, and push the aircraft in and out. It all proved you were willing to put the time in. I became airfield manager there for a short while as well. Flying-wise I started off in April 1995 on the Tiger Moth and Magister, and slowly worked my way through the collection. Although I love the adrenaline of flying fast and doing aerobatics in something like a Spitfire, there's also a great adrenaline rush from flying the Boxkite around the pattern and getting it back on the ground safely, because it's on the verge of its stability and control, and if you push it too far it's going to say no.

"For me, the 'Edwardians' were the most interesting aeroplanes there.

BELOW: September 1995, and Hunter FGA9 XE601 was Dave's mount for his final RAF flight. VIA DAVE MACKAY

BELOW RIGHT: The LVG C.VI was interesting, but not pleasant to fly. BEN DUNNELL

LEFT: In Plane Sailing's Tigercat, Dave leads The Fighter Collection's Hellcat and Bearcat at the 1992 Great Warbirds show, the first to be staged at Wroughton.
PETER R. MARCH

There was so much experimentation: triplanes, biplanes, monoplanes, lifting tail surfaces, foreplanes, wing-warping. People were test-flying them with very little practical experience of aviation, and nothing like the same understanding of stability and control as we like to think we have today. They were very brave individuals. Having read about that era, to sample it first-hand was fantastic.

"It was an achievement just to get the Blériot airborne, and to fly the world's oldest original aeroplane and engine combination was tremendous, but they were just straight 'hops'. But the Avro Triplane and Bristol Boxkite replicas you could really display if the conditions were right, and get a better feel for the flight envelope. The Vne [never exceed speed] on the Boxkite, for example, I think was 55kt. You knew it was 55kt because if you crept up on that, you'd get a progressive lifting force from the tail which you couldn't overcome, and you knew not to go that fast again. In both the Boxkite and the Triplane, we'd typically set a maximum 15° angle of bank. You'd get to 15° angle of bank, and you wouldn't want to go any further because it doesn't feel good.

"The Triplane has virtually no directional stability. The only directional stability it gets is from the rudder, which is under the control of your feet. There's nothing else to keep the thing pointing straight. You've got no indication of sideslip, except that the engine is sitting ahead of you and is blowing warm air back over your face, so if you've got an equal temperature on both cheeks you know you're flying pretty straight. If your left or right cheek is cold, you know you're flying with left or right sideslip. That works! It's just the sort of thing you've got to do.

"On the Boxkite, of course, you're sitting on the leading edge of the wing, so you can look straight down and see the ground, which isn't going very fast. It's got a longitudinal instability because the foreplane is pretty effective and you've got an elevator behind you, so it's very easy to end up in a rocking motion. It feels like you're in a rocking chair on your veranda, looking down, rocking gently and hardly moving.

> ***"At Shuttleworth you get such an insight into stability and control"***

"I'm always fascinated by stability and control and handling characteristics. Those are what really interest me in aviation. You get such an insight into basic stability and control and handling qualities in aircraft like that. Modern aircraft are all engineered to fly beautifully and to minimise the workload for the pilot, but in those days they were flying by the seat of their pants a lot of the time, with basic handling skills."

One of the other Shuttleworth aircraft that stands out in his memories is the LVG C.VI, still the last original German aeroplane from the 1914-18 war to have flown in Britain. Dave got to fly the RAF Museum-owned reconnaissance two-seater "quite a lot" before it was grounded in 2003. Because others were reluctant, perhaps? "Funny you should say that! I had that suspicion for quite a while. It wasn't a nice aeroplane to fly.

"One of the things that was really unsettling about it was, I believe, due to its wing not being rigid enough. If you got to high speed and put in an aileron deflection, the wing twisted in the opposite direction. So, if you wanted to roll right at high speed and you put in a right roll input, the wing twisted because of the aileron deflection, and you ended up rolling the wrong way. It was the first aircraft I ever flew — and maybe the only one I've ever flown — where I thought, 'I'm losing control of this'. I got to it on a couple of occasions in a display. Not a nice feeling. The way out of it was to power back and slow down, and it had so much drag it would slow down and recover pretty quickly."

During 2011 Dave flew his last displays at Shuttleworth, much to his regret. But the opportunity to fulfil the last element of his dream was too good to pass up. Moving to the US, and taking up the role of chief pilot with Virgin Galactic, had been a few years in the making. It originally came about through fellow Virgin Atlantic pilot Alex Tai. One day, in a chance flightdeck meeting with company founder Richard Branson, Tai suggested a location in Morocco as a potential launch site for Branson's planned round-the-world hot-air balloon flight — the eventually abortive Virgin Global Challenger. That precipitated

ABOVE: A spirited performance in the Shuttleworth Sopwith Pup.
DARREN HARBAR

a deeper involvement with Steve Fossett's Virgin-sponsored, Scaled Composites-built GlobalFlyer.

One day in 2003, Dave and his crew were in a Hong Kong bar when they came across Tai. "I said to Alex, 'How's it going with the GlobalFlyer?' He said, 'Interesting you should ask, Dave, because I was thinking of getting in touch with you. I've got this technical document from Scaled — I'd like you to have a look at it and see what you think.' He sent me this document, I wrote a report on it, and I went to Gatwick to present it to the team. Alex said, 'This is great. You need to come out to Mojave and have a look at it.'

"Myself and Alex went to Mojave to look at the GlobalFlyer, to talk to the engineers and the test pilots. At the same time, Scaled Composites was testing SpaceShipOne. The GlobalFlyer was an amazing aeroplane" — it went on to set a new world record for the fastest non-stop, unrefuelled circumnavigation, with Tai piloting the chase-plane — "and very, very interesting. Even more interesting was this little rocket, which was also sitting in a hangar. We managed to talk our way into flying the simulator. Having done that we spoke to the test pilots, and I talked to Pete Siebold who'd built the simulator.

"Then Alex and I went into a meeting with [Scaled boss] Burt Rutan, where we talked about what was going to happen with SpaceShipOne and what could be done. I'll always remember Burt Rutan saying, 'Well, you know, I could build a six-place spaceship. I'd be interested in doing that, but I'm not interested in running it. Maybe your boss would be?' Alex went back to Richard Branson, and that's how Galactic got going. As soon as it did, and they wanted a test pilot, I was in the right place at the right time."

> ***"That's the moment I love, when the vehicle comes alive"***

Meanwhile, the SpaceShipOne concept had been proved. Launched from its White Knight carrier aircraft, during 2004 it completed the inaugural private human spaceflight and won the Ansari X-Prize for the first private-sector organisation to successfully put a reusable, crewed spacecraft into space twice within a two-week period. Retired afterwards, SpaceShipOne today resides in the Smithsonian's National Air and Space Museum. But it led straight on to the SpaceShipTwo programme, the basis for Virgin Galactic's pioneering launch of commercial passenger spaceflights.

SpaceShipTwo is a six-place spaceplane powered by a single hybrid rocket motor, capable of carrying a combination of passengers and/or payloads alongside two crew. Two have been built, the first being lost during testing. Virgin Galactic has given its second example the fleet name VSS *Unity*, VSS standing for Virgin Space Ship. It requires a mother-ship, White Knight Two, to take it to its launch altitude of around 45,000ft. "Therefore, we're already above most of the atmosphere. There's very little drag up there, because the air is so thin, and therefore we don't have to burn the motor for very long to achieve sufficient energy to get to space.

"This little machine is very simple. The design philosophy of the mother-ship and the spaceship was simplicity. There's very little in the way of pilot aids, which, as a pilot, I love. Any input you make is not being filtered by a computer anywhere. It's being transmitted to the control surfaces, so you are feeling everything that the aeroplane's feeling. It's a great pilot's machine. It's really an aeroplane with a rocket motor attached. The nozzle doesn't gimbal; it's fixed, so your control is the normal stability and control you get from the airframe itself and the control inputs you're making.

"We launch at about Mach 0.55, only about 130kt or so at that altitude. You're under the four-engined mother-ship aircraft for the best part an hour, so it's like being on an airliner with the noise of those engines. At the point of release, the mother-ship is releasing almost half of its payload instantaneously, so it springs up. The spaceship, on the other hand, is below flying speed, so it just falls away at about 0.8g. It feels like going over the top of a rollercoaster. The noise on release is loud, because the hooks are deliberately designed to release very quickly indeed. As you can imagine, you don't want the hooks coming off slowly and the spacecraft releasing asymmetrically, so there's a loud mechanical noise, this lightness in your stomach, and then silence. It's now a glider at a very high altitude.

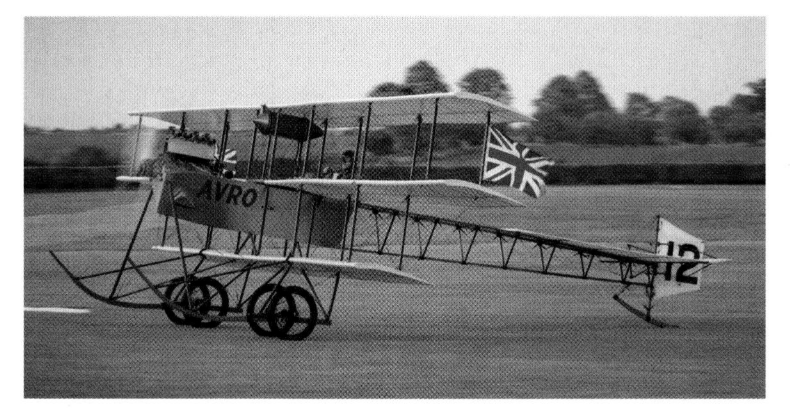

TOP LEFT: **Rolling out in the replica Avro Triplane.** DARREN HARBAR

ABOVE LEFT: **Airborne for quite a high 'hop' of the Shuttleworth Deperdussin.** DARREN HARBAR

ABOVE: **The hybrid rocket motor engages on VSS *Unity* as Dave pilots the spacecraft on its 11 July 2021 test mission, which had Richard Branson on board.** VIRGIN GALACTIC

"But there's only silence for about three seconds, because as soon as we know it's flying properly we say 'Fire' — that's the command to fire the motor. It's not a sudden kick in the back, but it very quickly comes up to full thrust. That's the moment I love, when this vehicle comes alive with the motor burning at full thrust. The acceleration is tremendous. It builds up to 3g, so you've got a 3g push in your back. As we pass Mach 1, which takes about eight seconds, there's a little 'bump in the road' as it goes through the sound barrier and the shockwaves are becoming fully formed.

"Once we're through that we start pitching it up into the vertical. We pull about a 4g turn there, as well as the 3g in the back, until we're in the vertical. We then stabilise it in the vertical, so now you're on your back and you're being pushed upwards, still with this 3g acceleration. The sky goes quickly from blue to dark blue to black. You're looking at a black night sky but you're bathed in very bright sunlight.

"You continue to fly it until the motor shuts down, which is after about 60 seconds. It's a smooth shut-down — you don't get thrown forward in your straps, because you're effectively already outside the atmosphere. We're at Mach 3 at 140,000ft, and you're in weightlessness. At that point we allow our customers to unstrap and float around in the cabin. We continue upwards, and we raise the 'feather' — basically, the aft end of the unit, the tail boom, both tailplanes and the aft flap, all move together as one unit up through 60°. We pitch over into the inverted position and we go up upside-down. You can go up at any angle at all because you're outside the atmosphere. We control that through the reaction control system.

"We continue up towards the apogee inverted. As we start to come back down to meet the atmosphere again, we pitch it round into the upright position to get a smooth re-entry interface with the atmosphere. The 'feather' system controls that attitude, like a badminton shuttlecock. As you meet the atmosphere, the air is exactly hitting the underside of the vehicle, slowing us down, almost acting like a parachute. We ride it down. It comes down in that configuration, peaking at Mach 2.7 — it's an incredible configuration to be in, going at that speed. When we get to 53,000ft we lower the 'feather' and become a glider again, to glide down and land.

"It's an astonishing machine. It launches at a very slow speed; I've had it at Mach 3.2. It folds itself in half; it unfolds itself and it's a glider. And it flies really well. Last year we had six spaceflights and, as they say out here, they were like 'cookie-cutters'. They were almost identical."

That's the desired product of painstaking development, whether the subject is a spacecraft or an everyday aeroplane. And in this process, the human element remains as crucial a link in the chain as ever it has since the days of the early pioneers. Dave's career, uniquely, provides a connection between the two. "To me", he says, "it doesn't seem very long ago that I was looking up at the sky in Helmsdale at those aeroplanes flying by. But going back to the early '60s, which is when I became aware of and hugely interested in aviation, 60 years before that man hadn't even flown. All my grandparents were born before man flew. I do feel very privileged to have been able to sample everything from the oldest flying aeroplane to a piloted spaceship. The speed of progression in aviation has been astonishing, and to me it's been an exciting adventure the whole way."

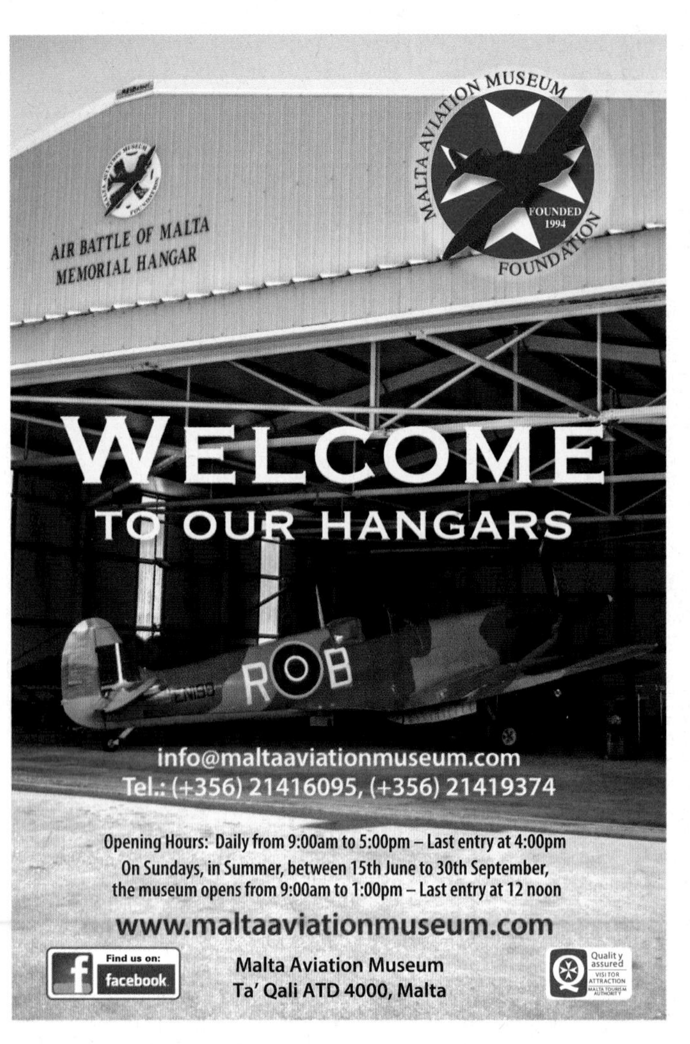
MALTA AVIATION MUSEUM
FOUNDED 1994
FOUNDATION
AIR BATTLE OF MALTA
MEMORIAL HANGAR
WELCOME
TO OUR HANGARS
info@maltaaviationmuseum.com
Tel.: (+356) 21416095, (+356) 21419374
Opening Hours: Daily from 9:00am to 5:00pm – Last entry at 4:00pm
On Sundays, in Summer, between 15th June to 30th September,
the museum opens from 9:00am to 1:00pm – Last entry at 12 noon
www.maltaaviationmuseum.com
Find us on: facebook
Malta Aviation Museum
Ta' Qali ATD 4000, Malta

BRAVO DELTA MODELS
THE WORLD'S FINEST HAND CARVED MAHOGANY MODELS
Hawker Hurricane
Z4018/FH-41
Signed By Flt Sgt Eric Carter
Who Flew this aircraft in 1941on a secret mission
Code named "Force Benedict"
Limited Edition
Hand Carved, hand painted highly detailed model.
1/25 Scale • Length 38.74cm • Wingspan 49.53cm
SPECIAL OFFER for Year Book readers 10% OFF this
model or any other stock desktop model
QUOTE BBMF2025
www.bravodeltamodels.com
+44 (0) 1884 861011

Aircraft Covers &
Ground Equipment
Cambrai Covers
IS09001 Accredited
Aerospace Approved
3 Year Warranty
Refurbishment Service
Reduce your flying costs - Call us to find out how!
+44 (0)1377 267426 info@cambraicovers.com www.cambraicovers.com